Java™
For Kids

A Computer Programming Tutorial

Philip Conrod & Lou Tylee

KIDWARE SOFTWARE, LLC
PO Box 701
Maple Valley, WA 98038
www.computerscienceforkids.com
www.kidwaresoftware.com

Copyright © 2013 by Kidware Software LLC. All rights reserved

Published by:
Kidware Software, LLC
PO Box 701
Maple Valley, Washington 98038
1.425.413.1185
www.kidwaresoftware.com
www.biblebytebooks.com
www.computerscienceforkids.com

All Rights Reserved. No part of the contents of this book may be reproduced or transmitted in any form or by any means without the written permission of the publisher.

Printed in the United States of America

ISBN-13: 978-1-937161-60-6

Copy Editor: Jessica Conrod
Book Cover by Stephanie Conrod
Book Cover Illustration: Kevin Brockschmidt

Previous edition published digitally as "Java For Kids – JDK6 Edition"

This copy of the Java For Kids Tutorial and the associated software is licensed to a single user. Copies of the course are not to be distributed or provided to any other user.
Multiple copy licenses are available for educational institutions. Please contact Kidware Software for school site license information.

This guide was developed for the course, "Java For Kids" produced by Kidware Software LLC, Maple Valley, Washington. It is not intended to be a complete reference to the Java language. Please consult the Oracle website for detailed reference information.

This guide refers to several software and hardware products by their trade names. These references are for informational purposes only and all trademarks are the property of their respective companies and owners.

Java is a trademark product of Oracle Corporation. JCreator is a trademark product of XINOX Software. Microsoft Word, Excel, and Windows are all trademark products of the Microsoft Corporation.

The example companies, organizations, products, domain names, e-mail addresses, logos, people, places, and events depicted are fictitious. No association with any real company, organization, product, domain name, e-mail address, logo, person, place, or event is intended or should be inferred.

This book expresses the author's views and opinions. The information in this book is distributed on an "as is" basis, without and expresses, statutory, or implied warranties. Neither the author(s) nor Kidware Software LLC shall have any liability to any person or entity with respect to any loss nor damage caused or alleged to be caused directly or indirectly by the information contained in this book.

About The Authors

Philip Conrod holds a BS in Computer Information Systems and a Master's certificate in the Essentials of Business Development from Regis University. Philip has been programming computers since 1978. He has authored, co-authored and edited numerous beginning computer programming books for kids, teens and adults. Philip has also held various Information Technology leadership roles in companies like Sundstrand Aerospace, Safeco Insurance Companies, FamilyLife, Kenworth Truck Company, and PACCAR. Today, Philip serves as the Chief Information Officer for a large manufacturing company based in Seattle, Washington. In his spare time, Philip serves as the President of Kidware Software, LLC. Philip makes his home with his three lovely and "techie" daughters in Maple Valley, Washington.

Lou Tylee holds BS and MS degrees in Mechanical Engineering and a PhD in Electrical Engineering. Lou has been programming computers since 1969 when he took his first Fortran course in college. He has written software to control suspensions for high speed ground vehicles, monitor nuclear power plants, lower noise levels in commercial jetliners, compute takeoff speeds for jetliners, locate and identify air and ground traffic and to let kids count bunnies, learn how to spell and do math problems. He has written several on-line texts teaching Visual Basic, Visual C# and Java to thousands of people. He taught a beginning Visual Basic course for over 15 years at a major university. Currently, Lou works as an engineer at a major Seattle aerospace firm. He is the proud father of five children and proud husband of his special wife. Lou and his family live in Seattle, Washington.

Acknowledgements

I would like to thank my three wonderful daughters - Stephanie, Jessica and Chloe, who helped with various aspects of the book publishing process including software testing, book editing, creative design and many other more tedious tasks like textbook formatting and back office administration. I could not have accomplished this without all your hard work, love and support. I also want to thank my best friend Jesus who always stands by my side giving me wisdom and guidance.

Last but definitely not least, I want to thank my multi-talented co-author, Lou Tylee, for doing all the real hard work necessary to develop, test, debug, and keep current all the 'kid-friendly' applications, games and base tutorial text found in this book. Lou has tirelessly poured his heart and soul into so many previous versions of this tutorial and there are so many beginners who have benefited from his work over the years. Lou is by far one of the best application developers and tutorial writers I have ever worked with.   Thanks Lou for collaborating with me on this book project.

Forward By Alan Payne

What is "Java for Kids" ... and how it works.

The tutorial "Java for Kids" is a highly organized and well-indexed set of lessons meant for children aged 10 and above. Xinox JCreator, a specific IDE (Integrated Development Environment) for beginners is used throughout the lessons.

The tutorial provides the benefit of completed age-appropriate applications for children and fully documented projects from the teacher's or parents' point of view. That is, while full solutions are provided for the adults' (and child learner's) benefit, the projects are presented in an easy-to-follow set of lessons explaining the rational for the form layout, coding design and conventions, and specific code related to the problem. Child-learners may follow the tutorials at their own pace. Every bit of the lesson is remembered as it contributes to the final solution of a kid-friendly application. The finished product is the reward, but the student is fully engaged and enriched by the process. This kind of learning is often the focus of teacher training. Every computer science teacher knows what a great deal of preparation is required for projects to work for kids. With these tutorials, the research behind the projects is done by an author who understands the classroom and parenting experience. That is extremely rare!

Graduated Lessons for Every Project ... Lessons, examples, problems and projects. Graduated learning. Increasing and appropriate difficulty... Great results.

With these projects, there are lessons providing a comprehensive, kid-friendly background on the programming topics to be covered. Once understood, concepts are easily applicable to a variety of applications. Then, specific examples are drawn out so that a young learner can practice with the JCreator environment. Then specific Java coding for the example is provided so that the student can see all the parts of the project come together for the finished product.

By presenting lessons in this graduated manner, students are fully engaged and appropriately challenged to become independent thinkers who can come up with their own project ideas and design their own forms and do their own coding. Once the process is learned, then student engagement is unlimited! I have seen literacy improve dramatically because students cannot get enough of what is being presented.

Indeed, lessons encourage *accelerated* learning - in the sense that they provide an enriched environment to learn computer science, but they also encourage *accelerating* learning because students cannot put the lessons away once they start! Computer science provides this unique opportunity to challenge students, and it is a great testament to the authors that they are successful in achieving such levels of engagement with consistency.

My History with Kidware Software products.

I have used Kidware's Programming Tutorials for over a decade to keep up my own learning. By using these lessons, I am able to spend time on things which will pay off in the classroom. I do not waste valuable time ensconced in language reference libraries for programming environments with help screens which can never be fully remembered! These projects are examples of how student projects should be as final products - thus, the pathway to learning is clear and immediate in every project.

If I want to use or expand upon some of the projects for student use, then I take advantage of site-license options. I have found it very straight forward to emphasize the fundamental computer science topics that form the basis of these projects when using them in the classroom. I can list some computer science topics which everyone will recognize, regardless of where they teach – topics which are covered expertly by these tutorials:

- Data Types and Ranges
- Scope of Variables
- Naming Conventions
- Decision Making
- Looping
- Language Functions – String, Date, Numerical
- Arrays
- Writing Your own Methods (subroutines) and more… it's all integrated into the tutorials.

In many States or Provinces, the above-listed topics would not be formally introduced in Middle School computer studies, but *would* form the basis of most projects undertaken by students. With these tutorials, you as the teacher or parent may choose where to put the emphasis, to be sure to cover the curricular expectations of your curriculum documents.

Any further Middle school computer programming topics derive directly from those listed above. Nothing is forgotten. All can be integrated with the lessons provided.

Quick learning curve for teachers! How teachers can use the product:

Having projects completed ahead of time can allow the teacher to present the design aspect of the project FIRST, and then have students do all of their learning in the context of what is required in the finished product. This is a much faster learning curve than if students designed all of their own projects from scratch. Lessons concentrating on a unified outcome for all makes for much more streamlined engagement for students (and that is what they need, in Middle school, and in grades 9 and 10), as they complete more projects within a short period of time and there is a context for everything that is learned.

With the Java for Kids tutorials, sound advice regarding generally accepted coding strategies ("build and test your code in stages", "learn input, output, formatting and data storage strategies for different data types" etc..) encourage independent thought processes among learners. After mastery, then it is much more likely that students can create their own problems and solutions from scratch. Students are ready to create their own summative projects for your computer science course – or just for fun, and they may think of projects for their other courses as well! And what could be wrong with asking the students' other teachers what they would like to see as project extensions?

Meets State and Provincial Curriculum Expectations and More

Different states and provinces have their own curriculum requirements for computer science. With the Kidware Software products, you have at your disposal a series of projects which will allow you to pick and choose from among those which best suit your curriculum needs. Students focus upon design stages and sound problem-solving techniques from a computer-science, problem-solving perspective. In doing so, they become independent problem-solvers, and will exceed the curricular requirements of Middle schools and Secondary schools everywhere.

Useable projects - Out of the box!

The specific projects covered in the *Java for Kids* tutorials are suitable for students aged 10 and above.

Specific kid-friendly tutorials and projects are found in the Contents document, and include:

- Sub-Sandwich Party
- Savings Calculator
- Guess the Number Game
- Lemonade Stand
- Card Wars
- Blackboard Fun (GUI, meaning it has a Graphical User Interface)
- Balloons (GUI)

And, from the final chapter,

- Computer Stopwatch
- Dice Rolling
- State Capitals
- Tic-Tac-Toe (GUI)
- Memory Game (GUI)
- Pong (GUI)

As you can see, there is a high degree of care taken so that projects are age-appropriate.

You as a parent or teacher can begin teaching the projects on the first day. It's easy for the adult to have done their own learning by starting with the solution files. Then, they will see how all of the parts of the lesson fall into place. Even a novice could make use of the accompanying lessons.

How to teach students to use the materials.

In a Middle school situation, parents or teachers might be tempted to spend considerable amounts of time at the projector or computer screen going over the tutorial – but the best strategy is to present the finished product first! That way, provided that the adult has covered the basic concepts listed in the table of contents first, the students will quickly grasp how to use the written lessons on their own. Lessons will be fun, and the pay-off for younger students is that there is always a finished product which is fun to use!

Highly organized reference materials for student self-study!

Materials already condense what is available from MSDN *(which tends to be written for adults)* and in a context and age-appropriate manner, so that younger students remember what they learn.

The time savings for parents, teachers and students is enormous as they need not sift through pages and pages of on-line help to find what they need.

How to mark the projects.

In a classroom environment, it is possible for teachers to mark student progress by asking questions during the various problem design and coding stages. In the early grades (grades 5 to 8) teachers can make their own oral, pictorial review or written pop quizzes easily from the reference material provided as a review strategy from day to day. I have found the requirement of completing projects (mastery) sufficient for gathering information about student progress - especially in the later grades (grades 10 to 12).

Lessons encourage your own programming extensions.

Once concepts are learned, it is difficult to NOT know what to do for your own projects. This is true even at the Middle school level – where applications can be made in as short as 10 minutes (a high-low guessing game, or a temperature conversion program, for example), or 1 period in length – if one wished to expand upon any of the projects using the "Other Things to Try" suggestions.

Having used Kidware Software tutorials for the past decade, I have to say that I could not have achieved the level of success which is now applied in the variety of many programming environments which are currently of considerable interest to kids! I thank Kidware Software and its authors for continuing to stand for what is right in the teaching methodologies which work with kids - even today's kids where competition for their attention is now so much an issue.

Regards,

Alan Payne
Computer Science Teacher
T.A. Blakelock High School
Oakville, Ontario
http://chatt.hdsb.ca/~paynea

1. Introducing Java

Preview 1-1
What is Java? 1-2
Why Learn Java? 1-4
A Brief History of Programming Languages 1-5
Let's Get Started 1-7
Downloading and Installing Java 1-9
JCreator – A Java Development Environment 1-13
Starting JCreator 1-21
Opening a Java Project 1-24
Compiling and Running a Java Project 1-26
Stopping JCreator 1-28
Java Programming without a Development Environment 1-29
Summary 1-32

2. Java Program Basics

Review and Preview 2-1
Structure of a Java Program 2-2
The Welcome Project (Revisited) 2-4
Some Rules of Java Programming 2-8
Creating Java Projects with JCreator 2-10
Saving Java Projects with JCreator 2-20
Compiling and Running a Java Program 2-21
JCreator and Java Files 2-23
Summary 2-25

3. Your First Java Program

Review and Preview 3-1
Creating a Java Program 3-2
Java - The First Lesson 3-6
    Variables 3-6
    Variable Names 3-7
    Variable Types 3-8
    Declaring Variables 3-10
    Assignment Statement 3-12
    Arithmetic Operators 3-14
    String Concatenation 3-18
    Comments 3-19
    Program Output 3-20
Project - Sub Sandwich Party 3-23
    Project Design 3-23
    Project Development 3-24
    Run the Project 3-30
    Other Things to Try 3-31
Summary 3-33

4. Java Project Design, Input Methods

Review and Preview 4-1
Project Design 4-2
Java – The Second Lesson 4-4
    Variable Initialization 4-4
    Mathematical Functions 4-6
Program Input Methods 4-10
    Input Methods Example 4-13
Project – Savings Calculator 4-20
    Project Design 4-20
    Project Development 4-21
    Run the Project 4-24
    Other Things to Try 4-26
Summary 4-27

5. Debugging, Decisions, Random Numbers

Review and Preview 5-1
Debugging a Java Project.. 5-2
    Syntax Errors 5-3
    Run-Time Errors... 5-7
    Logic Errors 5-9
Java – The Third Lesson 5-10
    Logical Expressions 5-10
    Comparison Operators 5-12
    Comparing Strings 5-15
    Logical Operators 5-16
    Decisions – The if Statement 5-21
    Random Number Generator 5-27
Project – Guess the Number Game..5-31
    Project Design..5-32
    Project Development 5-33
    Run the Project 5-37
    Other Things to Try..5-39
Summary 5-41

6. Java Looping, Methods

Review and Preview 6-1
Java – The Fourth Lesson 6-2
    Java Loops 6-2
A Brief Interlude – Guess the Number Game (Revisited) 6-8
Java – The Fourth Lesson (Continued)...6-11
    Java Methods 6-11
Project – Lemonade Stand..6-18
    Project Design..6-19
    Project Development 6-20
    Run the Project 6-29
    Other Things to Try..6-31
Summary 6-32

7. Arrays, More Java Looping

Review and Preview 7-1
Java – The Fifth Lesson 7-2
    Variable Arrays 7-2
    Java for Loops 7-5
"Shuffle" Method 7-11
Project – Card Wars 7-19
    Project Design 7-19
    Project Development 7-20
    Run the Project 7-30
    Other Things to Try 7-31
Summary 7-32

8. Java Graphics, Mouse Methods

Review and Preview 8-1
Graphic User Interfaces (GUI) 8-2
Java Graphics 8-9
    Frames 8-9
    Event Methods 8-12
Java – The Sixth Lesson 8-14
    Mouse Events 8-14
    mousePressed Event 8-14
    mouseDragged Event 8-18
    Class Level Scope Variables 8-21
More Java Graphics 8-23
    Graphics Coordinates 8-23
    Colors 8-25
    drawLine Method 8-28
    drawRect Method 8-34
    fillRect Method 8-37
Project – Blackboard Fun 8-41
    Project Design 8-41
    Project Development 8-42
    Run the Project 8-54
    Other Things to Try 8-56
Summary 8-59

9. Timers, Animation, Keyboard Methods

Review and Preview 9-1
Timer Class 9-2
Java – The Final Lesson 9-15
    drawstring Method.. 9-15
    Animation 9-18
    Object Disappearance 9-25
    Border Crossing 9-29
    Object Erasure 9-34
    Collision Detection 9-36
    Keyboard Methods 9-42
    keyPressed Event 9-43
Project – Balloons 9-48
    Project Design.. 9-48
    Project Development 9-49
    Run the Project 9-69
    Other Things to Try.. 9-70
Summary 9-72

10. More Topics, More Projects

Preview 10-1
Project 1 – Computer Stopwatch 10-2
    New Topic – Timing.. 10-2
Project 2 – Dice Rolling 10-8
    New Topic – Switch Structure... 10-9
Project 3 – State Capitals... 10-18
Project 4 – Tic-Tac-Toe 10-28
Project 5 – Memory Game 10-41
Bonus – Pong! 10-60

Course Description:

Java for Kids is an interactive, self-paced tutorial providing a complete introduction to the Java programming language. The tutorial consists of 10 lessons explaining (in simple, easy-to-follow terms) how to build a Java application. Numerous examples are used to demonstrate every step in the building process. The tutorial also includes detailed computer projects for kids to build and try. **Java for Kids** is presented using a combination of course notes and many Java examples and projects.

Course Prerequisites:

To use **Java for Kids**, you should be comfortable working within the Windows (or other operating system) environment, knowing how to find files, move windows, resize windows, etc. No programming experience is needed. The course material should be understandable to kids aged 10 and up. You will also need the ability to view and print documents saved in the Acrobat PDF format. Finally, and most obvious, you need to have Java. This is a FREE product that can be downloaded from:

> http://www.oracle.com/technetwork/java/index.html

This site contains complete downloading and installation instructions for the latest version of Java. You can also download all Java documentation from this same site. Look for the development kit (current version is **JDK 7**) for the Standard Edition of Java (**Jave SE**).

Our tutorials use **JCreator 5.0** as the IDE (Integrated Development Environment) for building and testing Java applications. JCreator is availabefor download at the Xinox website:

> http://www.jcreator.com

A Brief Word on the Course:

Though this course is entitled "Java for Kids," it is not necessarily written in a kid's vocabulary. Computer programming has a detailed vocabulary of its own and, since adults developed it, the terminology tends to be very adult-like. In developing this course, we discussed how to address this problem and decided we would treat our kid readers like adults, since they are learning what is essentially an adult topic. We did not want to 'dumb-down' the course. You see this in some books. We, quite frankly, are offended by books who refer to readers as dummies and idiots simply because they are new to a particular topic. We didn't want to do that here. Throughout the course, we treat the kid reader as a mature person learning a new skill. The vocabulary is not that difficult, but there may be times the kid reader needs a little help from a parent or teacher. Hopefully, the nearest adult can provide that help.

Installing the Downloadable Multimedia and Solution Files

If you purchased this directly from our website you received an email with a special and individualized internet download link where you could download the compressed Program Solution Files. If you purchased this book through a 3rd Party Book Store like Amazon.com, the solutions files for this tutorial are included in a compressed ZIP file that is available for download directly from our website (after registration) at:

http://www.kidwaresoftware.com/javakids-registration.html

Complete the online web form at the webpage above with your name, shipping address, email address, the exact title of this book, date of purchase, online or physical store name, and your order confirmation number from that store. After we receive all this information we will email you a download link for the multimedia and source code solution files associated with this book.

Warning: If you purchased this book "used" or "second hand" you are not licensed or entitled to download the Program Solution Files. However, you can purchase the Digital Download Version of this book at a highly discounted price which allows you access to the digital source code solutions files required for completing this tutorial.

Installing Java for Kids:

The course notes and code for **Java for Kids** are included in one or more ZIP files. Use your favorite 'unzipping' application to write all files to your computer. The course is included in the folder entitled **JavaKids**. This folder contains two other folders: **JK Notes** and **JK Code**. The **JK Code** folder includes all the Java projects developed during the course.

How To Take the Course:

Java for Kids is a self-paced course. The suggested approach is to do one class a week for ten weeks. Each week's class should require about 3 to 6 hours of your time to grasp the concepts completely. Prior to doing a particular week's work, open the class notes file for that week and print it out. Then, work through the notes at your own pace. Try to do each example as they are encountered in the notes. Work through the projects in Classes 3 through 10. If you need any help, all completed projects are included in the **JK Code** folder.

1. Introducing Java

Preview

You are about to start a new journey. Writing programs that ask a computer to do certain tasks is fun and rewarding. Like any journey, you need to prepare before starting.

In this first class, we do that preparation. You will learn what Java is and why you might want to learn Java. You will download and install the Java development software and download and install the software that will help you create Java programs. Once the preparation is done, you will run your first Java application to check that you have prepared properly. Let's get started.

What is Java?

Java is a computer **programming language** developed by Sun Microsystems. A programming language is used to provide instructions to a computer to do specific tasks. Java is a new language that is less than 10 years old (being created in 1995) and has been very successful for many reasons.

The first reason for Java's popularity is its cost – absolutely FREE!! Many other programming languages sell for hundreds and thousands of dollars, which makes it difficult for many people to start learning programming. A second reason for the popularity of Java is that a Java program can run on almost any computer. I'm sure you've seen programs that only run on Macintosh computers or Windows-based computers. With Java, there is no such thing as a Mac version or a Windows version of a program. We say that Java programs are **platform-independent**.

Java can be used to develop many types of applications. There are simple text-based programs called **console applications**. These programs just support text input and output to your computer screen. You can also build **graphical user interface** (GUI, pronounced 'gooey') **applications**. These are applications with menus, toolbars, buttons, scroll bars, and other controls which depend on the computer mouse for input. Examples of GUI applications you may have used are word processors, spreadsheet programs and computer games. A last application that can be built with Java are **applets**. These are small GUI applications that can be run from within a web page. Such applets make web pages dynamic, changing with time. I think you can see the versatility of Java. In this class, we work mainly with simple **console applications**. This allows us to concentrate on learning the basics of Java without getting lost in the world of GUI's.

Another popular feature of Java is that it is **object-oriented**. This is a fancy way of saying that Java programs are many basic pieces that can be used over and over again. What this means to you, the Java programmer, is that you can build and change large programs without a lot of additional complication. As you work through this course, you will hear the word **object** many, many times.

A last advantage of Java is that it is a simple language. Compared to other languages, there is less to learn. This simplicity is necessary to help insure the platform-independence (ability to run on any computer) of Java applications. But, just because it is a simple language doesn't mean it lacks capabilities. You can do anything with Java that you can with any of the more complicated languages.

Why Learn Java?

We could very well just ask the question – **Why Learn a Programming Language?** There are several reasons for doing this. First, if you know how to program, you will have a better understanding of just how computers work. Second, writing programs is good exercise for your thinking skills – you must be a very logical thinker to write computer programs. You must also be something of a perfectionist – computers are not that smart and require exact, perfect instructions to do their jobs. Third, computer programmers are in demand and make a lot of money. And, last, writing computer programs is fun. It's rewarding to see your ideas for a certain computer program come to life on the computer screen.

So, why learn **Java**? We've already seen some of the advantages of using and learning Java – it's free, it's platform-independent, it can be used to write a wide variety of applications and it is object-oriented. And, another reason for learning Java is that it is one of the easiest languages to learn. Recall Java is a simple language with not a lot of instructions to learn. Because of its simplicity, you can learn to write Java programs very quickly. But, just because you can write your first program quickly doesn't mean you'll learn everything there is to know about Java. This course just introduces Java. There's still a lot to learn – there's always a lot to learn. So, consider this course as a first step in a journey to becoming a proficient Java programmer.

A Brief History of Programming Languages

We're almost ready to get started. But, first I thought it would be interesting for you to see just where the Java language fits in the history of some other computer languages. You will see just how new Java is!

In the early 1950's most computers were used for scientific and engineering calculations. The programming language of choice in those days was called **FORTRAN** (**FOR**mula **TRAN**slator). FORTRAN was the first modern language and is still in use to this day (after going through several updates). In the late 1950's, bankers and other business people got into the computer business using a language called **COBOL** (the letter **B** stands for business, I can't remember what the other letters mean). Within a few years after its development, COBOL became the most widely used data processing language. And, like FORTRAN, it is still being used today.

In the 1960's, two professors at Dartmouth College decided that "everyday" people needed to have a language they could use to learn programming. They developed **BASIC** (**B**eginner's **A**ll-Purpose **S**ymbolic **I**nstruction **C**ode). BASIC (and its successors, GW-BASIC, Visual Basic, Visual Basic .NET) is probably the most widely used programming language. Many dismiss it as a "toy language," but BASIC was the first product developed by a company you may have heard of - Microsoft! And, BASIC has been used to develop thousands of commercial applications.

Java had its beginnings in 1972, when AT&T Bell Labs developed the **C** programming language. It was the first, new scientific type language since FORTRAN. If you've every seen a C program, you will notice many similarities between Java and C. Then, with object-oriented capabilities added, came **C++** in 1986 (also from Bell Labs). This was a big step.

On May 23, 1995, Sun Microsystems released the first version of the **Java** programming language. It represented a streamlined version of C and C++ with capabilities for web and desktop applications on <u>any</u> kind of computer. No language before it had such capabilities. Since this introduction, just a few years ago, millions of programmers have added Java capabilities to their programming skills. Improvements are constantly being made to Java and there is a wealth of support to all programmers, even beginners like yourself, from the vast Java community. Let's start your journey to join this young, vital community.

Introducing Java

Let's Get Started

Learning how to use Java to write a computer program (like learning anything new) involves many steps, many new terms, and many new skills. We will take it slow, describing each step, term, and skill in detail. Before starting, we assume you know how to do a few things:

- You should know how to start your computer and use the mouse.
- You should have some knowledge on working with your particular operating system (Windows 7, 2000, XP, NT, Vista, Linux, Mac OS). In these notes, we use Windows XP and Windows Vista. If you are using another operating system, your screens may appear different than those shown here.
- You should know how to resize and move windows around on the screen.
- You should know how to run an application on your computer by using the **Start Menu** or some other means.
- You should know how to fill in information in dialog boxes that may pop up on the screen.
- You should know about folders and files and how to create and find them on your computer.
- You should know what file extensions are and how to identify them. For example, in a file named **Example.ext**, the three letters **ext** are called the extension.
- You should know how to click on links to read documents and move from page to page in such documents. You do this all the time when you use the Internet.
- You should know how to access the Internet and download files.

You have probably used all of these skills if you've ever used a word processor, spreadsheet, or any other software on your computer. If you think you lack any of these skills, ask someone for help. They should be able to show you how to do them in just a few minutes. Actually, any time you feel stuck while trying to learn this material, never be afraid to ask someone for help. We were all beginners at one time and people really like helping you learn.

Let's get going. And, as we said, we're going to take it slow. In this first class, we will learn how to install Java on your computer, how to load a Java program (or project), how to run the program, and how to stop the program. It will be a good introduction to the many new things we will learn in the classes to come.

Downloading and Installing Java

To write and run programs using Java, you need the **Java Development Kit** (JDK). This is a free product that you can download from the Internet. This simply means we will copy a file onto our computer to allow installation of Java. Follow these steps:

1. Start up your web browser (Internet Explorer, Chrome, Firefox, Safari or other) and go to Java web site:

    http://www.oracle.com/technetwork/java/index.html

    This web site has lots of useful Java information. As you become more proficient in your programming skills, you will go to this site often for answers to programming questions, interaction with other Java programmers, and lots of sample programs.

2. On this web page, you should see a link that allows downloading something called the **Java SE** (Java Standard Edition). Click this link to see on the next web page:

Java SE Downloads

Latest Release   Next Release (Early Access)   Embedded Use   Previous Releases

Java Platform (JDK) 7u13   JavaFX 2.2.5   JDK 7 + NetBeans

You want to download the Java Development Kit (**JDK**). There may be several versions – you want to download the latest version. As of this writing the latest version is **JDK 7, Update 13**. Click the **Download JDK** button. Once on the page with the JDK download links, choose the link corresponding to your computer's operating system. In these notes, we will be downloading and installing the Windows 64 bit version of the JDK. Instructions for installing Java on other platforms (Linux, Mac OS) can be found at the Java website.

Introducing Java   1-11

3. Continue to the next window and click on the link with the **Java SE Development Kit** executable file. You will be asked if you want to **Run** a file. Click **Yes**. Installation begins.

4. The Java installer will unpack some files and an introductory window will appear:

![Java SE Development Kit 7 Update 13 (64-bit) - Setup window showing "Welcome to the Installation Wizard for Java SE Development Kit 7 Update 13. This wizard will guide you through the installation process for the Java SE Development Kit 7 Update 13. The JavaFX SDK is now included as part of the JDK." with Next > and Cancel buttons.]

Click **Next** to start the installation. Several windows will appear. Accept the default choices by clicking **Next** at each window.

When complete, you will see this window:

Click **Close** and you are done with the installation.

JCreator – A Java Development Environment

The process of creating and running a Java program has three distinct steps:

- **Type** the program
- **Compile** the program (generate a file your computer can understand)
- **Run** the program.

Don't worry too much about what goes on in each of these steps right now. One way to complete these three steps is to first type the program using a basic editor and save the resulting file. Next, the compile and run steps can be completed by typing separate commands to your computer. Very few Java programmers write programs in this manner. Nearly all programmers develop their programs using something called an **Integrated Development Environment** (IDE). There are many IDE's available for Java development purposes, some very elaborate, some very simple. In these notes, we will use an IDE called **JCreator**. It is a very easy-to-use interface that we can download from the Internet. We strongly recommend its use – it will make your job as a programmer easier, allowing you to concentrate on learning the elements of the Java language.

Before downloading and installing **JCreator**, we have to confront a problem. JCreator only works for Windows-based computers. Does this mean if you are using Linux or a Macintosh computer that you need to stop using these notes right now? No, it just means you have to resort to other means to implement the above mentioned three steps in building a Java application. One solution for you would be to find an IDE that works with your particular operating system. Then, you should be able to easily find similar capabilities to the capabilities of JCreator discussed in these notes. You could do the same thing if you are a Windows user and don't want to use JCreator - find another IDE and use its capabilities to write, compile and run programs. Search the Internet for such an IDE. Examples of other IDE's are **NetBeans**, **Eclipse** and **IntelliJ**. We like JCreator for its ease of use.

Or, for Linux, Macintosh and even Windows machines, you can use the barebones approach to Java programming referred to earlier - use a simple editor and typed commands to generate running Java programs. Check the Internet for ways to do this.

If you use Windows and choose to use **JCreator**, let's start the download process. JCreator is developed by a company called Xinox Software. There are two versions of **JCreator LE** (light edition) and **Pro** (professional edition). We will be using JCreator LE. As you progress in your programming skills, we encourage you to look into JCreator Pro as a more advanced IDE. To download, follow these steps:

1. Go to our website at:

    http://www.kidwaresoftware.com/downloads/jcrea500_setup.exe

    IMPORTANT NOTE: This is a special download link for a free shareware version of the JCreator 5.00.008 Integrated Development Environment (IDE). If you like their their clean and simple IDE as much as we do, we encourage to purchase the Professional version from the JCreator website after you complete the course if you decide to become a professional Java developer. The special 5.00.008 version of the Xinox JCreator IDE software that we provide you above from our website does not expire and is more compatible with our Java tutorials than the version that is currently available on the vendor's website.

2. After clicking the program link, select **Run**. A progress window will appear (your window may differ slightly):

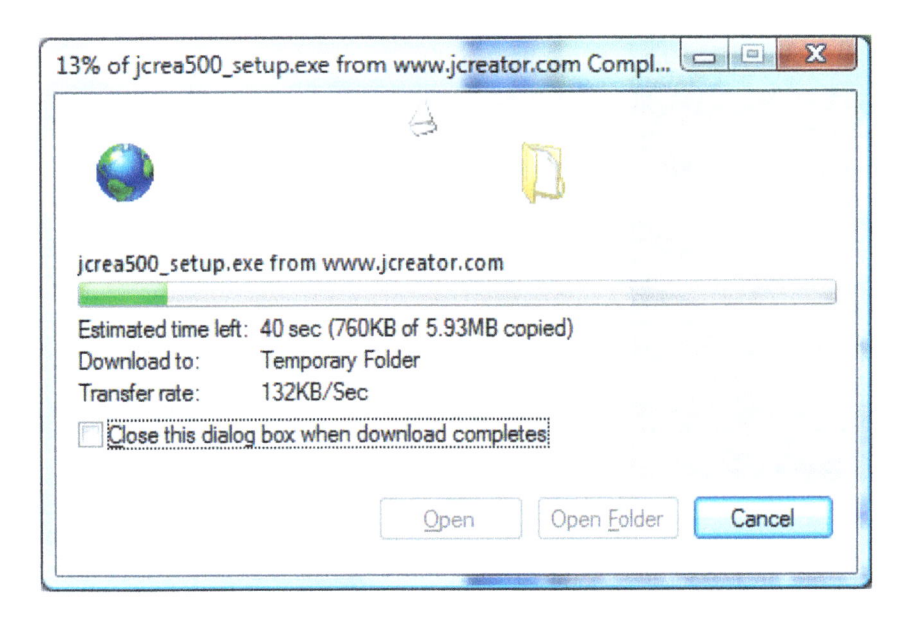

This window will eventually appear:

Click **Next** and you will see a licensing agreement (agree to it or you can't finish).

Introducing Java 1-17

A few screens asking where you want JCreator files installed and how you want it to appear on your Desktop will follow. We suggest clicking **Next** on each screen until you see:

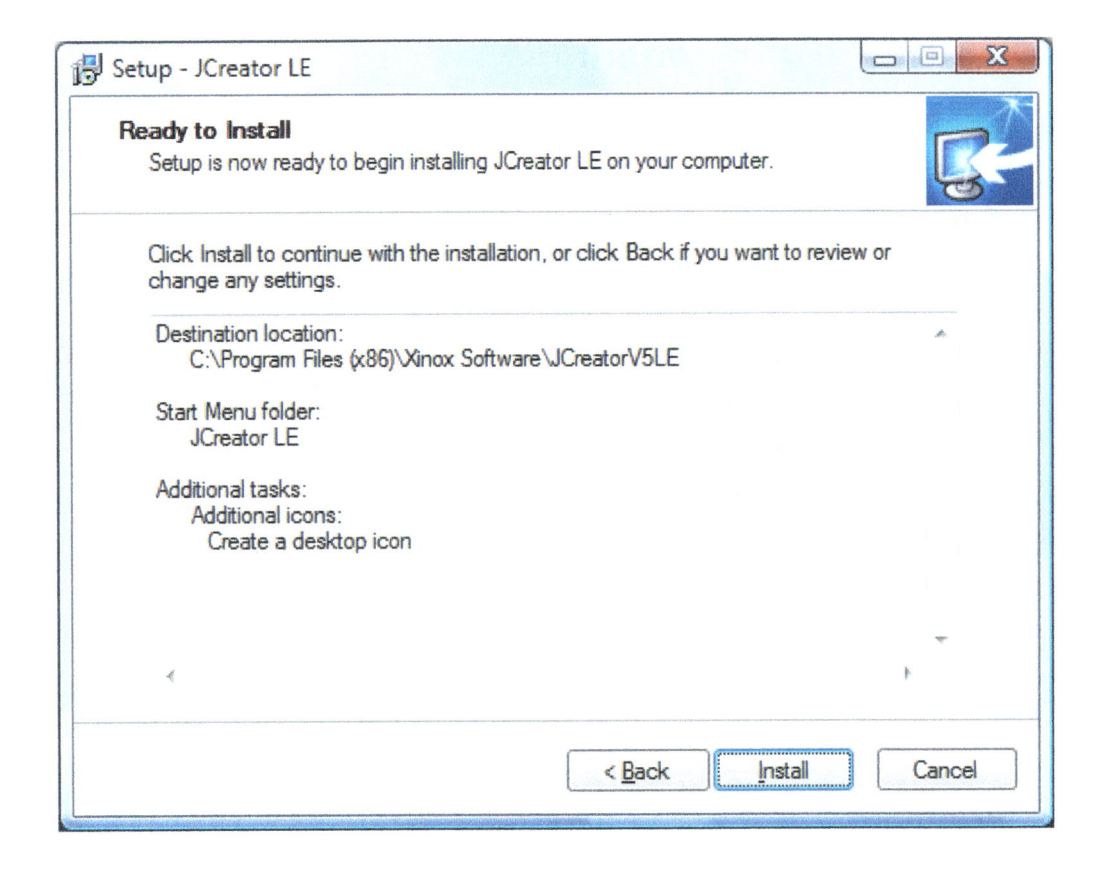

Setup - JCreator LE

Ready to Install
Setup is now ready to begin installing JCreator LE on your computer.

Click Install to continue with the installation, or click Back if you want to review or change any settings.

Destination location:
  C:\Program Files (x86)\Xinox Software\JCreatorV5LE

Start Menu folder:
  JCreator LE

Additional tasks:
  Additional icons:
    Create a desktop icon

[< Back] [Install] [Cancel]

Click **Install** at this point to begin the installation.

When finished, you will see:

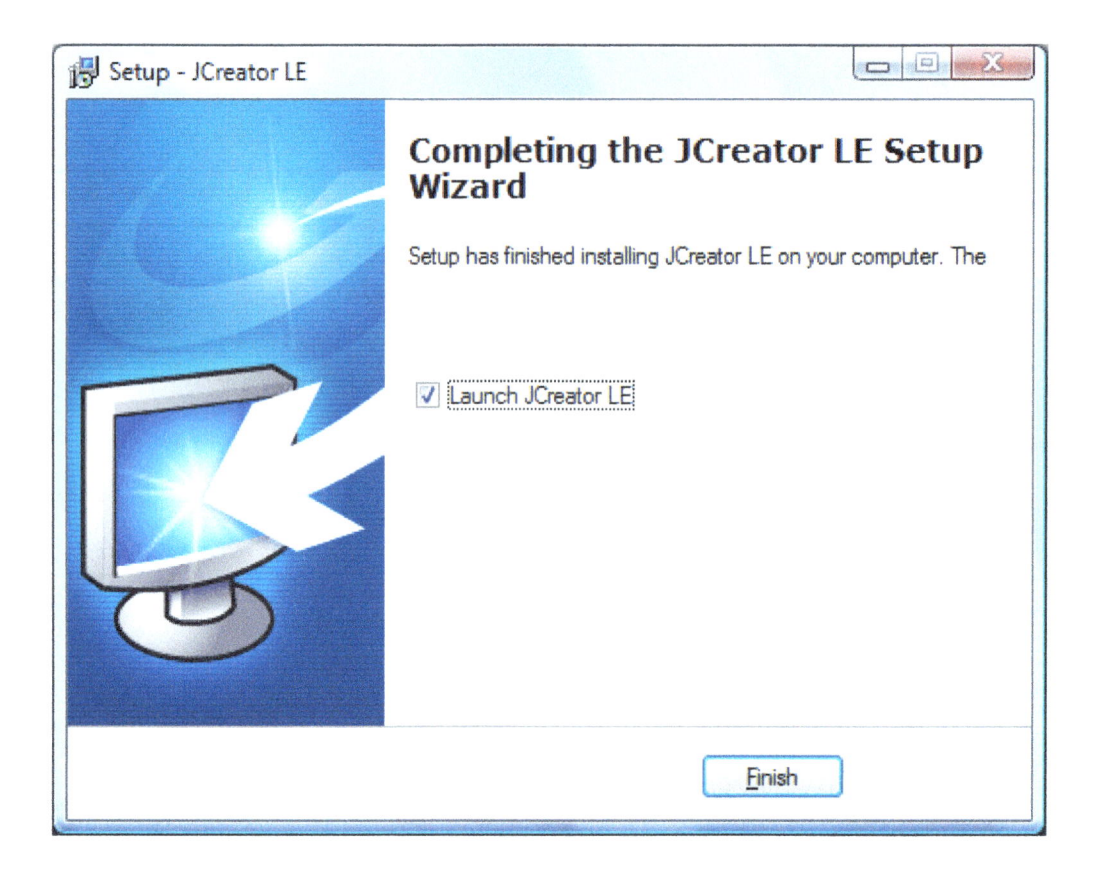

Click the **Finish** button (make sure you leave the check mark next to **Launch JCreator LE**).

Introducing Java 1-19

JCreator will start up and ask a few more questions. Accept the defaults in the first couple of windows by clicking **Next**. Now the most important dialog – you see:

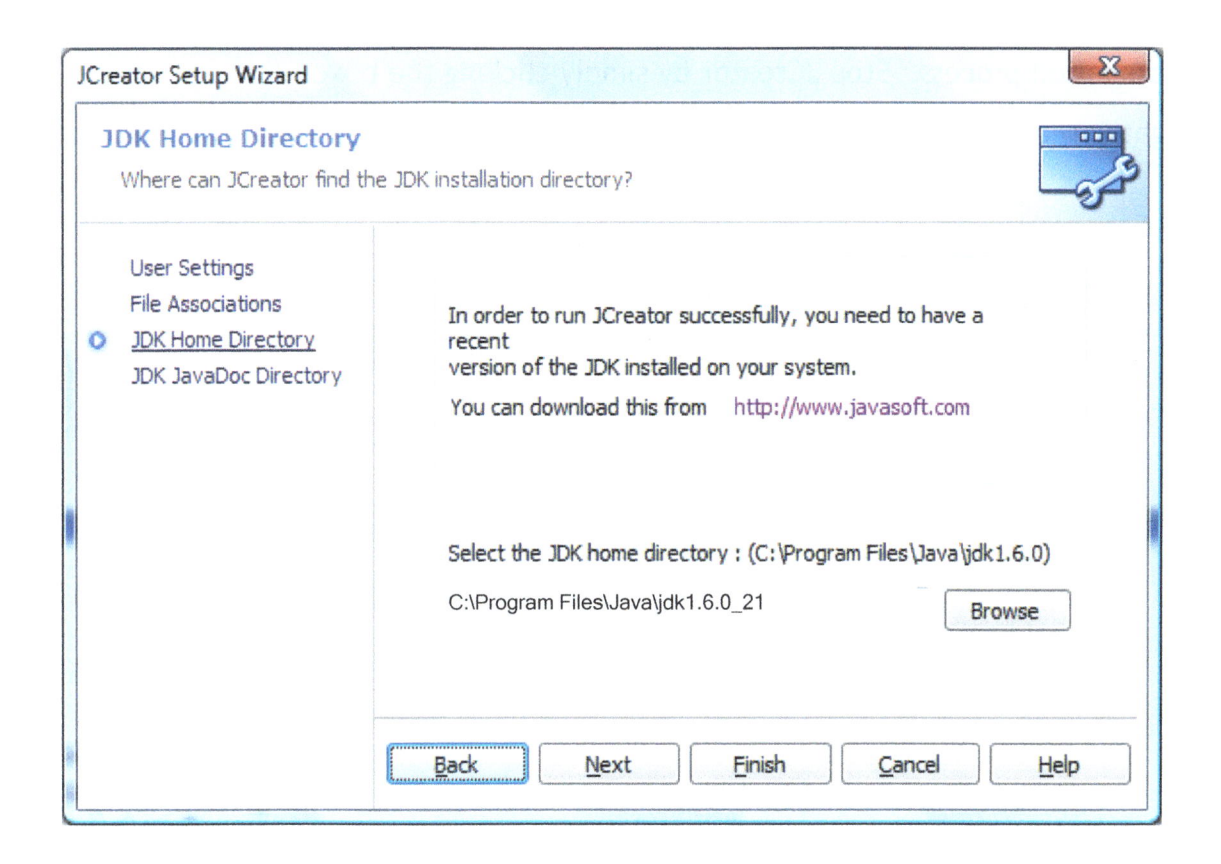

[JCreator Setup Wizard - JDK Home Directory dialog showing: "Where can JCreator find the JDK installation directory?" with options User Settings, File Associations, JDK Home Directory (selected), JDK JavaDoc Directory. Text reads: "In order to run JCreator successfully, you need to have a recent version of the JDK installed on your system. You can download this from http://www.javasoft.com   Select the JDK home directory : (C:\Program Files\Java\jdk1.6.0)   C:\Program Files\Java\jdk1.6.0_21   [Browse]" Buttons: Back, Next, Finish, Cancel, Help]

Here, you tell JCreator where you have installed the Java Development Kit (JDK). Click **Browse** (if necessary), make sure the Java home directory (the current default location is **c:\Program Files\Java\jdk1.7.0_13** in this case) is correct and click **Next**.

A last window will appear asking where you put the SDK documentation. We didn't download the SDK. And, for this class, we don't need it. The Java website has a wealth of such documentation if you ever need it. So, just click **Finish** at this point and JCreator should start. If it doesn't, try repeating the installation process. Stop JCreator by simply clicking the boxed **X** in the upper right corner of the window (or select **File** from the main menu and choose **Exit**).

Starting JCreator

At long last, we're ready to try out all the new files we've installed on our computer. We'll learn how to start **JCreator**, how to load a Java project, how to compile a project and how to run a project. This will give us some assurance we have everything installed correctly. This will let us begin our study of the Java programming language.

Once installed, to start JCreator:

- Click on the **Start** button on the Windows task bar.
- Select **Programs**, then **JCreator LE**
- Click on **JCreator LE 5.00**

(Some of the headings given here may differ slightly on your computer, but you should have no trouble finding the correct ones.) If you put a shortcut on your desktop in the installation, you can also start JCreator by double-clicking the correct icon. The JCreator program should start. Several windows will appear on the screen.

Upon starting, my screen shows a **Start Page** with lots of helpful information. You can spend some time looking through these if you wish. For now, close the this page by clicking the **X** on the tab:

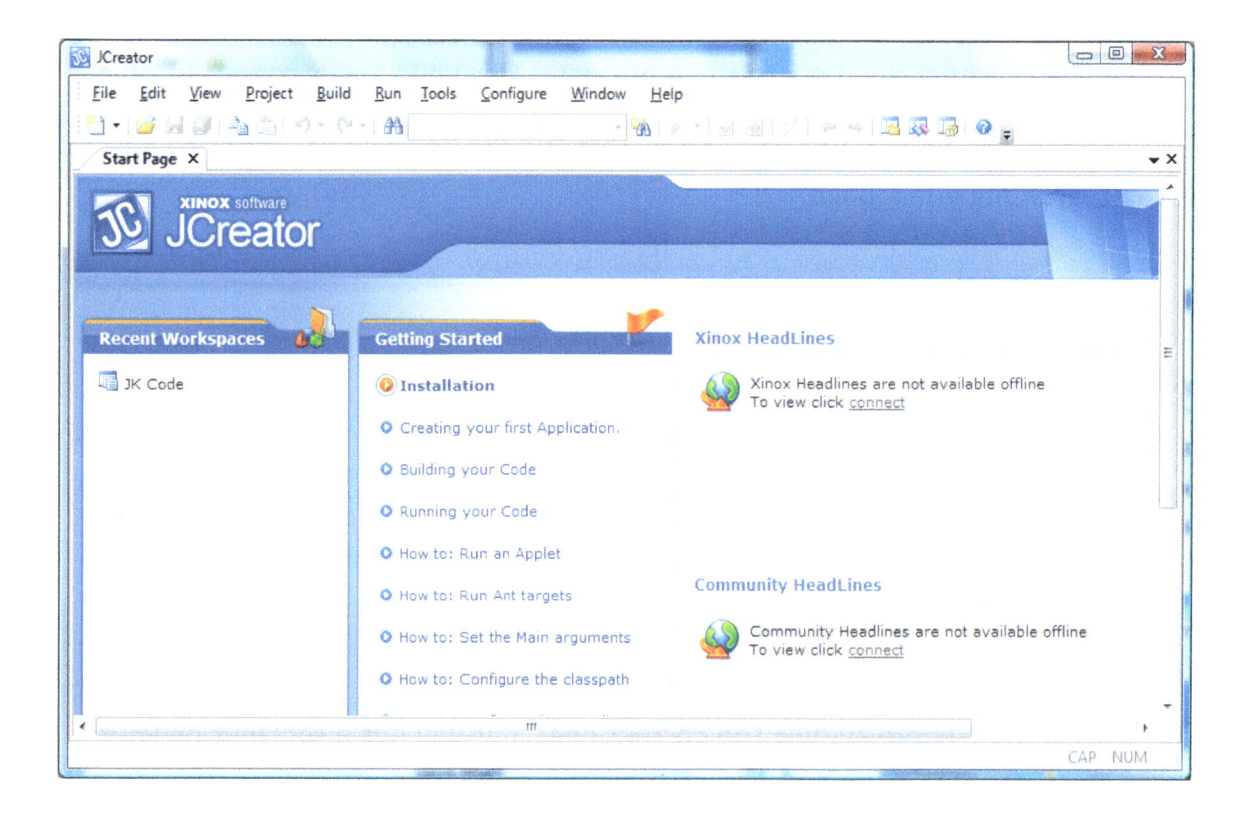

Next, choose the **View** menu option and select **File View**.

Introducing Java 1-23

The window should now look like this (this is where we will always start to build and run Java programs):

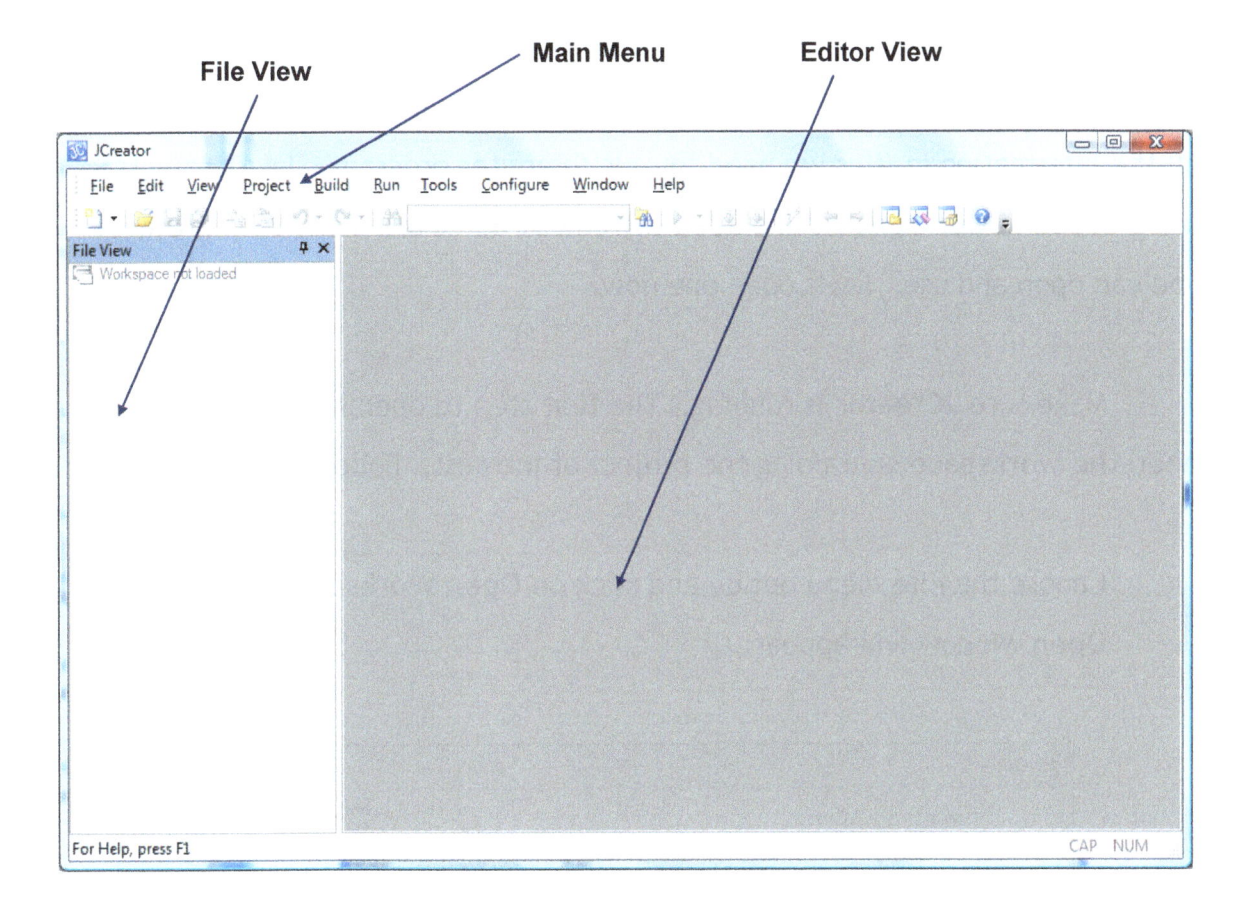

[Screenshot of JCreator IDE with labels pointing to **File View**, **Main Menu**, and **Editor View**]

This screen displays the JCreator **Integrated Development Environment (IDE)**. We will learn a lot more about this IDE in Class 2. Right now, we're just going to use it to test our Java installation and see if we can get a program up and running. Note the location of the **file view** area, **editor view** area and the **main menu**. The file view tells you what Java programs are available, the editor view area is used to view the actual code and the main menu is used to control file access and file editing functions. It is also used to compile and run the program.

Opening a Java Project

What we want to do right now is **open a project**. Computer programs (applications) written using Java are referred to as **projects**. Projects include all the information in **files** we need for our computer program. Java projects are grouped in **workspaces**. Included with these notes are many Java projects you can open and use. Let's open one now.

Make sure **JCreator** is running. The first step to opening a project is to **open the workspace** containing the project of interest. Follow these steps:

Choose the **File** menu option and click on **Open Workspace** option. An **Open** window will appear:

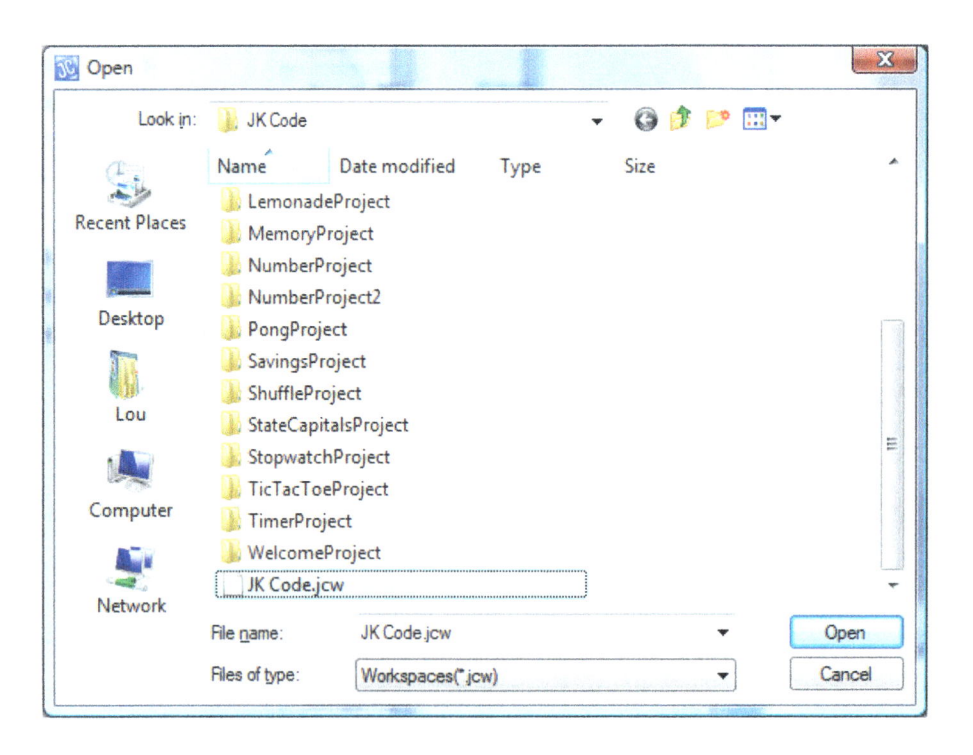

Introducing Java

- All projects in these notes are saved in a workspace named **\JavaKids\JK Code**. Move to that folder and choose the **JK Code** workspace as shown. Click **Open**.

- There will be many projects listed in the file view area in JCreator. Find the project named **WelcomeProject**. Right-click that project name and choose **Sets as Active Project**. Expand the WelcomeProject node by clicking the plus sign. Note there is one file in WelcomeProject named **Welcome.java**. If the file contents do not appear in the editor view area, double-click that file to open it.

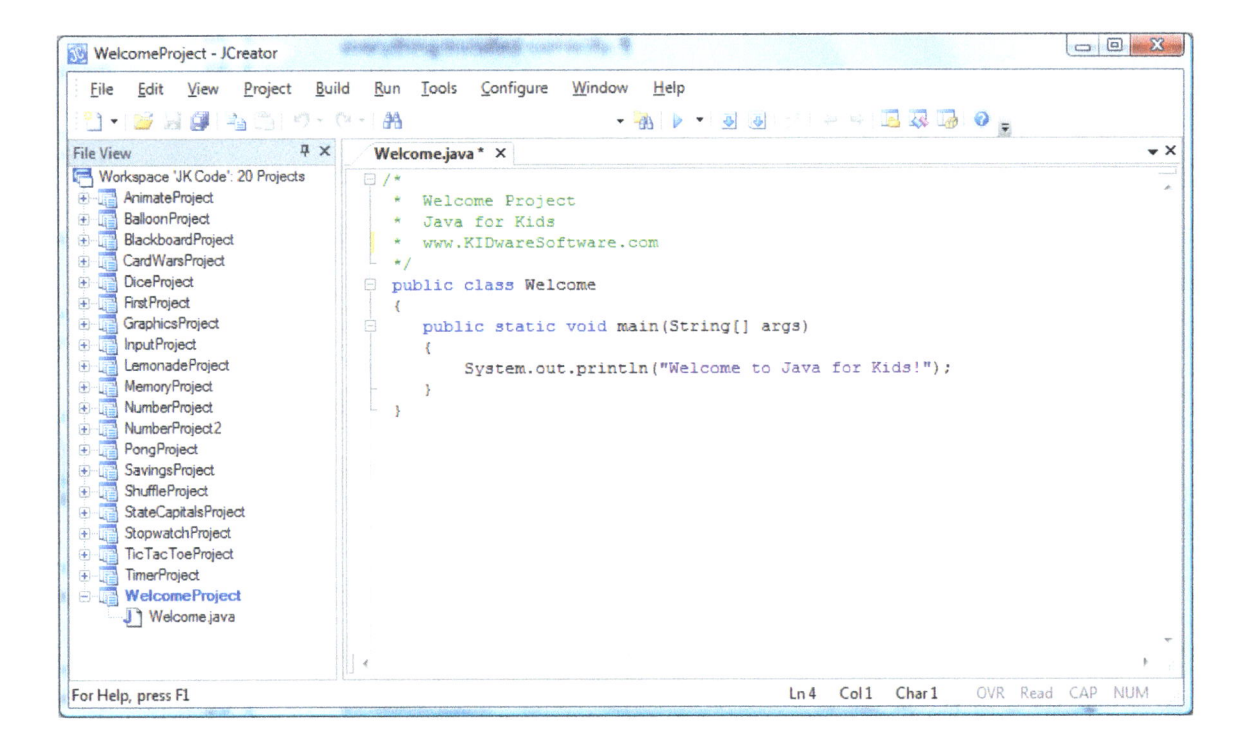

You now finally see your first Java program: We'll learn what these few lines of code do in the next class. Right now, we just want to see if we can get this program running.

Compiling and Running a Java Project

After developing a Java project, you want to start or run the program. There are two steps: **building** (also called **compiling**) and **running**. Again, you'll learn more about what this means in the next class. Right now, we're checking if we have everything installed correctly.

To compile the **Welcome** project, choose **Build** in the main menu and select **Build Project**. Alternately, you can just press the **<F7>** key on your keyboard. A new window should open and you should see:

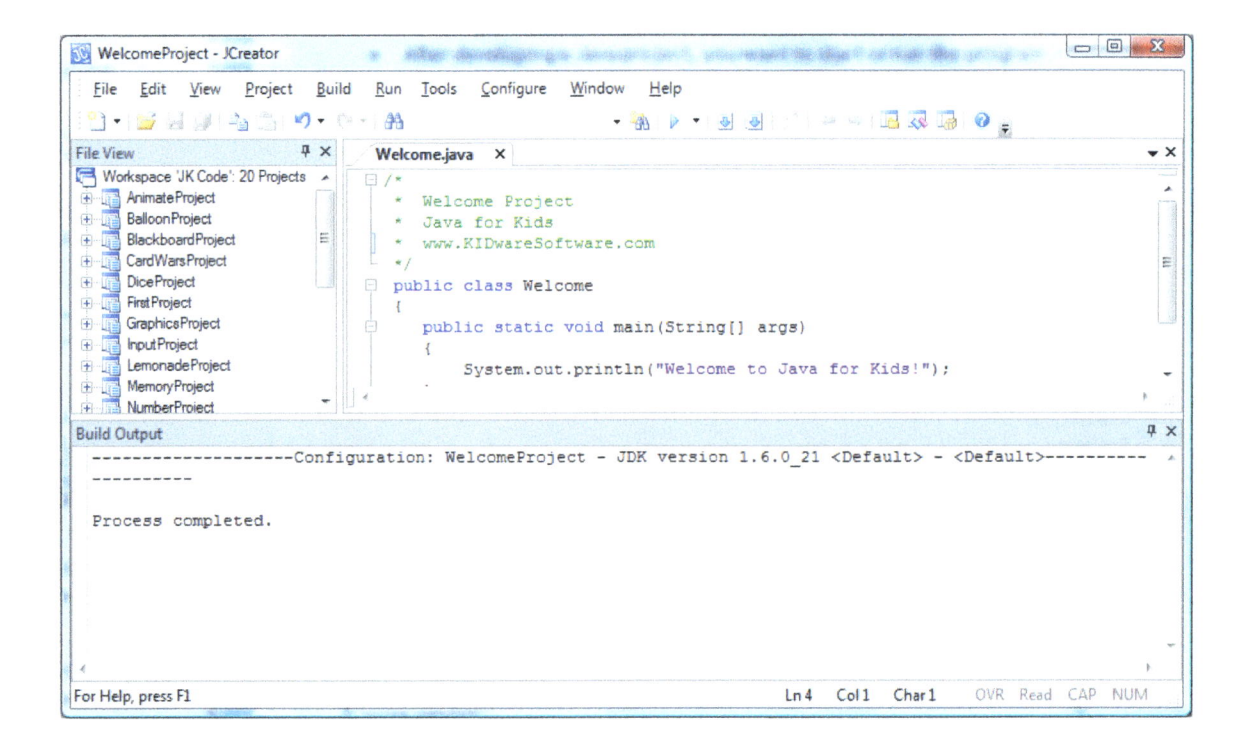

If everything has been installed correctly, the lower window should have the words **Process completed**. This tells us the project has successfully compiled.

If the program does not compile, the most likely problem is JCreator can't find the Java Development Kit. To make sure JCreator knows where the JDK is, try this:

- Click **Configure** in main menu
- Choose **Options**
- Click **JDK Profiles** in **Options** dialog box

In the window should be the directory (Home Path) where you installed Java. If it is not there, choose **New** and follow instructions to point to the correct directory. If it is there and incorrect, select the listed directory and click **Edit**. Make the needed changes.

Are you ready to finally run your first project? To do this, choose **Run** from the menu and select **Run Project** (or alternately press **<F5>** on your keyboard). A **General Output** window should open and you should see the following Welcome message:

```
General Output
-------------------Configuration: WelcomeProject - JDK version 1.6.0_21 <Default> - <Default>----------
----------
Welcome to Java for Kids!

Process completed.
```

If you've gotten this far, everything has been installed correctly. If you don't see the Welcome message, something has not been installed correctly. You should probably go back and review all the steps involved with installing Java and JCreator and make sure all steps were followed properly.

Stopping JCreator

It's been a lot of work just to get to this point. We finally have our first Java project running and now we're just going to stop it and move on. We'll dig into many more details in Class 2.

When you are done working with a Java project, you want to leave the JCreator design environment. It is the same procedure used by nearly all Windows applications:

- Select **File** in the main menu.
- Select **Exit** (at the end of the File menu).

Stop JCreator now. JCreator will close all open windows and you will be returned to the Windows desktop. You may be asked if you would like to save the workspace modifications. Like with stopping a project, an alternate way to stop JCreator is to click on the close button in the upper right hand corner of the main window. It's the button that looks like an **X**.

Java Programming without a Development Environment

We strongly suggest using a development environment (like JCreator) to build and run your Java projects. It will save you lots of effort. However, if you can't or don't want to use JCreator or another IDE, you need to overlook specific references to the development environment in these notes and perform needed programming tasks using a more "barebones" approach.

This alternate approach is covered in detail on the Sun (now Oracle) website for Windows, Linux, and Macintosh machines. The current link for this information is:

http://java.sun.com/docs/books/tutorial/getStarted/cupojava/index.html

The basic approach has three steps: (1) type your code using a text editor, (2) move to the folder holding your program file and compile the file using the **javac** command, (4) run the file using the **java** command.

Creating a Java Project

Your Java projects will be made up of one or more files. We suggest creating a separate folder (directory) for each project you build. Then, edit your program files in a text editor (Notepad or Wordpad for Windows, Pico or VI for Linux or SimpleText for Macintosh) of your choice. Once your source file is done, save it with a **.java** extension in the project folder.

Compiling a Java Project

Compiling a project using Windows and Linux is a very similar process. [Compiling and running a project using the MacOS is a bit different (it involves dragging files to different locations) – see Sun's old website for all the details.] For Windows and Linux, you need to open a prompt window (**command prompt window** for Windows, a **shell window** for Linux). Once, the prompt window is open, change the directory to your project folder. Capitalization usually matters, so use proper case when typing anything.

Say you want to compile the Welcome project we used with JCreator. First move to the proper directory (**\JavaKids\JK Code\WelcomeProject**). Then, to compile the single Java file (**Welcome.java**) in the project file:

javac Welcome.java

If the prompt reappears without any message, the compile was successful. If a message returns, saying it doesn't recognize the command **javac**, recheck that you have followed all instructions for proper installation of Java. On my Windows machine, I see:

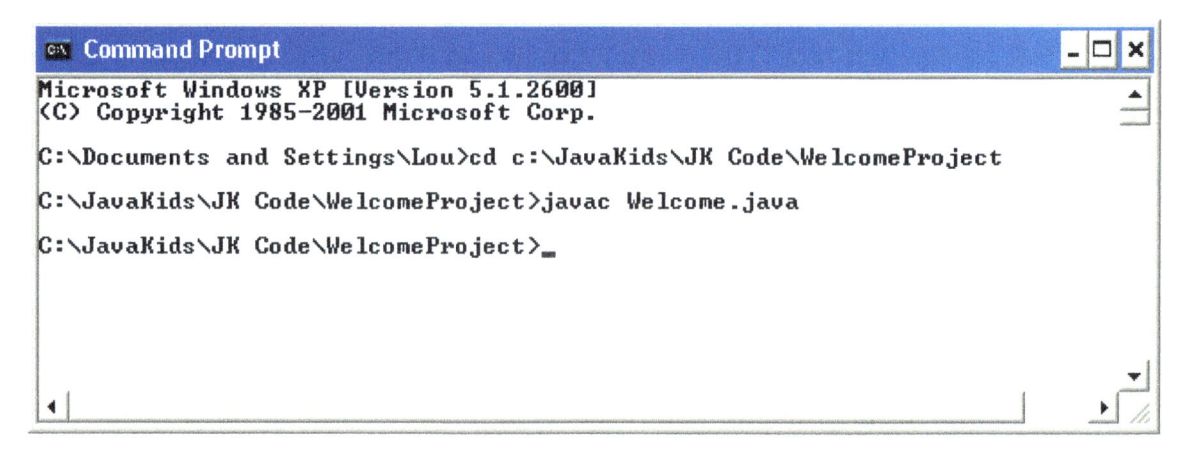

```
Microsoft Windows XP [Version 5.1.2600]
(C) Copyright 1985-2001 Microsoft Corp.

C:\Documents and Settings\Lou>cd c:\JavaKids\JK Code\WelcomeProject

C:\JavaKids\JK Code\WelcomeProject>javac Welcome.java

C:\JavaKids\JK Code\WelcomeProject>_
```

Running a Java Project

At this point, the compiler has created a file named **Welcome.class** in the projects folder. Check the folder – you will see such a file. This is the file you can run. To do this, type:

java Welcome

In my Windows world, I see:

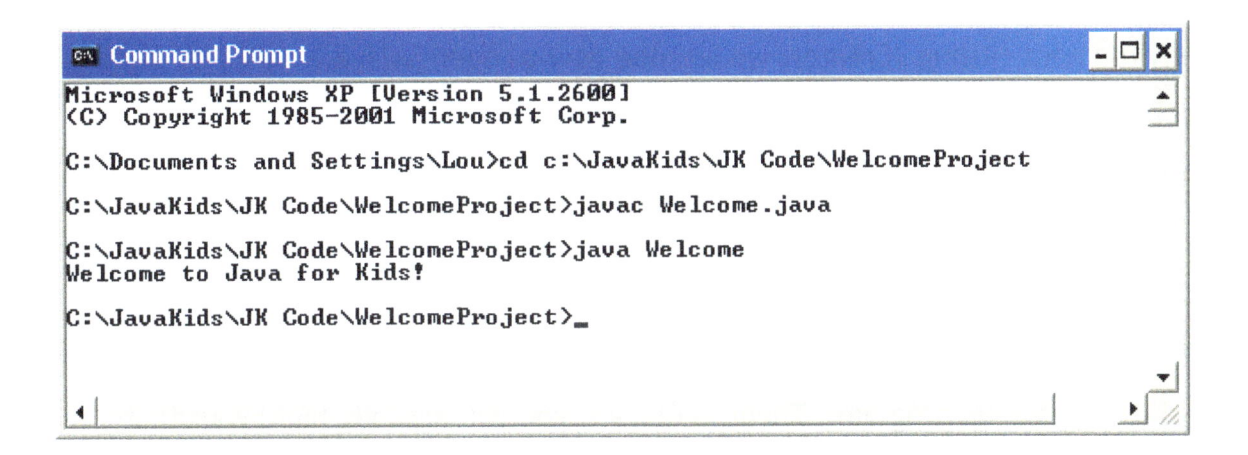

```
Command Prompt

Microsoft Windows XP [Version 5.1.2600]
(C) Copyright 1985-2001 Microsoft Corp.

C:\Documents and Settings\Lou>cd c:\JavaKids\JK Code\WelcomeProject

C:\JavaKids\JK Code\WelcomeProject>javac Welcome.java

C:\JavaKids\JK Code\WelcomeProject>java Welcome
Welcome to Java for Kids!

C:\JavaKids\JK Code\WelcomeProject>_
```

If your project is made up of more than one file, you still follow the same steps for compiling and running (referring to the file with the **main** method) the project. You need to make sure the compiled **class** files for all other files are in the project folder to obtain a successful compilation and running of your project.

Summary

Whew! Are you tired? We covered a lot of new material here, so if you are, that's OK. As we said earlier, you learned a lot of new words and concepts. Don't worry if you don't remember everything we talked about here. You will see the material many times again. It's important that you just have some concept of what goes into a Java project. And you know how to start and stop the JCreator development environment.

In summary, we installed the Java Development Kit and the JCreator environment. Using JCreator, we learned how to open a Java workspace and a corresponding project. We learned how to compile and run a project. In the next class, you will learn (in detail) what each of these steps really means. And, you will begin to acquire the skills that allow you to start building your own Java projects. You will see how the parts of a project fit together. Using the **Welcome** project as an example, you will learn about important concepts related to a Java program. Then, in Class 3, you will actually build your first project!

2. Java Program Basics

Review and Preview

In the first class, we spent all of our time just preparing our computer for creating and running Java programs. In this second class, we will look further into some of the tasks we have done.

We will learn the basic structure of a Java program by reexamining the Welcome Project from Class 1. We will learn some of the basic rules for writing Java programs. We will create and save a project using JCreator, our development environment. And, we will learn just what goes on when you compile and run a Java program. This will give us the skills needed to create our first Java program in Class 3.

Structure of a Java Program

Java, like any language (computer or spoken), has a terminology all its own. Let's look at the structure of a Java program and learn some of this new terminology. A Java program (or project) is made up of a number of files. These files are called **classes**. Each of these files has Java code that performs some specific task(s). Each class file is saved with the file extension **.java**. The filename used to save a class must match the class name. One class in each project will contain something called the **main method**. Whenever you run a Java program, your computer will search for the **main** method to get things started. Hence, to run a program, you refer directly to the class containing this **main** method.

Let's see how this relates to **Welcome Project** we saw in Class 1. Start **JCreator**. Click **JK Code** under **Recent Workspaces**. The Welcome Project should still be the active project. If it isn't, right-click the **WelcomeProject** folder in the file view and choose **Sets as Active Project**. You should see:

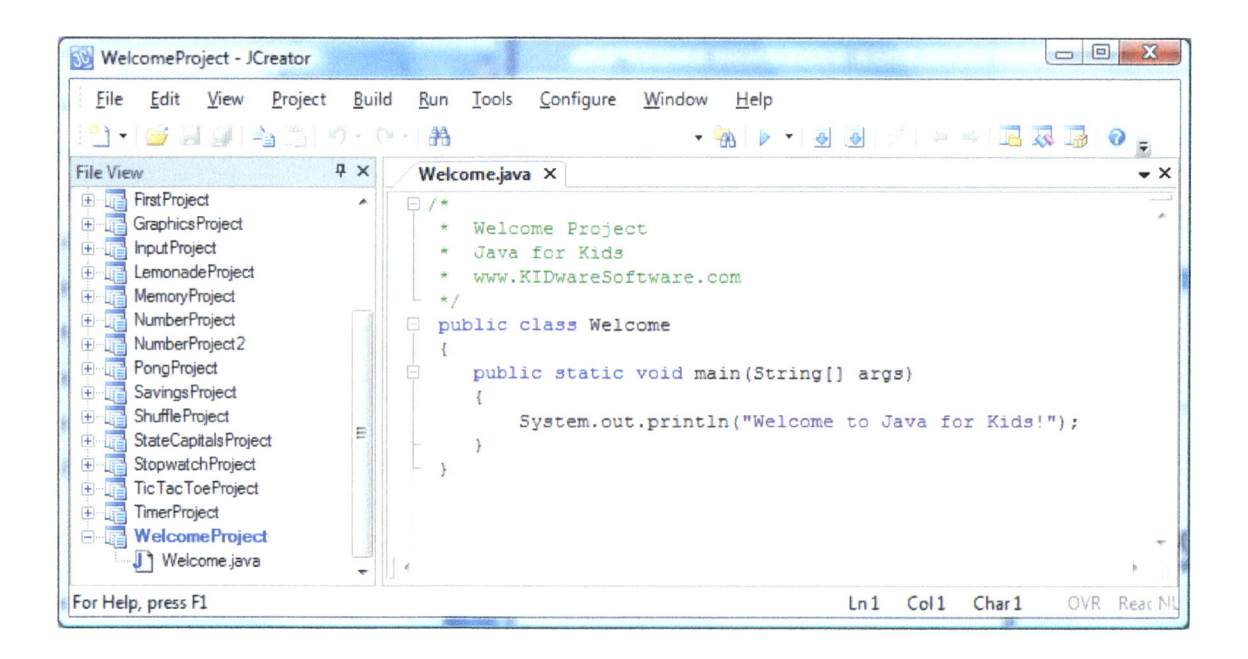

This particular project has a single file named **Welcome.java**. Notice, as required, the name **Welcome** matches the class name seen in the code (public class **Welcome**). If no code is seen, simply double-click on the filename **Welcome.java**. If the project had other classes, they would be listed under the **WelcomeProject** folder. Notice too in the code area the word **main**. This is the **main** method we need in one of the project's classes.

That's really all we need to know about the structure of a Java program. Just remember a **program** (or project, we'll use both terms) is made up of files called **classes** that contain actual Java code. One class is the **main** class where everything starts. And, one more thing to remember is that projects are grouped in **workspaces**. With this knowledge, we can dissect the **Welcome** program line by line to start understanding what Java programming is all about.

The Welcome Project (Revisited)

You should still have **JCreator** running with the **Welcome** program displayed. If not, start JCreator, make **WelcomeProject** your active project (right-click the project name and select **Set as Active Project**) and double-click the **Welcome.java** file. Here's the code you will see:

```
/*
 *  Welcome Project
 *  Java for Kids
 *  www.KIDwareSoftware.com
 */
public class Welcome
{
  public static void main(String[] args)
  {
    System.out.println("Welcome to Java for Kids!");
  }
}
```

Let's go through this code line by line to explain its structure.

Java Program Basics

The first several lines of the program are:

```
/*
 *   Welcome Project
 *   Java for Kids
 *   www.KIDwareSoftware.com
 */
```

These lines are a **comment**. They simply provide some information about what the program is and provides some contact information. The comment begins with the symbol /* and ends with symbol */. These lines are also known as a **program header**. It's a good idea to always put a header on your Java programs to give someone an idea of what your program does and who wrote it. The Java compiler ignores any comments – their only use is provide explanation.

The first non-comment line is:

```
public class Welcome
{
```

This line is the definition of our class named **Welcome**. The keyword **public** determines if other parts of the program can access this class. **Keywords** are part of every programming language – these are reserved words and cannot be used in any regular Java expression. The left curly brace ({) is used to start the definition of the class. You will see lots of curly braces are used in Java!

The next line is:

```
public static void main(String[] args)
{
```

This line creates the **main method** discussed earlier. Don't worry what all the words mean right now. Just notice that this begins the **main** method where we write the Java code we want to execute once the program starts. For most of this course, we will put all of our code in the **main** method. Notice another left curly brace is used to start defining the method.

The single **Java statement** in the **main** method is:

```
System.out.println("Welcome to Java for Kids!");
```

Remember when you ran the Welcome project back in Class 1? When you ran it, you saw a message that said **Welcome to Java for Kids!** in the output window. The above line of code printed that message. In this line, **System** is a class built into Java, **out** is the object of the class (referring to the output window). The word **println** (pronounced print line) displays a single text line. The text to be displayed is in double-quotes. Notice the statement ends with a semicolon (;) - there are lots of semicolons in Java too! In this simple example, the **main** method only has a single statement. Of course, later examples will have many more statements. **Methods** are where Java programs perform tasks. In addition to writing our own methods, you can use any of the many methods built into the Java language. You will learn about such methods as you progress through this course.

Following this line of code are two more lines, each with a right curly brace (}). The first brace ends the **main** method, the second ends the class definition. You will always need to make sure that every time you use a left curly brace in a Java program, that there is a matching right curly brace.

Though this is a very short, very simple program, it illustrates the major components in a Java program. You need a program header, a class definition and a **main** method. And, you need to remember to save the class file with the same name as used in the class definition. That file will have a **.java** extension.

Some Rules of Java Programming

Let's look at the **Welcome** code one more time to point out some basic rules of Java programming. Here's that code:

```
/*
 *  Welcome Project
 *  Java for Kids
 *  www.KIDwareSoftware.com
 */
 public class Welcome
 {
   public static void main(String[] args)
   {
     System.out.println("Welcome to Java for Kids!");
   }
 }
```

And, here's the rules:

- Java code requires perfection. All keywords must be spelled correctly. If you type **printline** instead of **println**, a human may know what you mean, but a computer won't.
- Java is case-sensitive, meaning upper and lower case letters are considered to be different characters. When typing code, make sure you use upper and lower case letters properly. In Java, the words **Main** and **main** are completely different.
- Java ignores any **"white space"** such as blanks. We will often use white space to make our code more readable.
- Curly **braces** are used for grouping. They mark the beginning and end of programming sections. Make sure your Java programs have an equal number of left and right braces. We call the section of code between matching braces a **block**.

- It is good coding practice to **indent** code within a block. This makes code easier to follow. Notice in the example, each block is indented 3 spaces. If you use JCreator, it automatically indents code in blocks for you.
- Every Java statement will end with a semicolon. A **statement** is a program expression that generates some action (for example, the **Println** statement above). Note that not all Java expressions are statements (for example, the line defining the **main** method has no semicolon).

We'll learn a lot more Java programming rules as we progress.

Creating Java Projects with JCreator

In Class 3, we will begin learning the Java language and start writing our own Java programs. In preparation for this, you'll need to know how to create a new project with JCreator. And, you'll need to know how to add files to your project. Let's do that now. What we'll do is re-create the **Welcome** project in your very own workspace. We will put the workspace in a folder named **JKWorkspace**. Create that folder now. If using Windows, you can use **Windows Explorer** or **My Computer** to that task.

If it's not already running, start **JCreator**. The workspace containing the Welcome project should still be there. We are going to remove this workspace and create a new one. (You should only use the **JK Code** workspace when you want to refer to the code included with the class notes. For all your projects, you will use your own workspace). To remove the workspace there, in the file view area, highlight the current workspace (**JK Code**). Choose **File** from the main menu and select **Close Workspace**.

Java Program Basics

Now, create your workspace – we'll name it **MyJavaWorkspace**. Choose **File** from the main menu and select **New**, then **Blank Workspace**. The New Workspace Wizard appears:

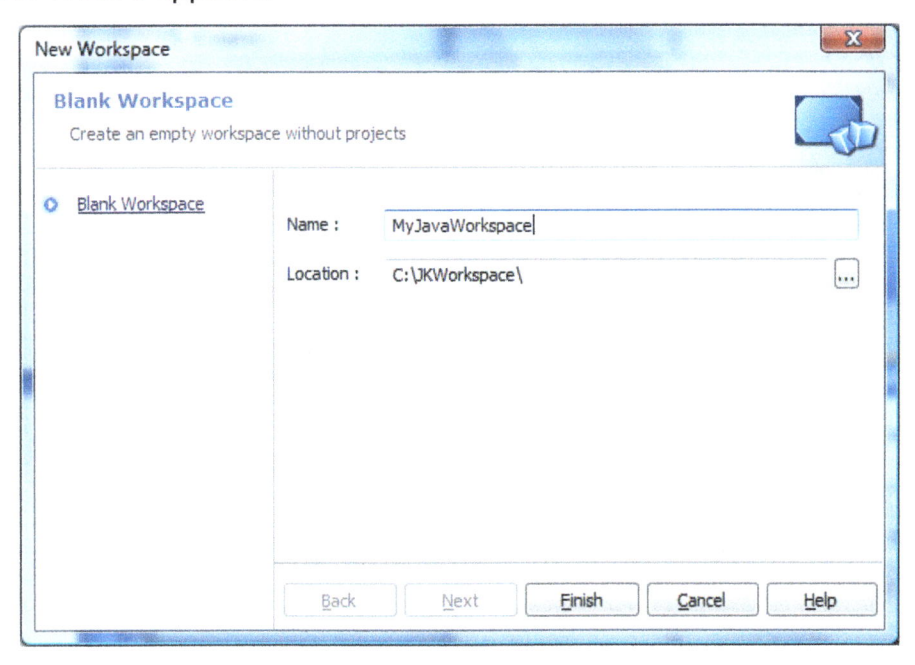

Click the ellipsis (...) next to the **Location** box and browse to the folder (**JKWorkspace** in this example) you want to hold the workspace. Type **MyJavaWorkspace** in the **Name** box as shown. Click **Finish** and the empty workspace will be created in a folder named **JKWorkspace** on your **c:** drive. This new workspace will appear in the file view area of JCreator:

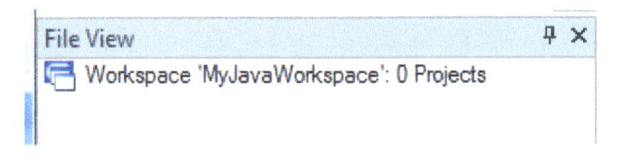

Now, we want to add a project to the workspace. Pay close attention to these steps because you will repeat them every time you need to create a new Java project. Right-click the workspace in the file view and choose **Add new Project** to see:

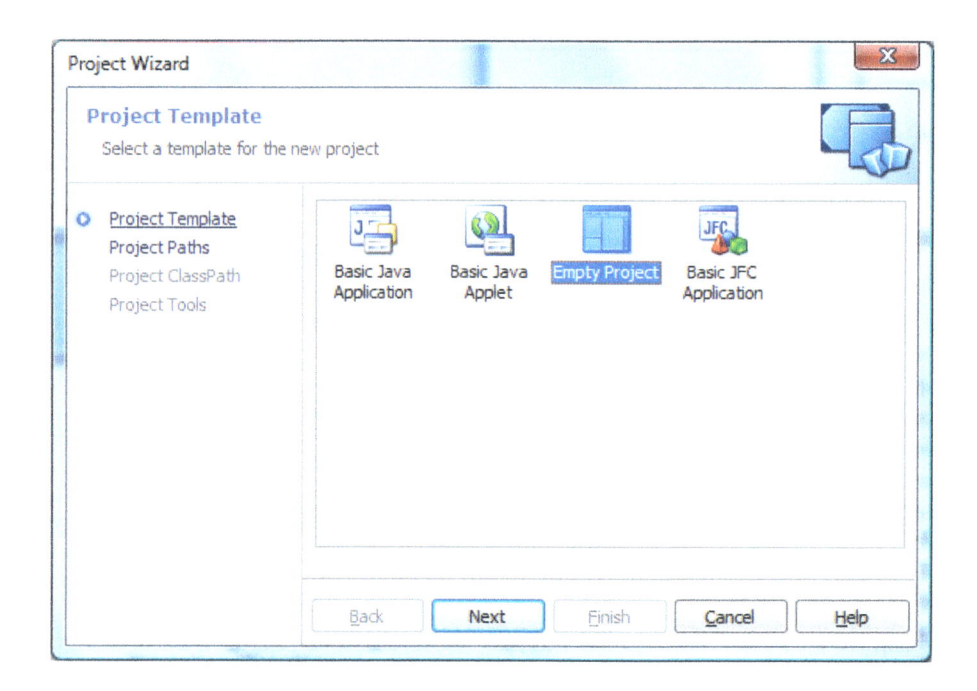

Select **Empty Project** (as shown) and click **Next**.

Java Program Basics

The **Project Paths** window appears:

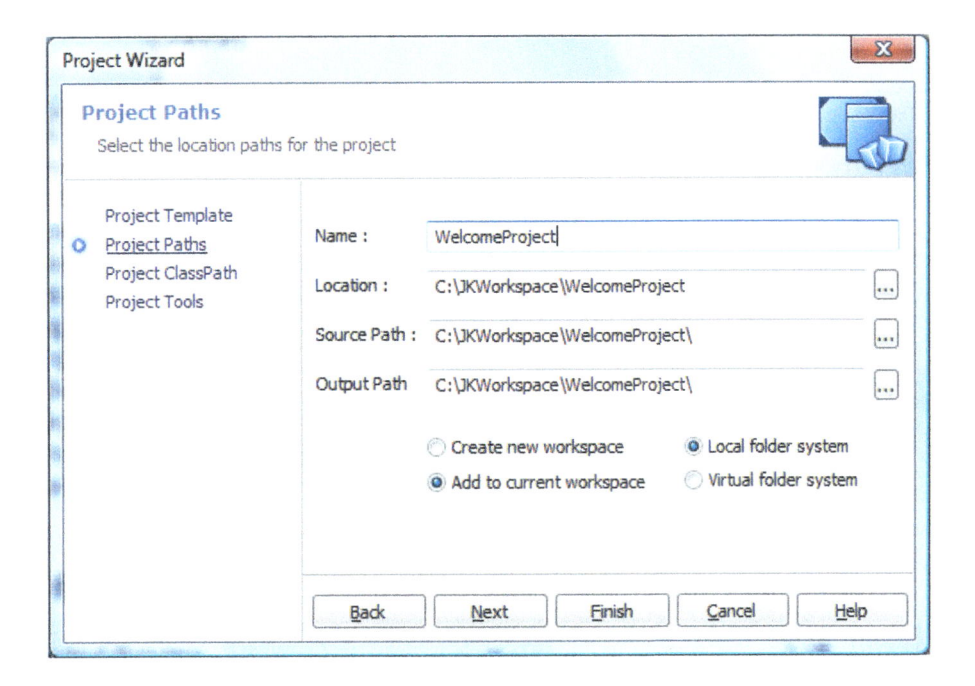

Type **WelcomeProject** in the **Name** box (as shown above). Click **Finish** to create the project. Once created, click **Finish** in the resulting window.

The workspace view window should now show a project (**WelcomeProject**) in the workspace:

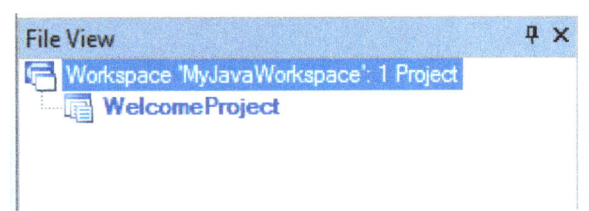

Now, we need to add a file (our Java program file) to the project.

Right-click **WelcomeProject** in the file view. Select **Add** from the drop-down menu, then choose **New File**. This window appears:

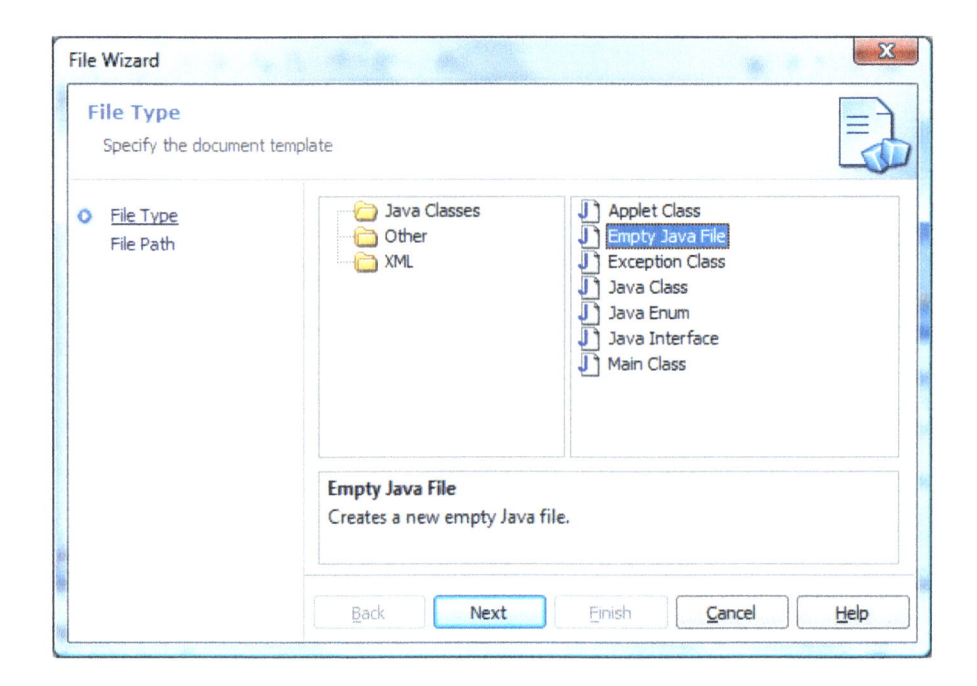

As shown, choose **Empty Java File**, then click **Next**.

The **File Path** window appears:

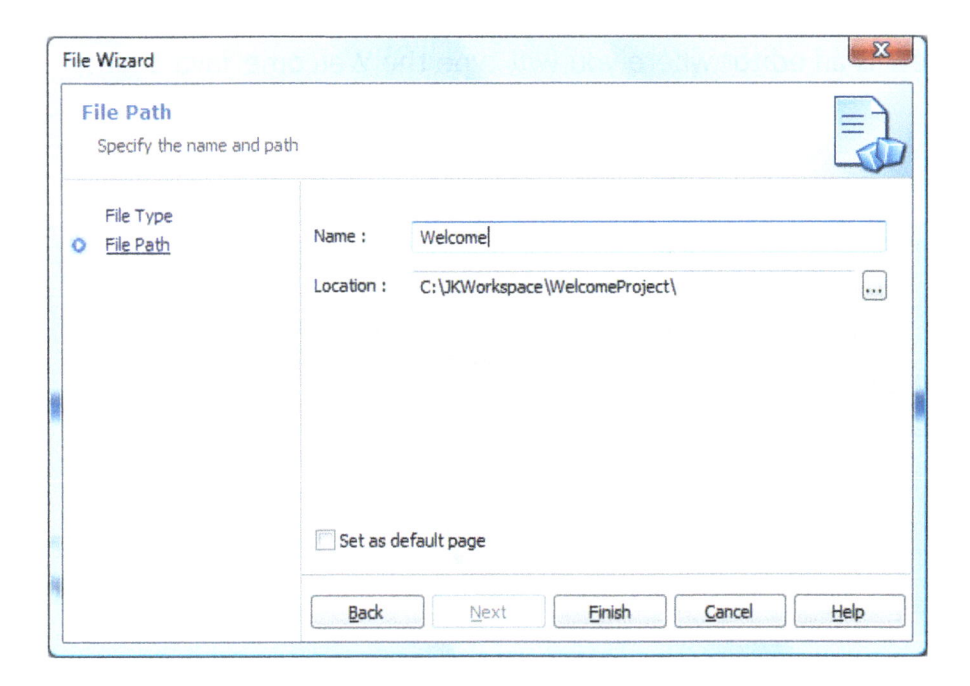

Type **Welcome** in the **Name** box (it is good practice to make sure your file names are different than you project folder and workspace folder names). Click **Finish**.

Expand **WelcomeProject** (click the plus sign) and you will see the file **Welcome.java** is added to the project. In the editor view area to the right of the file view is an editor where you will type the Welcome.java code:

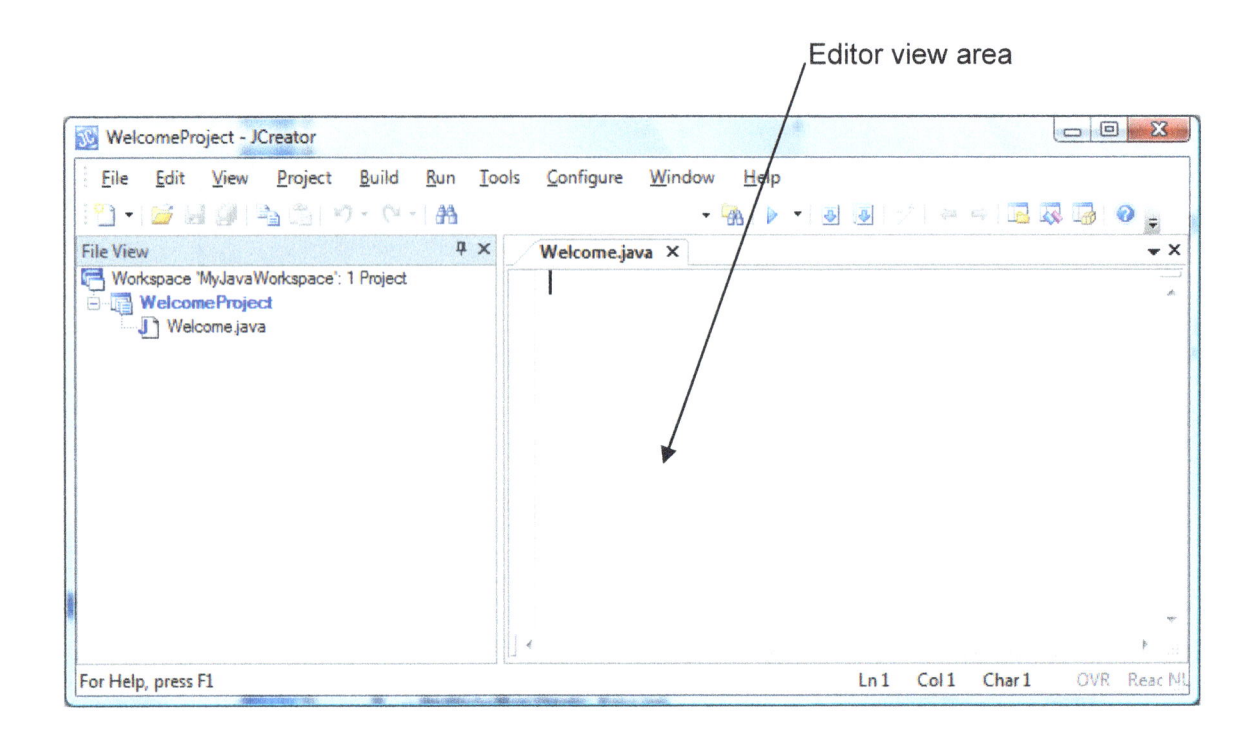

Editor view area

Type one line at a time, paying close attention that you type everything as shown (pay attention to the rules seen earlier). Here, again, is the code:

```java
/*
 *  Java for Kids Welcome Program
 */
public class Welcome
{
  public static void main(String[] args)
  {
    System.out.println("Welcome to Java for Kids!");
  }
}
```

As you type, notice after you type each left brace ({), the JCreator editor automatically adds the matching right brace (}). And, when you hit <**Enter**>, JCreator automatically indents the next line. This follows the rule of indenting each code block. By default, the JCreator indents 4 characters at each level. To change this value, choose **Configure** from the main menu and choose **Options**. Select the **Java Editor** and type a new value for **Tabs Size**. In these notes, we use a value of 2 rather than 4 (just personal preference). Similarly, each time you type a left parenthesis, a matching right parenthesis is added.

In JCreator, the automatic addition of a matching right brace following a left brace can sometimes be a headache, especially when modifying existing code. You decide whether you like the feature or not – we will use it in these notes while writing code. To turn this feature off, follow these steps:

- Select **Configure** from JCreator menu, then **Options**.
- In **Options** window, under **Editor** heading, select **Java**.
- In **Compatibility** frame, remove check next to **Auto insert brackets**.

Reverse the above features to restart automatic brace matching.

Another thing to notice is that the editor uses different colors for different things in the code. Green text represents comments. Code is in black and keywords are in blue. This coloring sometimes helps you identify mistakes you may have made in typing.

When done typing, you should see:

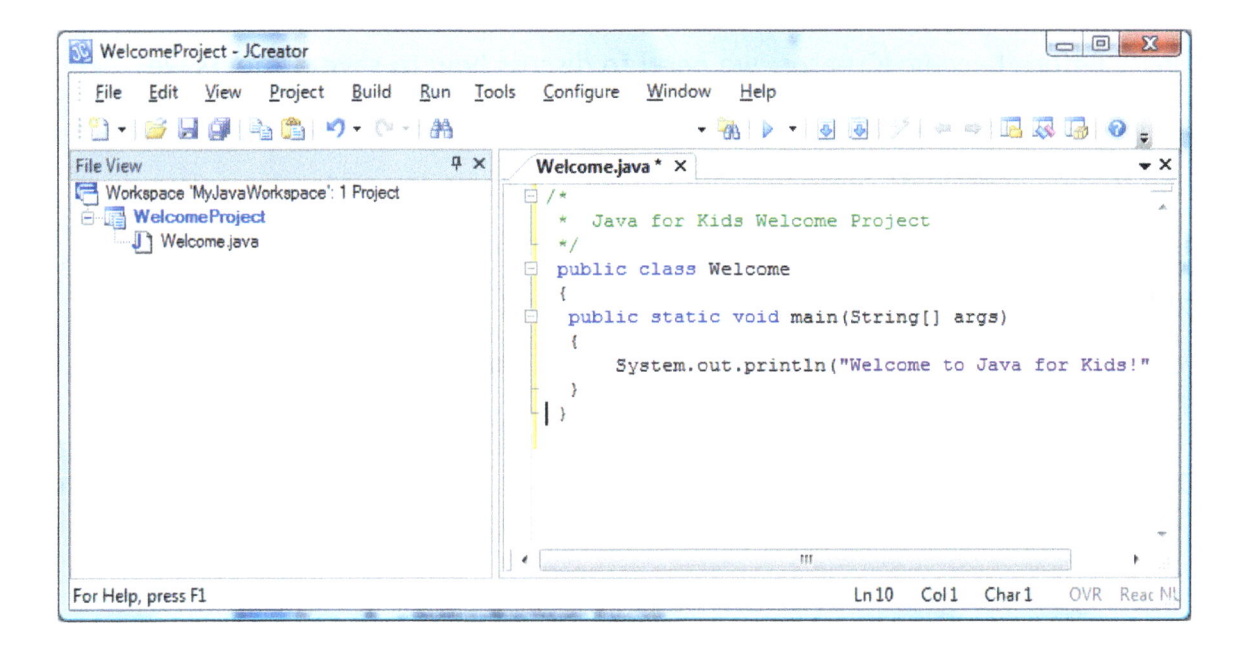

```
/*
 *  Java for Kids Welcome Project
 */
public class Welcome
{
  public static void main(String[] args)
  {
      System.out.println("Welcome to Java for Kids!")
  }
}
```

Try compiling your program (choose **Build**, then click **Build Project**, or press <**F7**>). You should see the words **Process completed** just like you did in Class 1. If you don't, make sure everything is typed exactly as shown above. Remember, no errors can be tolerated.

Once your program compiles, you can run it by choosing **Run**, then **Run Project** (or press <**F5**>). You should once again see the **Welcome to Java for Kids!** message. You should also see that it's really kind of easy to get a Java program going using JCreator.

Saving Java Projects with JCreator

Before leaving JCreator, we need to discuss how to save projects we create. There are two things to consider: saving projects and saving workspaces (the folders containing projects). Whenever you compile and/or run a Java project, JCreator automatically saves both the source files and the compiled code files for you. So, most of the time, you don't need to worry about saving your projects - it's taken care of for you. If you want to save code you are typing (before compiling), simply choose **File** from the main menu and click **Save All**. Or, just click the **Save All** button on the toolbar:

You do need to save the workspace anytime you make a change, for example, if you add/delete files from a project or add/delete projects. To save a workspace, select **File** from the main menu and click **Save Workspace**. If you try to exit JCreator and have not saved projects or workspaces, JCreator will pop up dialog boxes to inform you of such and give you an opportunity to save files before exiting.

Java Program Basics

Compiling and Running a Java Program

In the example we just did, we followed three steps to follow to create and run a Java program:

- **Write** the code
- **Compile** the code
- **Run** the code

We see that writing code involves following the established rules (and we'll actually start writing our own code in Class 3). And, we know how to compile and run a program, but what exactly is going on when we do these two steps. We'll look at that now.

Remember one of the big advantages of Java is that a Java program will run on a variety of machines with no changes in the code. We say that Java is **platform-independent.** This independence is possible because a Java program does not run directly on your computer, but on a 'pretend' computer installed on your computer with the Java Software Development Kit (SDK). This pretend computer is called the **Java virtual machine.** Before the Java virtual machine can understand your Java program, it must be converted or translated into a language it understands. This conversion is done when you compile your Java program. Compiling a Java program creates an **object code** file that the Java Virtual Machine can understand. This file will have a **.class** extension. The compile process is:

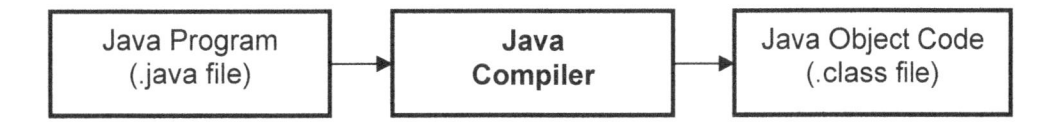

Java Program (.java file) → **Java Compiler** → Java Object Code (.class file)

When you run a Java program, these **.class** files are processed by something called a **Java interpreter** within the virtual machine. This interpreter talks to your computer and translates your Java statements into desired results. It's like magic! The program running process:

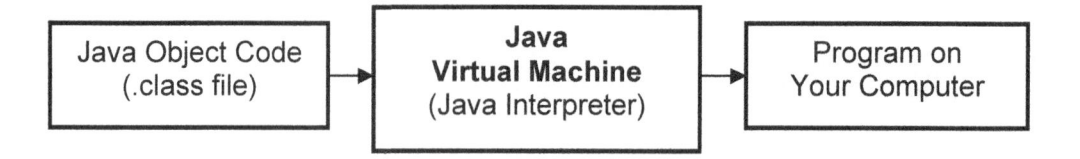

Java Object Code (.class file) → **Java Virtual Machine** (Java Interpreter) → Program on Your Computer

Java Program Basics

JCreator and Java Files

So, how does all this information about program structure, files, compiling and running fit in with JCreator, our development environment. We have seen that Java projects are grouped in workspaces. And projects are made up of **.java** files.

Using My Computer or Windows Explorer (if using Windows), go to the folder containing the **Welcome Project** you just built, compiled and ran. You should see the following files:

Welcome.java
Welcome.class
WelcomeProject.jcp
src_welcomeproject.txt

Welcome.java is the source code that appears in the editor view area of JCreator. **Welcome.class** is the compiled version of Welcome.java (this is the file needed by the Java virtual machine). **WelcomeProject.jcp** is the JCreator project file used to keep track of what files make up the project and **src_welcomeproject.txt** is another JCreator file needed for organization. In addition, in your workspace folder will be some or all of these:

MyJavaWorkspace.jcw
MyJavaWorkspace.jcd
MyJavaWorkspace.jcu

(This assumes you named the workspace MyJavaWorkspace, of course). These are other JCreator files used to keep track of what projects are in the **JK Code** workspace.

Be aware that the only true Java files here are the ones with **.java** and **.class** extensions. The other files are created and modified by our particular development environment, JCreator. If you want to share your Java program with a friend or move your Java program to another development environment, the only files you really need to transfer are the **.java** files. These files can be used by any Java programmer or programming environment to create a running program.

Summary

After all the downloading and installing done in the first class, this second class must have seemed like a breeze. You deserve the break. In this class, we looked at several important concepts that will let us start building our own Java programs.

In this class, we studied the structure of a program, knowing it is built from classes. We learned how to use JCreator to create and run a new Java program. We looked briefly at some of the rules used in writing Java code and we saw just what happens when we compile and run a Java program. In the next class, we finally get started learning the Java language. And, we'll write and run our first Java program.

This page intentionally not left blank.

3. Your First Java Program

Review and Preview

In the first two classes, you've learned about the structure of a Java program, some rules for typing code, and how to compile and run a Java program. Do you have some ideas of projects you would like to build using Java? If so, great. Beginning with this class, you will start to develop your own programming skills. In each class to come, you will learn some new features of the Java language. In this class, you will write your first Java program. To do this, you first need to learn about some of the basic components of the Java language. You will learn about variables, assignment statements and some simple operators.

Creating a Java Program

Recall from Class 2 that a **Java statement** does something. In the **Welcome** example, we saw a statement that printed some information ("Welcome to Java for Kids!"). Each program we build in this class will be made up of many Java statements for the computer to process. Creating a computer program using Java (or any other language) is a straightforward process. You have a particular task you would like the computer to do for you. You tell the computer in a logical, procedural set of steps how to accomplish that task.

It's relatively easy to write out solution steps to a problem in our language (English, in these notes). The difficult part is you have to talk to the computer in its own language. It would be nice if we could just write "Hey computer, here's two numbers – add them together and tell me the sum." A human might understand these instructions, but a computer won't. Why? First, the computer needs to be told how to do tasks in very specific, logical steps. For this little addition example, the steps would be:

1. Give a value to the first number.
2. Give a value to the second number.
3. Add the first number to the second number, resulting in the sum, a third number.
4. Tell me the sum.

Next, we need to talk to the computer in its own language. We translate each solution step into a statement (or statements) in the computer's language. And, in this course, the computer's language is **Java**. To be able to tell the computer how to do any task, you need to have a thorough understanding of the Java language. Your understanding of Java will allow you to translate your programming steps into a language the computer can understand.

Another thing to remember as you write Java programs is that you need to be logical and exact. A computer will follow your instructions – even if they're wrong! So, as you learn Java, we will emphasize the need to be exact. Once you write exact and logical Java code, the computer is very good and fast at doing its job. And, it can do some pretty amazing things. Let's look at a couple of other examples of writing out a programming task as a series of steps to illustrate some things a computer can do.

What if your principal asks you to average the test scores of the 352 students in your school? Those steps are:

1. Determine the score of each student.
2. Add up the 352 scores to get a sum.
3. Divide the sum by 352 to get the average value.
4. Tell your principal the average.

Not too hard, huh? Notice here that the second step can be further broken down into smaller steps. To add up 352 scores, you would:

1. Start with the first score.
2. Add in the second score, then the third score, then the fourth score, etc.
3. Stop when all scores have been added.

In these steps, the computer would do the same task (adding a number) 352 times. Computers are very good at repeating tasks – we will see that this process of repetition is called **looping**. You will build code for this example in Class 7.

Computers are also very good at playing games with you (that's why video games are so popular). Have you ever played the card game "War?" You and another player take a card from a standard playing deck. Whoever has the 'highest' card wins the other player's card. You then each get another card and continue the comparison process until you run out of cards. Whoever has the most cards once the game stops is declared the winner. Playing this game would require steps similar to these:

1. Shuffle a deck of cards.
2. Give a card to the first player.
3. Give a card to the second player.
4. Determine which card is higher and declare a winner.
5. Repeat the process of giving cards to players until you are out of cards.

Things are a bit more complicated here, but the computer is up to the task. The first step requires the computer to shuffle a deck of cards. How do you tell a computer how to do this? Well, before this course is over, you will know how. For now, just know that it's a series of several programming steps. We will put the Java program for such a specific task in its own area called a **method** (similar to the **main** method seen in our little **Welcome** example). This makes the program a little easier to follow and also allows use this code in other programs, an advantage of **object-oriented programming**. Notice Step 4 requires the computer to make a **decision** - determining which card is higher. Computers are very good at making decisions. Finally, Step 5 asks us to repeat the handing out of cards - another example of **looping**. You will also build this program in Class 7.

If all of these concepts are not clear at the moment, that's okay. They will become clearer as you progress through this course. I just wanted you to have some idea of what you can do with Java programs. Just remember, for every Java program you create, it is best to first write down a series of logical steps you want the computer to follow in performing the tasks needed by your program. Then, converting those steps into the Java language will give you your Java program - it's really that simple. This class begins instruction in the elements of Java. And, in subsequent classes, you learn more and more Java, adding to your Java vocabulary. We'll start slow. By the end of this course, you should be pretty good at "talking Java."

Java - The First Lesson

At long last, we are ready to get into the heart of a Java project - the Java language. In this class, we will discuss variables (name, type, declaring), assignments, arithmetic operations, and techniques for working with a particular type of variable called strings. In each subsequent class in this course, you will learn something new about the Java language.

Variables

All computer programs work with information of one kind or another. Numbers, text, dates and pictures are typical types of information they work with. Computer programs need places to store this information while working with it. What if we need to know how much ten bananas cost if they are 25 cents each? We would need a place to store the number of bananas, the cost of each banana, and the result of multiplying these two numbers together. To store such information, we use something called **variables**. They are called variables because the information stored there can change, or vary, during program execution. Variables are the primary method for moving information around in a Java project. And, certain rules must be followed in the use of variables.

Variable Names

You must **name** every variable you use in your project. Rules for naming variables are:

- Can only use letters, numbers, and the underscore (_) character (though the underscore character is rarely used).
- The first character must be a letter.
- You cannot use a word reserved by Java (for example, you can't have a variable named **println** or one named **System**).

By convention, variable names begin with a lowercase letter. If a variable name consists of more than one word, the words are joined together, and each word after the first begins with an uppercase letter.

The most important rule is to use variable names that are meaningful. You should be able to identify the information stored in a variable by looking at its name. As an example, in our banana buying example, good names would be:

Quantity	Variable Name
Cost of each banana	bananaCost
Number of bananas purchased	numberBananas
Cost of all bananas	totalBananaCost

Notice the convention of beginning the variable name with a lower case letter and using upper case for each subsequent word in the name.

Variable Types

We need to know the **type** of information stored by each variable. Does it contain a number? Does the number have a decimal point? Does it just contain text information? Let's look at some variable types.

The first variable type is the **int** type. This type of variable is used to represent whole, non-decimal, numbers. Examples of such numbers are:

$$1 \quad -20 \quad 4000$$

Notice you write 4,000 as 4000 in Java – we can't use commas in large numbers. In our banana example, **numberBananas** would an **int** type variable.

What if the variable you want to use will have decimal points. In this course, such variables will be of **double** type. In techno-talk, we say such variables are double-precision, floating point numbers (the decimal point being the thing that "floats"). All you need to know about **double** type variables is that they are numbers with decimal points. Examples of such numbers:

$$-1.25 \quad 3.14159 \quad 22.7$$

In our banana example, the variables **bananaCost** and **totalBananaCost** would be **double** type variables.

Another variable type used all the time in Java programming is the **boolean** type. It takes its name from a famous mathematician (Boole). It can have one of two values: **true** or **false**. We will see that such variables are at the heart of the computer's decision making capability. If wanted to know if a banana was rotten, we could name a **boolean** variable **isBananaRotten**. If this was true, the banana is indeed rotten.

The next variable "type" we use is not really a type at all. More correctly, it is a Java class – the **String** class (the fact it begins with an upper case letter, rather than lower case indicates it is a class). A **String** variable is just that – one that stores a string (list) of various characters. A string can be a name, a string of numbers, a sentence, a paragraph, any characters at all. And, many times, a string will contain no characters at all (an empty string). We will use lots of strings in Java, so it's something you should become familiar with. Strings are always enclosed in quotes ("). Examples of strings:

"I am a Java programmer"   "012345"   "Title   Author"

Declaring Variables

Once we have named a variable and determined what type we want it to be, we must relay this information to our Java project. We need to **declare** our variables. The Java statement used to declare a variable named **variableName** as type **type** is:

```
type variableName;
```

Don't forget the semicolon (;) – every Java statement ends with one. We need a declaration statement like this for every variable in our project. This may seem like a lot of work, but it is worth it. Proper variable declaration makes programming easier, minimizes the possibility of program errors, and makes later program modification easier.

So, where do we put variable declarations? In our first several projects, we will only be writing code within the **main method** of a Java project. So, variable declarations will be placed after the line defining the **main** method. This gives the variables **local scope**, meaning they are available only in the method they are defined in. This level of scope is fine for our first few projects. Examples of variable declarations:

```
int numberBananas;
double bananaCost;
double totalBananaCost;
boolean isBananaRotten;
String myBananaDescription;
```

Notice the **int**, **double** and **boolean** declarations are lower case letters, **String** is upper case.

Java allows you to declare several variables of the same type on a single line by separating the variable names with commas. For example, we could combine two of the above declarations (for the **double** variables) into:

```
double bananaCost, totalBananaCost;
```

In a **main** method of a Java program, these variable declarations would appear at the top:

```
public static void main(String[] args)
{
   int numberBananas;
   double bananaCost, totalBananaCost;
   boolean isBananaRotten;
   String myBananaDescription;

      [Rest of main method]

}
```

Now, let's look at how to assign values to variables.

Assignment Statement

The simplest, and most widely used, statement in Java is the **assignment** statement. Such a statement appears as:

`variableName = variableValue;`

Note that only a single variable can be on the left side of the assignment operator (=). Some simple assignment examples using our "banana" variables:

```
numberOfBananas = 22;
bananaCost = 0.27;
isBananaRotten = false;
myBananaDescription = "Yes, we have no bananas!";
```

The actual values assigned to variables here are called **literals**, since they literally show you their values.

You may recognize the assignment operator as the equal sign you use in arithmetic, but it's not called an equal sign in computer programming. Why is that? Actually, the right side (**variableValue** in this example) of the assignment operator is not limited to literals. Any legal Java expression, with any number of variables or other values, can be on the right side of the operator. In such a case, Java computes **variableValue** first, then assigns that result to **variableName**. This is an important programming concept to remember – "compute the right side, assign to the left side." Also important to remember is that if the **type** of **variableValue** does not match the **type** of **variableName**, Java will convert (if it can) **variableValue** to the correct type. For example, if **variableName** is of type **int** (an integer) and **variableValue** is computed to be **25.6**, **variableName** will have the value of **25** (chopping off the decimal portion). Let's start looking at some operators that help in evaluating Java expressions.

Arithmetic Operators

One thing computer programs are very good at is doing arithmetic. They can add, subtract, multiply, and divide numbers very quickly. We need to know how to make our Java projects do arithmetic. There are five **arithmetic operators** we will use from the Java language.

Addition is done using the plus (+) sign and **subtraction** is done using the minus (-) sign. Simple examples are:

Operation	Example	Result
Addition	7 + 2	9
Addition	3 + 8	11
Subtraction	6 - 4	2
Subtraction	11 - 7	4

Multiplication is done using the asterisk (*) and **division** is done using the slash (/). Simple examples are:

Operation	Example	Result
Multiplication	8 * 4	32
Multiplication	2 * 12	24
Division	12 / 2	6
Division	42 / 6	7

I'm sure you've done addition, subtraction, multiplication, and division before and understand how each operation works. The other arithmetic operator may not familiar to you, though.

The other arithmetic operator we use is called the remainder operator (%). This operator gives you the remainder that results from dividing two whole numbers. It may not be obvious now, but the remainder operator is used a lot in computer programming. Examples:

Example	Division Result	Remainder Result
7 % 4	1 Remainder 3	3
14 % 3	4 Remainder 2	2
25 % 5	5 Remainder 0	0

Study these examples so you understand how the remainder operator works in Java.

What happens if an assignment statement contains more than one arithmetic operator? Does it make any difference? Look at this example:

7 + 3 * 4

What's the answer? Well, it depends. If you work left to right and add 7 and 3 first, then multiply by 4, the answer is 40. If you multiply 3 times 4 first, then add 7, the answer is 19. Confusing? Well, yes. But, Java takes away the possibility of such confusion by having rules of **precedence**. This means there is a specific order in which arithmetic operations will be performed. That order is:

1. Multiplication (*) and division (/)
2. Remainder (%)
3. Addition (+) and subtraction (-)

So, in an assignment statement, all multiplications and divisions are done first, then remainder operations, and lastly, additions and subtractions. In our example (7 + 3 * 4), we see the multiplication will be done before the addition, so the answer provided by Java would be 19.

If two operators have the same precedence level, for example, multiplication and division, the operations are done left to right in the assignment statement. For example:

24 / 2 * 3

The division (24 / 2) is done first yielding a 12, then the multiplication (12 * 3), so the answer is 36. But what if we want to do the multiplication before the division - can that be done? Yes - using the Java **grouping operators** - parentheses **()**. By using parentheses in an assignment statement, you force operations within the parentheses to be done first. So, if we rewrite our example as:

24 / (2 * 3)

the multiplication (2 * 3) will be done first yielding 6, then the division (24 / 6), yielding the desired result of 4. You can use as many parentheses as you want, but make sure they are always in pairs - every left parenthesis needs a right parenthesis. If you nest parentheses, that is have one set inside another, evaluation will start with the innermost set of parentheses and move outward. For example, look at:

((2 + 4) * 6) + 7

The addition of 2 and 4 is done first, yielding a 6, which is multiplied by 6, yielding 36. This result is then added to 7, with the final answer being 43. You might also want to use parentheses even if they don't change precedence. Many times, they are used just to clarify what is going on in an assignment statement.

As you improve your programming skills, make sure you know how each of the arithmetic operators work, what the precedence order is, and how to use parentheses. Always double-check your assignment statements to make sure they are providing the results you want.

Some examples of Java assignment statements with arithmetic operators:

```
totalBananaCost = numberBananas * bananaCost;
numberOfWeeks = numberOfDays / 7;
averageScore = (score1 + score2 + score3) / 3.0;
```

Notice a couple of things here. First, notice the parentheses in the **averageScore** calculation forces Java to add the three scores before dividing by 3. Also, notice the use of "white space," spaces separating operators from variables. This is a common practice in Java that helps code be more readable. We'll see lots and lots of examples of assignment statements as we build projects in this course.

String Concatenation

We can apply arithmetic operators to numerical variables (type **int** and type **double**). String variables can also be operated on. Many times in Java projects, you want to take a string variable from one place and 'tack it on the end' of another string. The fancy word for this is **string concatenation**. The concatenation operator is a plus sign (+) and it is easy to use. As an example:

```
newString = "Java for Kids " + "is Fun!";
```

After this statement, the string variable **newString** will have the value "Java for Kids is Fun!".

Notice the string concatenation operator is identical to the addition operator. We always need to insure there is no confusion when using both. String variables are a big part of Java. As you develop as a programmer, you need to become comfortable with strings and working with them.

Comments

You should always follow proper programming rules when writing your Java code. One such rule is to properly comment your code. You can place non-executable statements (ignored by the computer) in your code that explain what you are doing. These **comments** can be an aid in understanding your code. They also make future changes to your code much easier.

To place a comment in your code, use the comment symbol, two forward slashes (//). Anything written after the comment symbol will be ignored by the computer. You can have a comment take up a complete line of Java code like:

```
// Set number of bananas
numberBananas = 14;
```

Or, you can place the comment on the same line as the assignment statement:

```
numberBananas = 14; // Set number of bananas
```

You can also have a multiple line comment. Start the comment with the symbol (/*) and end it with the symbol (*/):

```
/*
  This is a very long comment
  Taking up two entire lines!!
*/
```

You, as the programmer, should decide how much you want to comment your code. We will try in the projects provided in this course to provide adequate comments.

Program Output

You're almost ready to create your first Java program. But, we need one more thing. We have ways to name and declare variables and ways to do math with them, but once we have results, how can those results be displayed? In this class, we will use the method seen in our little Welcome program, the Java **println** (recall, you pronounce it "print line") method. What this method does is print a string result on a single line:

```
System.out.println(stringValue);
```

In this expression, **stringValue** could be a **String** variable that has been evaluated somewhere (perhaps using the concatenation operator) or a literal (an actual value). In the **Welcome** example, we used a literal:

```
System.out.println("Welcome to Java for Kids!");
```

And saw that **Welcome to Java for Kids!** was output to the screen.

What if you want to output numeric information? It's really quite easy. The **println** method will automatically convert a numeric value to a string for output purposes. For example, look at this little code segment:

```
numberBananas = 45;
System.out.println(numberBananas);
```

If you run this code, a **45** will appear on the output window.

You can also combine text information with numeric information using the concatenation operator. For example:

```
numberBananas = 45;
System.out.println("Number of Bananas is " + numberBananas);
```

will print **Number of Bananas is 45** on the output screen. The numeric data (**numberOfBananas**) is converted to a string before it is concatenated with the text data

So, it's pretty easy to output text and numeric information. Be aware one slight problem could occasionally arise though. Recall the concatenation operator is identical to the arithmetic addition operator. Look at this little segment of code:

```
numberBananas = 32;
numberApples = 22;
System.out.println("Pieces of fruit " + numberBananas + numberApples);
```

You might think you are printing out the total number of fruit (**numberBananas + numberApples = 54**) with this statement. However, if you run this code, you will get **Pieces of fruit 3222**. What happens is that Java converts both pieces of numeric data to a string before the addition can be done. Then, the plus sign separating them acts as a concatenation operator yielding the 3222. To print the sum, we need to force the numeric addition by using parentheses:

```
numberBananas = 32;
numberApples = 22;
System.out.println("Pieces of fruit " + (numberBananas + numberApples));
```

In this case, the two numeric values are summed before being converted to a string and you will obtain the desired output of **Pieces of fruit 54**. So, we see the **println** method offers an easy-to-use way to output both text and numeric information, but it must be used correctly.

Notice one other thing about this example. The last line of code looks like it's two lines long! This is solely because of the word wrap feature of the word processor being used. In an actual Java program, this line will appear as, and should be typed as, one single line. Always be aware of this possibility when reading these notes. Let's build a project.

Your First Java Program   3-23

Project – Sub Sandwich Party

Your school class has decided to have a party. Two very long submarine sandwiches are being delivered and it is your job to figure out how much each student can eat. Sure, you could do this with a calculator, but let's use Java!! This project is saved as **FirstProject** in the course projects folder (**\JavaKids\JK Code**).

Project Design

Assume you know the length of each submarine sandwich. To make the cutting easy, we will say that each student will get a whole number of inches (or centimeters) of sandwich (no decimals). With this information, you can compute how many students can be fed from each sandwich. If the total number is more than the students you have in your class, everyone eats and things are good. If not, you may have to make adjustments. The program steps would be:

1. Set a value for the number of inches a student can eat.
2. Determine length of both sandwiches.
3. Determine how many students can eat from each sandwich.
4. Increase or decrease the number of inches until the entire class can eat.

Let's translate each of these steps into Java code as we build the project. Since this is your first project, we'll review many steps (creating a new project and adding a file) and we'll type and discuss the code one or two lines at a time.

Project Development

Start **JCreator** and make sure your workspace (**MyJavaWorkspace**) is opened. The **WelcomeProject** should be there. If your workspace is not there, click **File**, then **Open Workspace** to open it. Create a new project:

- Click **File**
- Choose **New**
- Choose **Project.**
- In **Project Template** window, select **Empty Project**, click **Next**.
- Name it: **FirstProject**

Your JCreator window should now appear as:

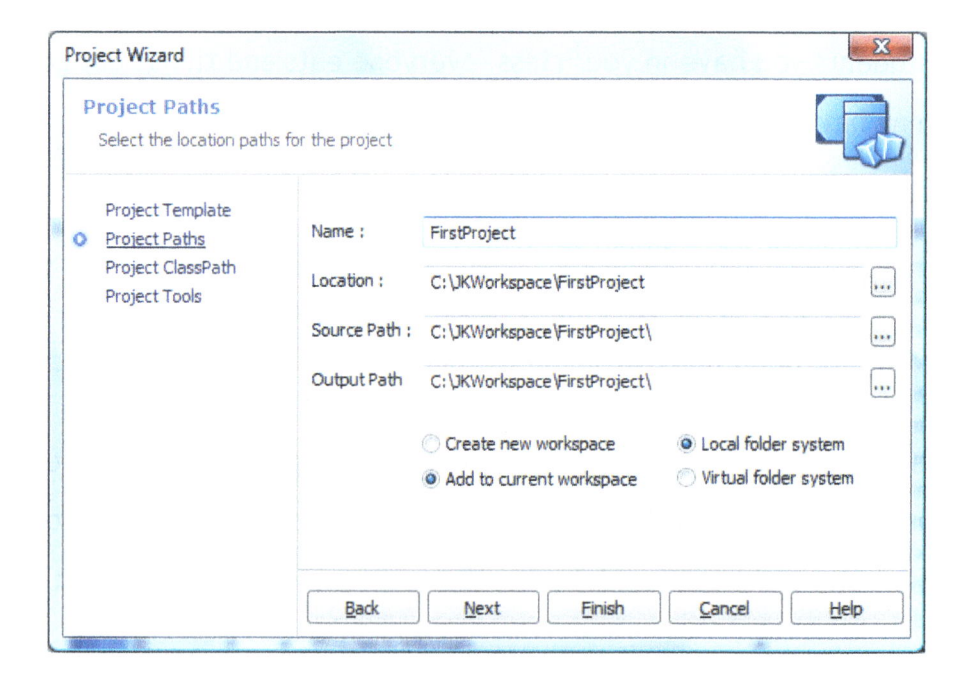

Your First Java Program

Click **Finish** in this window and the next. Right-click **FirstProject** in file view and select **Sets as Active Project**.

Add a file to your project:

- Click **File**
- Choose **New**
- Choose **File**
- In **File Type** window, select **Empty Java File**, click **Next**.
- Name it: **SubSandwich**

Your JCreator window should now appear as:

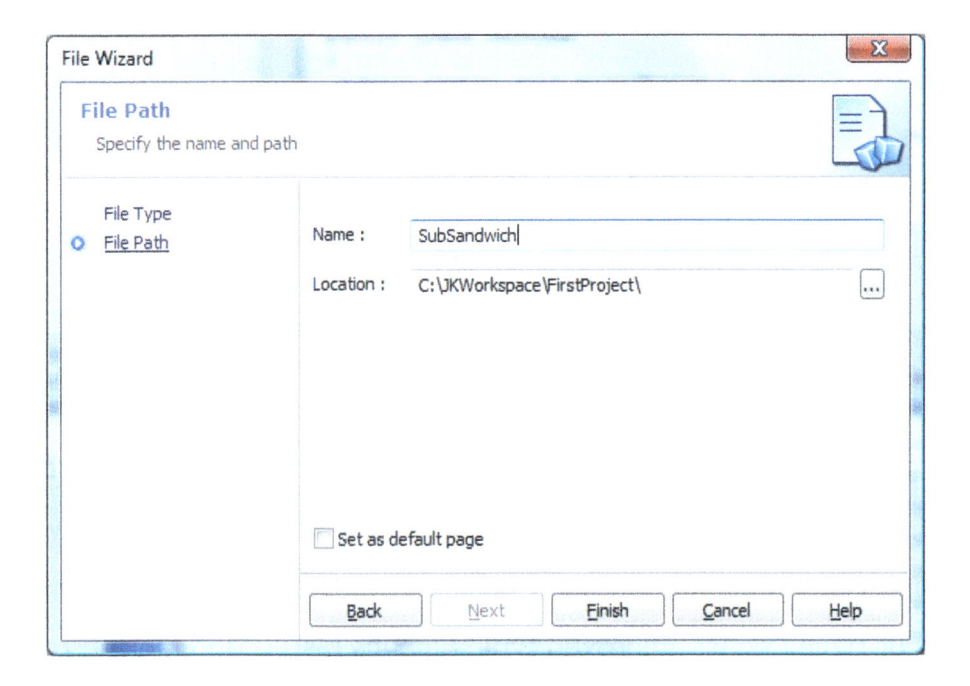

Click **Finish** and an empty file should appear in the editor view area. This is where we'll type our code.

First, type the following header information as a multi-line comment:

```
/*
 *   Sub Sandwich Project
 *   Java for Kids
 */
```

Now, type the class definition line and the opening left brace ({) - a right brace (}) will be added. Recall braces are used to define code blocks:

```
public class SubSandwich
{
}
```

Now, between the braces of the **SubSandwich** class, type the **main** method definition and its opening brace (a closing brace will be added). New code is shaded:

```
public class SubSandwich
{
  public static void main(String[] args)
  {
  }
}
```

Note, as you type new code blocks, JCreator indents the corresponding blocks. Make sure you type each line exactly as shown. There's lot of typing involved with computer programming - it might be useful to take a typing course to improve your typing skills. Improved typing means faster, and more error free, Java programs.

Your First Java Program

Now, you're ready to start typing the actual Java code. We will use five variables in this program: one for how much each student can eat, two for the sandwich lengths, and two for how many students can eat from each sandwich. These will all be integer (**int**) variables. <u>Between</u> the braces in the main method, type their declarations (make sure to end each declaration with a semicolon):

```
int inchesPerStudent;
int lengthSandwich1, lengthSandwich2;
int students1, students2;
```

Set values for some of the variables (also include a comment about what you are doing):

```
// set values
inchesPerStudent = 5;
lengthSandwich1 = 114;
lengthSandwich2 = 93;
```

These are just values we made up, you can use anything you like. Notice we assume each student can eat 5 inches of sandwich.

Next, we compute how many students can eat from each sandwich using simple division:

```
// determine how many students can eat each sandwich
students1 = lengthSandwich1 / inchesPerStudent;
students2 = lengthSandwich2 / inchesPerStudent;
```

Notice **students1** and **students2** will be (as desired) whole (integer) numbers. Display the results using the **println** method:

```
// print results
System.out.println("Letting each student eat " +
inchesPerStudent + " inches");
System.out.println((students1 + students2) + " students can
eat these two sandwiches!");
```

Notice how each of the string concatenations works. Notice, too, that we sum the number of students before printing it. Note the program finishes with two closing right braces (}), one to close the method and one to close the class:

The finished code in JCreator should look like this:

```java
/*
 *  Sub Sandwich Project
 *  Java for Kids
 */
public class SubSandwich
{
  public static void main(String[] args)
  {
    int inchesPerStudent;
    int lengthSandwich1, lengthSandwich2;
    int students1, students2;

    // set values
    inchesPerStudent = 5;
    lengthSandwich1 = 114;
    lengthSandwich2 = 93;

    // determine how many students can eat each sandwich
    students1 = lengthSandwich1 / inchesPerStudent;
    students2 = lengthSandwich2 / inchesPerStudent;

    // print results
    System.out.println("Letting each student eat " +
inchesPerStudent + " inches");
    System.out.println((students1 + students2) + " students
can eat these two sandwiches!");

  }
}
```

Double-check to make sure each line is typed properly.

Run the Project

Save your project (click the **Save All** toolbar button). Compile your code by pressing <**F7**>, or choose **Build** from the main menu and click **Build Project**. You should receive a **Process completed** message. If you don't, any error message that appears will help to point out a typing mistake. Again, double-check to make sure your code is exact – no missing semicolons, no missing quotes and no upper/lower case letter disagreements.

Once your code compiles, run it by pressing <**F5**>, or choose **Run**, then **Run Project**. The output window should show that 40 students can eat from this particular set of sandwiches:

```
General Output
   --------------------Configuration: FirstProject - JDK version
   -----------
   Letting each student eat 5 inches
   40 students can eat these two sandwiches!

   Process completed.
```

Congratulations – you have written your very first Java program!!

Other Things to Try

For each project in this course, we will offer suggestions for changes you can make and try. In this above run, we saw 40 students can eat. What if you need to feed more or less? Adjust the **inchesPerStudent** variable and determine the numbers of students who can eat for each value. After each adjustment, you will need to recompile and rerun the program. Assume the sandwiches cost so much per inch. Modify the program so it also computes the cost of the sandwiches. Determine how much each student would have to contribute to pay for their lunch. You might want to use **double** type variables to add decimal points. Give it a try!

Since we require each student to eat an integral (whole) number of inches, there might be leftover amounts in each sandwich. Can you figure out how to compute this amount? It's a neat little application of the remainder operator we saw in this class. There are just a couple of code modifications. First, define a variable that computes the leftover amount:

```
int inchesLeftOver;
```

Now, the code that computes that value:

```
// compute leftovers
inchesLeftOver = lengthSandwich1 % inchesPerStudent +
lengthSandwich2 % inchesPerStudent;
System.out.println("There are " + inchesLeftOver + " inches
left over.");
```

Add this code to your project, recompile and rerun. Do you see that there are a total of 7 inches remaining? Can you see why in computing **inchesLeftOver**, we just don't add both sandwiches length together before using the remainder operator?

Summary

Again, congratulations are due for completing your first Java project. You learned a lot about the Java statements and assignments and how to do a little bit of arithmetic. You should be comfortable with starting a new project with JCreator. In subsequent classes, we'll learn a little more Java and write increasingly more detailed Java projects.

This page intentionally not left blank.

4. Java Project Design, Input Methods

Review and Preview

You should now be fairly comfortable with creating, compiling and running simple Java projects. In this class, we continue learning new Java topics to expand our programming knowledge.

We'll look at some project design ideas, some new ways to declare variables, some mathematical functions and at ways to get input from users of your programs. And, we'll build a savings calculator project.

Project Design

You are about to start developing fairly detailed projects using Java. We will give you projects to build and maybe you will have ideas for your own projects. Either way, it's fun and exciting to see ideas end up as computer programs. But before starting a project, it's a good idea to spend a little time thinking about what you are trying to do. This idea of proper **project design** will save you lots of time and result in a far better project.

Proper project design is not really difficult. The main idea is to create a project that is easy to use, easy to understand, and free of errors. That makes sense, doesn't it? Spend some time thinking about everything you want your project to do. What information does the program need? What information does the computer determine? Decide what programming steps you need to follow to accomplish desired tasks.

Make the Java code in your methods readable and easy to understand. This will make the job of making later changes (and you will make changes) much easier. Follow accepted programming rules - you will learn these rules as you learn more about Java. Make sure there are no errors in your project. This may seem like an obvious statement, but many programs are not error-free.

The importance of these few statements about project design might not make a lot of sense right now, but they will. The simple idea is to make a useful, clearly written, error-free project that is easy to use and easy to change. Planning carefully and planning ahead helps you achieve this goal. For each project built in this course, we will attempt to give you some insight into the project design process. We will always try to explain why we do what we do in building a project. And, we will always try to list all the considerations we make.

One other consideration in project design is to always build your project in stages. Don't try to build your entire Java program and test it all at once. This just compounds the possibility of errors. We suggest always building your program in stages. Write a little code. Compile and test that little bit of code making sure it works correctly. Slowly add more and more code. Compile and test each code addition. Continue this approach until your program is complete. You will find that this "go slow" approach to creating a Java project will make your programming task much simpler. Give it a try in projects we build.

Java - The Second Lesson

We covered a lot of Java in the last class. This was necessary to introduce you to many basic concepts so you could write your first project. In this briefer second lesson, we look at a way to initialize variables and some mathematical functions.

Variable Initialization

In Class 3, we discussed the need to declare every variable used in a Java program. The general statement used to declare a variable is:

```
type variableName;
```

Here we say the variable **variableName** has been declared as type **type**. The types of variables we look at were **int** (whole numbers), **double** (decimal numbers), **boolean** (true or false values) and **String** variables. Some examples of variable declarations are:

```
int numberLightBulbsPerPack;
int numberPacks;
double costOfPack;
boolean anyBurnedOut;
String myQuestion;
```

When you declare a variable, it is assigned some location in your computer's memory and given whatever value happens to be at that memory location (some unpredictable value). Many times, this is sufficient, as long as you remember to assign a useful value to the variable at some point in your code. There are times you may want to assign an initial value to a variable when you declare it. It is actually pretty good programming practice to do such an initialization, if you happen to know the value (many times you won't). And, there will be times when Java will insist you initialize variables. In these cases, it is a simple extension of the declaration above to provide such initialization:

```
type variableName = variableValue;
```

In this declaration and initialization statement, a variable named **variableName** of type **type** is created and assigned an initial value of **variableValue**. Make sure the value assigned is of proper type. You cannot assign a decimal value to an integer variable! These statements are place along with the usual declarations at the top of a method to provide **local scope**.

Some examples of declaring and initializing variables in a Java program:

```
int numberLightBulbsPerPack = 8;
int numberPacks = 7;
double costOfPack = 2.45;
boolean anyBurnedOut = false;
String myQuestion = "How many Java programmers does it take
to change a light bulb?";
```

You should see how easy it is to use such statements. You, as a programmer, will need to decide when you want to initialize variables and when you don't.

Mathematical Functions

In Class 3, we saw the Java arithmetic operators that allow us to perform the basics of addition, subtraction, multiplication and division. Like other computer programming languages, Java also has the capability of doing very power mathematical computations. Java's built-in mathematical **functions** (also called **methods**) are often used in these computations.

We don't expect you to be a mathematical genius to work through these notes, so we will only look at three mathematical functions. First, just what is a **function**? A function is a routine that computes some value for you, given some information. The format for using a function is:

```
functionValue = functionName(argumentList);
```

functionName is the name of the function and **argumentList** is a list of values (**arguments**, separated by commas) provided to the function so it can do its work. In this assignment statement, **functionName** uses the values in **argumentList** to compute a result and assign that result to the variable we have named **functionValue**. We must insure the variable **functionValue** has the same type as the value computed by **functionName**.

How do you know what Java mathematical functions exist, what type of information they provide and what the arguments are? Check various Java references and the Sun Java website. As mentioned, we will look at three mathematical functions here. The methods that support mathematical functions are implemented in the Java class named **Math**. Hence, to refer to a particular function, you write **Math**, then a period, then the function name.

Java Project Design, Input Methods

The first function we examine is the **absolute value** function. In math, the absolute value is the positive part of a number. The Java function is:

`Math.abs(argument)`

where **argument** is number we want the absolute value of. The argument can be either an **int** or **double** type and the returned value will be the same type as the argument. Some examples:

Example	Result
`Math.abs(7)`	7
`Math.abs(-11)`	11
`Math.abs(-3.14)`	3.14
`Math.abs(72.1)`	72.1

Have you ever needed the **square root** of a number? A square root is a number that when multiplied by itself gives you the original number. For example, the square root of 4 is 2, since 2 times 2 is four. There's a button on your calculator (√) that will do this for you. In Java, the square root function is:

`Math.sqrt(argument)`

where **argument** is number we want the square root of. The argument must be a non-negative **double** number and the returned value is a **double**. Some examples:

Example	Result
`Math.sqrt(4.0)`	2.0
`Math.sqrt(36.0)`	6.0
`Math.sqrt(72.1)`	8.491

Java Project Design, Input Methods

The last function we will use in this class is the **exponentiation** method. In exponentiation, a number is multiplied times itself a certain number of times. If we multiply a number by itself 4 times, we say we raise that number to the 4th power. The Java function used for exponentiation is:

`Math.pow(argument1, argument2)`

Notice the **pow** (stands for power) function has two arguments. **argument1** is the number we are multiplying times itself **argument2** times. In other words, this function raises argument1 to the argument2 power. Each argument and the returned value are **double** type numbers. Some examples:

Example	Result
`Math.pow(4.0, 2.0)`	16.0
`Math.pow(-3.0, 3.0)`	-27.0
`Math.pow(10.0, 4.0)`	10000.0

In each example here, the arguments have no decimal parts. We have done this to make the examples clear. You are not limited to such values. It is possible to use this function to compute what happens if you multiply 7.654 times itself 3.16 times!! (The answer is 620.99, by the way.)

For the more mathematically inclined reader, you should know that there are many more Java functions available for your use. You might want to look into using them. There are trigonometric functions and inverse trig functions, functions to convert from radians to degrees and vice versa, functions to find extreme values, functions for rounding, logarithm and inverse logarithm functions and built-in values for pi and e. (If none of this means anything to you, don't worry – we won't be using them in this class).

Program Input Methods

In the example (Sub Sandwich Project) we built in the last class, we established variable values in code and ran the program to see the results. The results were printed by the Java output method **println**. If we want to use different values, we need to change the code, recompile and rerun. This is a pain! It would be nice, in such a program, to allow a user to type in values while the program is running and have the computer do the computations based on the inputs. This way no code changes or recompiling would be needed to get a new answer. We need such capabilities in our programs.

Java has several methods for input. These methods use the Java **Scanner** object. This object is not built into the basic Java language. It is stored in something called a Java API Package. Don't worry what this means – all you need to know is that we need to tell our program that we will be using something from the API Package named **java.util.Scanner**. To do this, we use an **import** statement:

```
import java.util.Scanner;
```

This statement goes <u>before</u> our program's class definition header. The class must be imported before anything else is done in the program.

Now, to use the **Scanner** object, it is first created using the object **constructor**:

```
Scanner myScanner = new Scanner(Program.in);
```

This statement is placed at the top of the main method. Once this is created, we can obtain user inputs using:

    `myScanner.nextInt()`   inputs an integer (**int**) number
    `myScanner.nextDouble()`   inputs a decimal (**double**) number
    `myScanner.nextLine()`   inputs a string (**String**) value

Each of these statements is usually preceded by a prompt asking the user for a particular input. Once the prompt appears, the user types the requested input and presses the **<Enter>** key to have the computer accept the value. Let's look at an example.

Say you have a program where you would like to know the user's age. Two lines of Java code that accomplish this task are:

```
System.out.print("What is your age? ");
ageUser = myScanner.nextInt();
```

For the prompt, we use a **print** statement instead of the **println** statement we have been using. What's the difference? The **println** statement starts a new line after printing, the **print** statement does not.

When this bit of code is run, the user will see the prompt message in the output window:

What is your age?

The user types an integer value and presses <**Enter**>. At this point, the input value is assigned to the variable **ageUser**. The **nextInt** method insures the user types only an integer value. Using the other two methods, **nextDouble** and **nextLine**, is similar. Let's work through an example to use each of the input methods.

Input Methods Example

Start JCreator, open the **MyJavaWorkspace** and follow the usual steps to create a new project named **InputProject**. Make **InputProject** the active project. Refer back to the **Sub Sandwich** project in Class 3 for steps in creating a project, if you need to. Add a file named **InputTest** to the project. This is the file where we will write our code to test the input routines.

Type the usual header information, the import statement for the **Scanner** object, the class definition and the main method definition:

```
/*
 *   Input Project
 *   Java for Kids
 */
import java.util.Scanner;

public class InputTest
{
  public static void main(String[] args)
  {
  }
}
```

In the main method (between the two braces), type this code to establish the **Scanner** object and to get a user's age:

```
Scanner myScanner = new Scanner(System.in);
int ageUser;
System.out.print("What is your age? ");
ageUser = myScanner.nextInt();
System.out.println("You typed " + ageUser);
```

The finished code should look like this in the JCreator file view area:

```java
/*
 *  Input Project
 *  Java for Kids
 */
import java.util.Scanner;

public class InputTest
{
  public static void main(String[] args)
  {
    Scanner myScanner = new Scanner(System.in);
    int ageUser;
    System.out.print("What is your age? ");
    ageUser = myScanner.nextInt();
    System.out.println("You typed " + ageUser);
  }
}
```

Compile the project (press <**F7**>). If the program does not compile, make sure your code is typed exactly as shown.

Run the project (press <**F5**>). You should see:

```
General Output
    --------------------Configuration: InputProject - JDK version 1.6.
    What is your age?
```

Notice how the prompt appears.

Java Project Design, Input Methods

Type in a value and press <**Enter**>. You should see:

```
General Output
    --------------------Configuration: InputProject - JDK version 1.6
What is your age? 14
You typed 14

Process completed.
```

The **nextInt** routine is working!!

Let's test the **nextDouble** method. Add a new variable declaration:

```
double myDouble;
```

After the code asking for the user's age, add these lines:

```
System.out.print("Type in a decimal number ");
myDouble = myScanner.nextDouble();
System.out.println("You entered " + myDouble);
```

Recompile and rerun. Enter your age when asked and you will see:

```
General Output
    --------------------Configuration: InputProject - JDK version 1.6.
What is your age? 14
You typed 14
Type in a decimal number
```

Type a value and press <**Enter**>. You will see your entry "mirrored" back to you:

```
General Output
--------------------Configuration: InputProject - JDK version 1.6.
What is your age? 14
You typed 14
Type in a decimal number 3.1415926
You entered 3.1415926

Process completed.
```

Finally, to test **nextLine** (for string input), add this variable declaration:

```
String myString;
```

and add these lines of code:

```
System.out.print("Type in some string ");
myString = myScanner.nextLine();
System.out.println("You entered " + myString);
```

Compile and run the program again. Type your age and type a decimal number. Look what happens:

```
General Output
--------------------Configuration: InputProject - JDK version 1.6.
What is your age? 14
You typed 14
Type in a decimal number 3.1415926
You entered 3.1415926
Type in some string You entered

Process completed.
```

The string input prompt appears, but you don't get a chance to type anything!

Java Project Design, Input Methods   4-17

The noted problem will occur any time the **nextLine** method is preceded by a **nextDouble** (or any kind of numeric input). Why? When a number is typed and you press <**Enter**>, there is still a new line character hanging around in that line of input. When the **nextLine** method is invoked, it reads this new line character as a string input and continues. To keep this from happening, we just put an extra **nextLine** method in the code to 'strip off' the straggling new line character. Then the subsequent **nextLine** method will get the string input you really want. Notice we only have to do this when a **nextLine** is preceded by a numeric input of some kind.

Add the shaded line to your 'string input' code:

```java
System.out.print("Type in some string ");
myScanner.nextLine();
myString = myScanner.nextLine();
System.out.println("You entered " + myString);
```

This line will read the new line character left after reading in the decimal number. Now, compile and run again. Enter an age and a decimal number. Now, the program is properly waiting for a string input:

```
General Output
    -------------------Configuration: InputProject - JDK version 1.6
    What is your age? 14
    You typed 14
    Type in a decimal number 3.1415926
    You entered 3.1415926
    Type in some string |
```

Type in a string and press <**Enter**>. Here's my output:

```
General Output
---------------------Configuration: InputProject - JDK version 1.6.
What is your age? 14
You typed 14
Type in a decimal number 3.1415926
You entered 3.1415926
Type in some string Java is fun!!
You entered Java is fun!!

Process completed.
```

It seems all the input methods are working just fine. Did you notice how building a project in stages (adding a few lines of code at a time) is good? Always follow such a procedure. As mentioned, we will use the **Scanner** object and its input methods in almost every application built in this class, so become familiar with its use. You may want to refer back to this example several times. This project has been saved as **InputProject** in the course projects folder (**\JavaKids\JK Code**).

Before leaving this example and building another project, let's take a quick look at one other useful Java concept. In the output window above, it would be nice if there was a blank line between each input request. This just makes your output appear a little cleaner, a quality of a well designed Java project. One way to insert a blank line in the output is to just use a **println** method with no argument:

```
System.out.println();
```

This can become a hassle if you need many blank lines.

An easier approach is to use the Java escape sequence for a new line (**\n**). You simply insert this two character sequence in any string output by **println**. Whenever the character is encountered, a new line is started. For example,

```
System.out.println("This is a line\n");
```

will print a blank line after printing **This is a line** on the output screen. Conversely,

```
System.out.println("\nThis is a line");
```

will print a blank line before printing **This is a line** on the output screen. You'll find the new line escape sequence (**\n**) will come in very handy.

Project - Savings Calculator

In this project, we will build a savings account calculator. We will input how much money we can put into an account each week and the number of weeks we put money in the account. The project will then compute how much we saved. This project is saved as **SavingsProject** in the course projects folder (**\JavaKids\JK Code**).

Project Design

The steps needed to do this calculation are relatively simple:

1. Obtain an amount for each week's deposit.
2. Obtain a number of weeks.
3. Multiply the two input numbers together.
4. Output the product, the total savings.

We will use the **Scanner** object input methods to get user input. The **println** method will be used to output the savings amount. We'll throw in an additional step to ask for the user's name (an example of using the **nextLine** method).

Java Project Design, Input Methods

Project Development

Start JCreator, open your workspace and create a new project named **SavingsProject**. Add a blank file named **Savings** (the .java extension will be added). Refer to the **Sub Sandwich** project in Class 3 if you need to review the steps to create a new project.

Open the empty **Savings.java** file. First, type the following header information, the needed import statement, the class definition line and the main method definition (along with needed braces):

```
/*
 *  Savings Project
 *  Java for Kids
 *  www.KIDwareSoftware.com
 */
import java.util.Scanner;
public class Savings
{
  public static void main(String[] args)
  {
  }
}
```

We will use four variables in this program: one for the user's name, one for the deposit amount, one for the number of weeks and one for the total amount. Type their declarations next (in the **main** method; also create the **Scanner** object):

```
Scanner myScanner = new Scanner(System.in);
// declare and initialize variables
String yourName;
double deposit = 0.0;
int weeks = 0;
double total = 0.0;
```

Now, we start the code, using the steps outlined under **Project Design**. At any time, after typing some code, you might like to stop, compile and run just to see if things are going okay. That is always a good approach to take. First, ask the user his/her name using this code:

```
// ask user name
System.out.print("Hello, what is your name? ");
yourName = myScanner.nextLine();
```

Notice **yourName** is a **String** type. Next, determine how much will be deposited in the savings account each week:

```
// get deposit amount
System.out.print("\nHow much will you deposit each week? ");
deposit = myScanner.nextDouble();
```

The deposit amount is a **double** type. Notice the use of the new line escape sequence (**\n**) to skip a line before printing the prompt. Finally, obtain the number of weeks, an **int** value:

```
// get number of weeks
System.out.print("For how many weeks? ");
weeks = myScanner.nextInt();
```

With this information, the total deposit can be computed and displayed using a **println** method:

```
// compute and display total
total = deposit * weeks;
System.out.println("\n" + yourName + ", after " + weeks + " weeks, you will have $" + total + " in your savings.\n");
```

Save your project by clicking the **Save All** button.

The finished code in the JCreator view window should appear as:

```java
/*
 *   Savings Project
 *   Java for Kids
 *   www.KIDwareSoftware.com
 */
import java.util.Scanner;
public class Savings
{
  public static void main(String[] args)
  {
    Scanner myScanner = new Scanner(System.in);
    // declare and initialize variables
    String yourName;
    double deposit = 0.0;
    int weeks = 0;
    double total = 0.0;

    // ask user name
    System.out.print("Hello, what is your name? ");
 yourName = myScanner.nextLine();

    // get deposit amount
    System.out.print("\nHow much will you deposit each week? ");
    deposit = myScanner.nextDouble();

    // get number of weeks
    System.out.print("For how many weeks? ");
    weeks = myScanner.nextInt();

    // compute and display total
    total = deposit * weeks;
    System.out.println("\n" + yourName + ", after " + weeks + " weeks, you will have $" + total + " in your savings.\n");
  }
}
```

Run the Project

Compile and run your project. If the project does not compile successfully, try to find out where your errors are using any error messages that may appear. We will cover some possible errors in the next class.

When the program runs successfully, you will see:

```
General Output
--------------------Configuration: SavingsProject - JDK version 1.6.
Hello, what is your name?
```

Type in your name, a deposit amount and a number of weeks. Your total will be given to you in a nicely formatted string output. Notice how the name, deposit, weeks and total are all put together (concatenated) in a single sentence, along with a dollar sign ($). Make sure the answer is correct. Remember, a big step in project design is making sure your project works correctly! If you say you want to save 10 dollars a week for 10 weeks and your computer project says you will have a million dollars by that time, you should know something is wrong somewhere!

When I tried the program, I got:

```
General Output
--------------------Configuration: SavingsProject - JDK version 1.6.0_2
Hello, what is your name? Lou

How much will you deposit each week? 40.52
For how many weeks? 10

Lou, after 10 weeks, you will have $405.20000000000005 in your savings.


Process completed.
```

Notice if I deposit 40.52 (you don't, and can't, enter the dollar sign) for 10 weeks, the program tells me I will have $405.20000000000005 in my savings account!! The many zeroes are due the computer's inability to do exact arithmetic – we get what is called round-off error. The answer should more correctly be displayed with just 2 decimal points ($405.20). It is easy to do this in Java, but beyond what we are discussing at the moment. Be aware in projects we use in this class that we may see round-off error when working with decimal numbers.

This project may not seem all that complicated. And it isn't. After all, we only multiplied two numbers together. But, the project demonstrates steps that are used in every Java project. Valuable experience has been gained in recognizing how to read input values, make sure they are the proper type, do the math to obtain desired results, and output those results to the user.

Other Things to Try

Most savings accounts yield interest, that is the bank actually pays you for letting them use your money. This savings account project has ignored interest. But, it is fairly easy to make the needed modifications to account for interest - the math is just a little more complicated. We will give you the steps, but not show you how, to change your project. Give it a try if you'd like:

- Define a variable **interest** to store the yearly savings interest rate. Interest rates are decimal numbers, so use the **double** type for this.
- Add code to allow the user to input this interest rate.
- Modify the code to use interest in computing **total**. The code for that computation is (get ready - it's messy looking):

```
total = 5200 * (deposit * (Math.pow((1 + interest /
5200), weeks) - 1) / interest);
```

Make sure you type this all on one line - as often happens, the word processor has made it look like it is on two. As we said, this is a pretty messy expression, but it's good practice in using parentheses and a mathematical function (**pow**). The number '5200' is used here to convert the interest from a yearly value to a weekly value.

Now, compile and run the modified project. Type in values for deposit, weeks, and interest. Make sure you get reasonable answers. (As a check, if you use a deposit value of 10, a weeks value of 20, and an interest value of 6.5, the total answer should be $202.39 (well, with round-off, I actually got $202.3929075...) - note you'd have $200 without interest, so this makes sense). Save your project.

Summary

Notice the projects are getting a little more detailed as you learn more Java. In this class, you learned about proper project design, mathematical functions and how to add input capabilities to your Java projects. You built a little savings account project. And, an important concept to remember as you continue through this course is to always try to build your projects a few lines of code at a time. A good mantra is "code a little, test a little." You will introduce fewer errors in your programs using this approach.

This page intentionally not left blank.

5. Debugging, Decisions, Random Numbers

Review and Preview

We continue our journey through the world of Java. Hopefully, creating and running a Java project is getting easier for you.

In this class, you will examine how to find and eliminate errors in your projects, how you can make decisions using Java, and look at a very fun function, the random number generator. You will build a 'Guess the Number' game project.

Debugging a Java Project

No matter how well you plan your project and no matter how careful you are in implementing your ideas in Java code, you will make mistakes. Errors, or what computer programmers call **bugs**, do creep into your project. You may have already encountered a few in the projects we've built so far. Perhaps you spelled a keyword wrong, forgot a semicolon, used an upper case letter when you should have used a lower case, or left off a curly brace somewhere. These are all examples of program bugs. You, as a programmer, need to have a strategy for finding and eliminating those bugs. The process of eliminating bugs in a project is called **debugging**. Unfortunately, there are not a lot of hard, fast rules for finding bugs in a program. Each programmer has his or her own way of attacking bugs. You will develop your ways. We can come up with some general strategies, though, and that's what we'll give you here.

Project errors, or bugs, can be divided into three types:

- **Syntax** errors
- **Run-time** errors
- **Logic** errors

Syntax errors occur when you make an error typing a line of Java code. Something is misspelled, an improper letter case is used or something is left out that needs to be there. Your project won't run if there are any syntax errors. **Run-time errors** occur when you try to run your project. It will stop abruptly because something has happened beyond its control. **Logic errors** are the toughest to find. Your project will run okay, but the results it gives are not what you expected. Let's examine each error type and address possible debugging methods.

Syntax Errors

Syntax errors are the easiest to identify and eliminate. The JCreator development environment is a big help in finding syntax errors. Syntax errors will occur as you're writing Java code.

To see how different bugs are identified, start a new project in your JCreator **MyJavaWorkspace**. Name it **BugProject**. Add a Java file named **Bugs**. Build a skeletal framework in this file with just an empty main method:

```
/*
 *   Debugging Project
 *   Java for Kids
 */
public class Bugs
{
  public static void main(String[] args)
   {
   }
}
```

Let's look at some typical errors. In the main method, type these two lines of code:

```
int myInt;
MyInt = 7;
```

We've used a different case on the variable name than we did in evaluating the variable.

Try compiling and this window will appear. Click **No**:

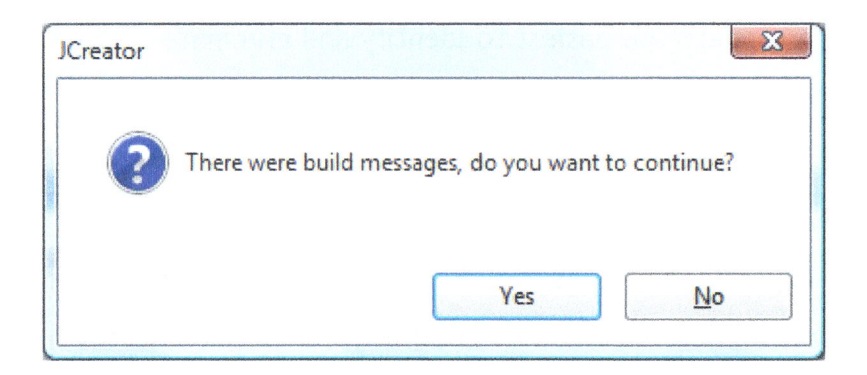

You will see in the **Build Output** window:

```
C:\JKWorkspace\BugProject\Bugs.java:10: cannot find symbol
symbol  : variable MyInt
location: class Bugs
         MyInt = 7;
         ^
1 error

Process completed.
```

The **10** tells you there is a problem in line 10 of your program. The message **'cannot find symbol'** is seen often in Java. It means Java does not recognize the name pointed to by the caret (^). In this case, Java does not recognize the variable **MyInt** because it was declared as **myInt** (different case on the letter m). Whenever you see a 'cannot find symbol' error, it means one of just a few things. If involving a variable, it means you have misspelled a properly declared variable or you have forgotten to declare a variable. If the message involves a method or function, it means you have misspelled the function name or have not provided it to your class. It is usually straightforward to correct such errors.

Now, change the second line to:

```
MyInt  7;
```

That is, leave out the assignment operator. Try compiling and you'll get two error messages:

```
C:\JKWorkspace\BugProject\Bugs.java:10: not a statement
        MyInt  7;
        ^
C:\JKWorkspace\BugProject\Bugs.java:10: ';' expected
        MyInt  7;
             ^
```

You are being told this (line 10 again) is not an acceptable statement. You should immediately see the problem and be able to fix it. Fix the errors.

Let's try one other example. Add this declaration line:

```
int anotherInt;
```

And add this line of code after the line establishing a value for **myInt**:

```
System.out.println(myInt / anotherInt);
```

Try compiling and you receive this message:

```
C:\JKWorkspace\BugProject\Bugs.java:12: variable anotherInt
might not have been initialized
          System.out.println(myInt / anotherInt);
                                    ^
```

Here's a case where Java wants you to initialize the new variable (there would be a potential for division by zero!). Again, it's clear what needs to be changed.

Other common syntax errors are forgetting semicolons, having unmatched parentheses and having unmatched curly braces. When you try to compile in such situations, the JCreator environment will kindly point out your errors to you so you can fix them. Note that syntax errors usually result because of incorrect typing, either misspellings or omissions - another great reason to improve your typing skills, if they need it.

Run-Time Errors

Once you have written your code and eliminated all identified syntax errors, obtaining a successful compilation, you try to run your project. If the project runs, great! But, many times, your project may stop and tell you it found an error - this is a run-time error. You need to figure out why it stopped and fix the problem. Again, the JCreator environment and Java will usually give you enough information to eliminate run-time errors. Let's look at some examples.

Change the **anotherInt** declaration to:

```
int anotherInt = 0;
```

Yes, I know we'll get a divide by zero, but that's the point here - to illustrate potential errors. Notice the program will compile (no more syntax errors). Try running the program and you should see:

```
General Output
--------------------Configuration: BugProject - JDK version 1.6.0_21
Exception in thread "main" java.lang.ArithmeticException: / by zero
    at Bugs.main(Bugs.java:12)

Process completed.
```

We obtain what is called an **exception** in Java. The exception in this case is a divide by zero error (**/ by zero**). And, we are told the problem is in line **12**. Such information will help us identify and correct the error.

Another common run-time error occurs when using one of Java's built-n functions. Errors result if you use the wrong type or value as one of the arguments. Change the **anotherInt** initialization to:

```
int anotherInt = -20;
```

And change the **println** line to:

```
System.out.println("Square root is " +
Math.sqrt(anotherInt));
```

Compile and run the program. You will see this:

```
General Output
--------------------Configuration: BugProject - JDK version 1.6.
Square root is NaN

Process completed.
```

The square root of -20 (an impossibility) is printed as **NaN**. In Java, **NaN** stands for **N**ot **a** **N**umber.

We've seen just a couple of possible run-time errors. There are others and you'll see them as you start building projects. But, you've seen that Java is pretty helpful in pointing out where errors are. One last thing about run-time errors. Java will not find all errors at once. It will stop at the first run-time error it encounters. After you fix that error, there may be more. You have to fix run-time errors one at a time.

Logic Errors

Logic errors are the most difficult to find and eliminate. These are errors that don't keep your project from running, but cause incorrect or unexpected results. The only thing you can do at this point, if you suspect logic errors exist, is to dive into your project and make sure everything is coded exactly as you want it. Finding logic errors is a time-consuming art, <u>not</u> a science. There are no general rules for finding logic errors. Each programmer has his or her own particular way of searching for logic errors.

With the example we have been using, a logic error would be setting a variable to an incorrect value. Or, perhaps you add two numbers together when you should have subtracted. Logic errors are mistakes you have inadvertently introduced into your Java code. And, unfortunately, these errors are not pointed out to you. Hence, eliminating logic errors is not always easy.

Advanced Java programmers use something called a **debugger** that helps in the identification of logic errors. Using a debugger lets you examine variable values, stop your code wherever and whenever you want, and run your project line-by-line. Use of a debugger is an advanced topic and will not be talked about in this course. If you want to improve your Java skills, you are encouraged to eventually learn how to use a debugger. For now, you need to learn to eliminate logic errors by paying close attention to your code. And, the best approach is to be so careful that you don't have any logic errors to worry about.

Java - The Third Lesson

In the Java lesson for this class, we learn about one of the more useful capabilities of a computer program - decision making. We will discuss expressions and operators used in decisions and how decisions can be made. We will also look at a new Java function - the random number generator. Such a function is at the heart of every computer game.

Logical Expressions

You may think that computers are quite smart. They appear to have the ability to make amazing decisions and choices. Computers can beat masters at chess and help put men and women into space. Well, computers really aren't that smart - the only decision making ability they have is to tell if something is **true** or **false**. But, computers have the ability to make such decisions very quickly and that's why they appear smart (and because, unlike the True or False tests you take in school, computers always get the right answer!). To use Java for decision making, we write all possible decisions in the form of **true or false?** statements, called **logical expressions**. We give the computer a logical expression and the computer will tell us if that expression is true or false. Based on that decision, we can take whatever action we want in our computer program. Note the result of a logical expression is a **boolean** type value.

Debugging, Decisions, Random Numbers

Say in a computer program we need to know if the value of the variable **aValue** is larger than the value of the variable **bValue**. We would ask the computer (by writing some Java code) to provide an answer to the true or false? statement: "aValue is larger than bValue." This is an example of a logical expression. If the computer told us this was true, we could take one set of Java steps. If it was false, we could take another. This is how decisions are done in Java.

To make decisions, we need to know how to build and use logical expressions. The first step in building such expressions is to learn about comparison operators.

Comparison Operators

In the Class 3, we looked at one type of Java operator - arithmetic operators. In this class, we introduce the idea of a **comparison operator**. Comparison operators do exactly what they say - they compare two values, with the output of the comparison being a **boolean** value. That is, the result of the comparison is either **true** or **false**. Comparison operators allow us to construct logical expressions that can be used in decision making.

There are six comparison operators. The first is the "**equal to**" operator represented by two equal (==) signs. This operator tells us if two values are equal to each other. Examples are:

Comparison	Result
6 == 7	false
4 == 4	true

A common error (a logic error) in Java is to only use one equal sign for the "equal to" operator. Using a single equal sign simply assigns a value to the variable making it always true!! **Note:** you cannot use this operator to compare two **String** variables – we'll see why after looking at all the comparison operators.

Debugging, Decisions, Random Numbers 5-13

There is also a **"not equal to"** operator represented by a symbol consisting of an exclamation point (called the **not** operator) followed by the equal sign (!=). Examples of using this operator:

Comparison	Result
6 != 7	true
4 != 4	false

There are other operators that let us compare the size of numbers. The **"greater than"** operator (>) tells us if one number (left side of operator) is greater than another (right side of operator). Examples of its usage:

Comparison	Result
8 > 3	true
6 > 7	false
4 > 4	false

The **"less than"** operator (<) tells us if one number (left side of operator) is less than another (right side of operator). Some examples are:

Comparison	Result
8 < 3	false
6 < 7	true
4 < 4	false

The last two operators are modifications to the "greater than" and "less than" operators. The **"greater than or equal to"** operator (>=) compares two numbers. The result is true if the number on the left of the operator is greater than or equal to the number on the right. Otherwise, the result is false. Examples:

Comparison	Result
8 >= 3	true
6 >= 7	false
4 >= 4	true

Similarly, the **"less than or equal to"** operator (<=) tells us if one number (left side of operator) is less than or equal to another (right side of operator). Examples:

Comparison	Result
8 <= 3	false
6 <= 7	true
4 <= 4	true

Comparison operators have equal precedence among themselves, but are lower than the precedence of arithmetic operators. This means comparisons are done <u>after</u> any arithmetic. Comparison operators allow us to make single decisions about the relative size of values and variables. What if we need to make multiple decisions? For example, what if we want to know if a particular variable is smaller than one number, but larger than another? We need ways to combine logical expressions - logical operators can do this. But, first we must look at a special case of comparing strings.

Comparing Strings

Remember we said you can't use the "equals to" operator (==) to compare **String** type variables. A common logic error is to forget this. The reason we can't use this operator is in how Java stores strings. Say we have two **String** type variables, **aString** and **bString**. Writing:

```
aString == bString
```

checks to see if each of these strings are stored in the same place in your computer's memory. That's not what we want to do. We want to see if each string has the same characters.

To properly compare two strings for equality, we use the **String** class **equals** method. This method does just what we want – compares two strings to see if they have the same characters in them. The code that does this comparison for our example strings is:

```
aString.equals(bString)
```

This method returns the **boolean** result of true if the **aString** and **bString** are the same length, that is have the same number of characters, and each character in one string is identical to the corresponding character in the other. And, the comparison is case-sensitive. To ignore case in the comparison, use:

```
aString.equalsIgnoreCase(bString)
```

Now, we can move on to looking at combining **boolean** results with logical operators.

Logical Operators

Logical operators are used to combine logical expressions built using comparison operators. Using such operators allows you, as the programmer, to make any decision you want. As an example, say you need to know if two variables named **aValue** and **bValue** are both greater than 0. Using the "greater than" comparison operator (>), we know how to see if **aValue** is greater than zero and we know how to check if **bValue** is greater than 0, but how do we combine these expressions and obtain one **boolean** result (true or false)?

We will look at two logical operators used to combine logical expressions. The first is the **and** operator represented by two ampersands (&&). The format for using this operator is (using two logical expressions, **x** and **y,** each with a **boolean** result):

```
x && y
```

This expression is asking the question "are x and y both true?" That's why it is called the and operator. The and operator (&&) will return a true value only if both x and y are true. If either expression is false, the and operator will return a false. The four possibilities for **and** (&&) are shown in this **logic table:**

x	y	x && y
true	true	true
true	false	false
false	true	false
false	false	false

Debugging, Decisions, Random Numbers

Notice the and operator would be used to solve the problem mentioned in the beginning of this section. That is, to see if the variables **aValue** and **bValue** are both greater than zero, we would use the expression:

```
aValue > 0 && bValue > 0
```

The other logical operator we will use is the **or** operator represented by two pipes (||). The pipe symbol is the shift of the backslash key (\) on a standard keyboard. The format for using this operator is:

```
x || y
```

This expression is asking the question "is x or y true?" That's why it is called the or operator. The or (||) operator will return a true value if either x or y is true. If both expressions are false, the or operator will return a false. The four possibilities for **or** (||) are:

x	y	x || y
true	true	true
true	false	true
false	true	true
false	false	false

The or operator is second in precedence to the and operator (that is, and is done before or), and all logical operators come after the comparison operators in precedence. Use of comparison operators and logical operators to form logical expressions is key to making proper decisions in Java. Make sure you understand how all the operators (and their precedence) work. Let's look at some examples to help in this understanding.

In these examples, we will have two integer variables **aInteger** and **bInteger**, with values:

```
aInteger = 14
bInteger = 7
```

What if we want to evaluate the logical expression:

```
aInteger > 10 && bInteger > 10
```

Comparisons are done first, left to right since all comparison operators share the same level of precedence. **aInteger** (14) is greater than 10, so **aInteger** > 10 is true. **bInteger** (7) is not greater than 10, so **bInteger** > 10 is false. Since one expression is not true, the result of the and (&&) operation is false. This expression 'aInteger > 10 && bInteger > 10' is false. What is the result of this expression:

```
aInteger > 10 || bInteger > 10
```

Can you see this expression is true (**aInteger** > 10 is true, **bInteger** > 10 is false; true || false is true)?

Debugging, Decisions, Random Numbers

There is no requirement that a logical expression have just one logical operator. So, let's complicate things a bit. What if the expression is:

```
aInteger > 10 || bInteger > 10 && aInteger + bInteger == 20
```

Precedence tells us the arithmetic is done first (**aInteger** and **bInteger** are added), then the comparisons, left to right. We know **aInteger** > 10 is true, **bInteger** > 10 is false, **aInteger** + **bInteger** == 20 is false. So, this expression, in terms of **boolean** comparison values, becomes:

```
true || false && false
```

How do we evaluate this? Precedence says the and (&&) is done first, then the or (||). The result of 'false && false' is false, so the expression reduces to:

```
true || false
```

which has a result of true. Hence, we say the expression '**aInteger** > 10 || **bInteger** > 10 && **aInteger** + **bInteger** = 20' is true.

Parentheses can be used in logical expressions to force precedence in evaluations. What if, in the above example, we wanted to do the or (||) operation first? This is done by rewriting using parentheses:

```
(aInteger > 10 || bInteger > 10) && aInteger + bInteger == 20
```

You should be able to show this evaluates to false [do the or (||) first]. Before, without parentheses, it was true. The addition of parentheses has changed the value of this logical expression! It's always best to clearly indicate how you want a logical expression to be evaluated. Parentheses are a good way to do this. Use parentheses even if precedence is not affected.

If we moved the parentheses in this example and wrote:

```
aInteger > 10 || (bInteger > 10 && aInteger + bInteger == 20)
```

the result (true) is the same as if the parentheses were not there since the and (&&) is done first anyway. The parentheses do, however, clearly indicate the and is performed first. Such clarity is good in programming.

Comparison and logical operators are keys to making decisions in Java. Make sure you are comfortable with their meaning and use. Always double-check any logical expression you form to make sure it truly represents the decision logic you intend. Use parentheses to add clarity, if needed.

Decisions - The if Statement

We've spent a lot of time covering comparison operators and logical operators and discussed how they are used to form logical expressions. But, just how is all this used in computer decision making? We'll address that now by looking at the Java **if** statement. Actually, the **if** statement is not a single statement, but rather a group of statements that implements some decision logic. It is conceptually simple.

The **if** statement checks a particular logical expression with a **boolean** result. It executes different groups of Java statements, depending on whether that expression is true or false. The Java structure for this logic is:

```
if (expression)
{
      [Java code block to be executed if expression is true]
}
else
{
      [Java code block to be executed if expression is false]
}
```

Let's see what goes on here. We have some logical **expression** which is formed from comparison operators and logical operators. **if** expression is true, then the first block of Java statements (marked by a pair of left and right curly braces) is executed. **else** (meaning expression is not true, or it is false), the second block of Java statements is executed. Each block of code contains standard Java statements, indented by some amount. Whether **expression** is true or false, program execution continues with the first line of Java code after the last right curly brace (}).

The **else** keyword and the block of statements following the **else** are optional. If there is no Java code to be executed if expression is false, the **if** structure would simply be:

```
if (expression)
{
    [Java code block to be executed if expression is true]
}
```

Let's try some examples.

Pretend you just opened a lemonade stand and you want to let the computer decide how much you should charge for each cup you sell. Define an **int** type variable **cost** (cost per cup in cents - our foreign friends can use some other unit here) and another **int** variable **temperature** (outside temperature in degrees F - our foreign friends would, of course, use degrees C). We will write an **if** structure that implements a decision process that establishes a value for cost, depending on the value of temperature. Look at the Java code:

```
if (temperature > 90)
{
  cost = 50;
}
else
{
  cost = 25;
}
```

We see that if temperature > 90 (a warm day, hence we can charge more), a logical expression, is true, the cost will be 50, else (meaning temperature is not greater than 90) the cost will be 25. Not too difficult. Notice that we have indented the lines of Java code in the two blocks (one line of code in each block here). This is common practice in writing Java code. It clearly indicates what is done in each case and allows us to see where an if structure begins and ends. The JCreator environment will actually handle the indenting for you.

We could rewrite this (and get the same result) without the **else** statement. Notice, this code is equivalent to the above code:

```
cost = 25;
if (temperature > 90)
{
   cost = 50
}
```

Here, before the **if** structure, cost is 25. Only if temperature is greater than 90 is cost changed to 50. Otherwise, cost remains at 25. Even though, in these examples, we only have one line of Java code that is executed for each decision possibility, we are not limited to a single line. We may have as many lines of Java code as needed in the code blocks of **if** structures.

What if, in our lemonade stand example, we want to divide our pricing structure into several different cost values, based on several different temperature values. The **if** structure can modified to include an **else if** statement to consider multiple logical expressions. Such a structure is:

```
if (expression1)
{
      [Java code block to be executed if expression1 is true]
}
else if (expression2)
{
      [Java code block to be executed if expression2 is true]
}
else if (expression3)
{
      [Java code block to be executed if expression3 is true]
}
else
{
      [Java code block to be executed if expression1, expression 2, and expression3 are all false]

}
```

Can you see what happens here? It's pretty straightforward - just work down through the code. If **expression1** is true, the first block of Java code is executed. If **expression1** is false, the program checks to see if **expression2** (using the **else if**) is true. If **expression2** is true, that block of code is executed. If **expression2** is false, **expression3** is evaluated. If **expression3** is true, the corresponding code block is executed. If **expression3** is false, and note by this time, **expression1**, **expression2**, and **expression3** have all been found to be false, the code in the **else** block (and this is optional) is executed.

You can have as many **else if** statements as you want. You must realize, however, that only one block of Java code in an if structure will be executed.

Debugging, Decisions, Random Numbers 5-25

This means that once Java has found a logical expression that is true, it will execute that block of code then leave the structure and execute the first line of code following the last right curly brace (}). For example, if in the above example, both **expression1** and **expression3** are true, only the Java statements associated with **expression1** being true will be executed. The rule for **if** structures is: only the code block associated with the <u>first</u> true expression will be executed.

How can we use this in our lemonade example? A more detailed pricing structure is reflected in this code:

```
if (temperature > 90)
{
   cost = 50;
}
else if (temperature > 80)
{
   cost = 40;
}
else if (temperature > 70)
{
   cost = 30;
}
Else
{
   cost = 25;
}
```

What would the cost be if **temperature** is 85? **temperature** is not greater than 90, but is greater than 80, so cost is 40.

What if this code was rewritten as:

```
if (temperature > 70)
{
  cost = 30;
}
else if (temperature > 80)
{
  cost = 40;
}
else if (temperature > 90)
{
  cost = 50;
}
Else
{
  cost = 25;
}
```

This doesn't look that different - we've just reordered some statements. But, notice what happens if we try to find cost for **temperature** = 85 again. The first if expression is true (**temperature** is greater than 70), so cost is 30. This is not the result we wanted and will decrease profits for our lemonade stand! Here's a case where the "first true" rule gave us an incorrect answer - a logic error.

This example points out the necessity to always carefully check any **if** structures you write. Make sure the decision logic you want to implement is working properly. Make sure you try cases that execute all possible decisions and that you get the correct results. The examples used here are relatively simple. Obviously, the **if** structure can be more far more complicated. Using multiple variables, multiple comparisons and multiple operators, you can develop very detailed decision making processes. In the remaining class projects, you will see examples of such processes.

Random Number Generator

Let's leave decisions for now and look at a fun concept - the random number. Have you ever played the Windows solitaire card game or Minesweeper or some similar game? Did you notice that every time you play the game, you get different results? How does this happen? How can you make a computer program unpredictable or introduce the idea of "randomness?" The key is the random number generator. This generator simply produces a different number every time it is referenced.

Why do you need random numbers? In the Windows solitaire card game, the computer needs to shuffle a deck of cards. It needs to "randomly" sort fifty-two cards. It uses random numbers to do this. If you have a game that rolls a die, you need to randomly generate a number between 1 and 6. Random numbers can be used to do this. If you need to flip a coin, you need to generate Heads or Tails randomly. Yes, random numbers are used to do this too.

Java has several methods for generating random numbers. We will use just one of them – a random generator of integers. The generator uses the Java **Random** object. Like the **Scanner** object seen in the last chapter, this object is not built into the basic Java language. It is in the API Package named **java.util.Random**. To use this package, we use an **import** statement:

```
import java.util.Random;
```

Recall, this statement goes <u>before</u> our program's class definition header.

Now, to use the **Random** object, it is first created using the object **constructor**:

```
Random myRandom = new Random();
```

This statement is placed with the variable declaration statements. Now, whenever you need a random integer value, use the **nextInt** method of this **Random** object we created:

```
myRandom.nextInt(Limit)
```

This statement generates a random integer value that is greater than or equal to 0 and less than **Limit**. Note it is less than **Limit**, not equal to. For example, the method:

```
myRandom.nextInt(5)
```

will generate random numbers from 0 to 4. The possible values will be 0, 1, 2, 3 and 4.

Let's see how this all works by building a quick application. Start **JCreator**, open your workspace (**MyJavaWorkspace**), start a new project named **RandomProject** and add a Java file named **RandomTest**. These steps should be second-nature by now.

Debugging, Decisions, Random Numbers

Type this little code snippet:

```java
/*
 *   Random Test
 *   Java for Kids
 */

import java.util.Random;

public class RandomTest
{
  public static void main(String[] args)
  {
    Random myRandom = new Random();
    System.out.println("Random number " + myRandom.nextInt(10));
  }
}
```

This code simply generates a random integer between 0 and 9 (**nextInt** uses a limit of 10) and prints it. Notice the placement of the **import** statement and the statement constructing the random number generator object **myRandom**. Compile and run the project. Some number should print:

```
General Output
    --------------------Configuration: Random Test - JDK version 1.6.
    Random number 5

    Process completed.
```

Stop the project and run it again. Most likely a different number will be printed; it could print the same number again, after all it is random. Continue stopping and running to see how each run results in a random result. The number printed should always be between 0 and 9.

So, the random number generator object can be used to introduce randomness in a project. This opens up a lot of possibilities to you as a programmer. Every computer game, video game, and computer simulation, like sports games and flight simulators, use random numbers. A roll of a die can produce a number from 1 to 6. To use our **myRandom** object to roll a die, we would write:

```
dieNumber = myRandom.nextInt(6) + 1;
```

For a deck of cards, the random integers would range from 1 to 52 since there are 52 cards in a standard playing deck. Code to do this:

```
cardNumber = myRandom.nextInt(52) + 1;
```

If we want a number between 0 and 100, we would use:

```
yourNumber = myRandom.nextInt(101)
```

Check the examples above to make sure you see how the random number generator produces the desired range of integers. Now, let's move on to a project that will use this generator.

Debugging, Decisions, Random Numbers 5-31

Project - Guess the Number Game

Back in the early 1980's, the first computers intended for home use appeared. Brands like Atari, Coleco, Texas Instruments, and Commodore were sold in stores like Sears and Toys R Us (sorry, I can't type the needed 'backwards' R). These computers didn't have much memory, couldn't do real fancy graphics, and, compared to today's computers, cost a lot of money. But, these computers introduced a lot of people to the world of computer programming (using the BASIC programming language). Many games appeared at that time and the project you will build here is one of those classics. This project is saved as **NumberProject** in the course projects folder (**\JavaKids\JK Code**).

Project Design

You've all played the game where someone said "I'm thinking of a number between 1 and 10" (or some other limits). Then, you try to guess the number. The person thinking of the number tells you if you're right or wrong, low or high, or provides some other clue and, sometimes, you guess again. We will develop a computer version of this game here. The computer will pick a number between 1 and 10 (using the random number generator). You will try to guess the number. Based on your guess, the computer will tell you if you are correct, too low or too high and tell you the answer. You only get one chance to guess it!!

The steps needed to do play this game are:

1. Computer picks a number between 1 and 10.
2. Computer asks your guess.
3. Computer analyzes your guess and outputs the result.

We will use the **Scanner** object to get user input. The **println** method will be used to output the result of your guess.

Project Development

Start JCreator, open your workspace and create a new project named **NumberProject**. Add a blank file named **GuessIt** (the .java extension will be added). Again, these steps should be getting easy for you.

Open the empty **GuessIt.java** file. First, type the following header information, the class definition line, the import statements needed for the **Random** and **Scanner** objects and the main method definition (along with needed braces):

```java
/*
 *  Guess the Number
 *  Java for Kids
 *  www.KIDwareSoftware.com
 */

import java.util.Random;
import java.util.Scanner;

public class GuessIt
{
  public static void main(String[] args)
  {
  }
}
```

We will use two variables in this program: one for the computer's number and one for your guess. We also need to construct the random number and scanner objects. Type their declarations next (in the main method):

```java
int computerNumber;
int yourGuess;
Random myRandom = new Random();
Scanner myScanner = new Scanner(System.in);
```

Now, we start writing the code, following the steps listed in **Project Design**. Again, after typing some code, you might like to stop, compile and run just to see if things are going okay. First, have the computer pick and print its random number:

```java
// get the computer's number between 1 and 10
computerNumber = myRandom.nextInt(10) + 1;
System.out.println("I'm thinking of a number between 1 and 10.");
```

Notice how the number selected is between 1 and 10. Next, you input your guess using the **nextInt** method:

```java
// get your guess
System.out.print("What do you think it is? ");
yourGuess = myScanner.nextInt();
```

With this information, your guess is next analyzed for correctness using a Java **if** structure:

```java
// analyze guess and print results
if (yourGuess == computerNumber)
{
  // you got it
  System.out.println("You got it!! That's my number!");
}
else if (yourGuess < computerNumber)
{
  // too low
  System.out.println("You are too low!! My number was " + computerNumber);
}
else
{
  // too high
  System.out.println("You are too high!! My number was " + computerNumber);
}
```

Debugging, Decisions, Random Numbers

You should be able to see how this works. Save your project by clicking the **Save All** button.

The finished code in the JCreator view window should appear as:

```
/*
 *  Guess the Number
 *  Java for Kids
 *  www.KIDwareSoftware.com
 */

import java.util.Random;
import java.util.Scanner;

public class GuessIt
{
  public static void main(String[] args)
  {
    int computerNumber;
    int yourGuess;
    Random myRandom = new Random();
    Scanner myScanner = new Scanner(System.in);

    // get the computer's number between 1 and 10
    computerNumber = myRandom.nextInt(10) + 1;
    System.out.println("I'm thinking of a number between 1 and 10.");

    // get your guess
    System.out.print("What do you think it is? ");
    yourGuess = myScanner.nextInt();

    // analyze guess and print results
    if (yourGuess == computerNumber)
    {
      // you got it
      System.out.println("You got it!! That's my number!");
    }
    else if (yourGuess < computerNumber)
    {
      // too low
      System.out.println("You are too low!! My number was " + computerNumber);
    }
```

```
    else
    {
      // too high
      System.out.println("You are too high!! My number was "
+ computerNumber);
    }
  }
}
```

Run the Project

Compile and run the project. Eliminate any syntax, run-time or logic errors you may encounter. You should now see:

```
General Output
    --------------------Configuration: NumberProject - JDK version 1.6.
    I'm thinking of a number between 1 and 10.
    What do you think it is?
```

Enter your guess and make sure the computer provides the correct analysis. Here's the results of my guess (I got it!):

```
General Output
    --------------------Configuration: NumberProject - JDK version 1.6.
    I'm thinking of a number between 1 and 10.
    What do you think it is? 7
    You got it!! That's my number!

    Process completed.
```

Run the program again and again until you know it can determine if a guess is correct, too low or too high. Here's another run I made:

```
General Output
--------------------Configuration: NumberProject - JDK version 1.6
I'm thinking of a number between 1 and 10.
What do you think it is? 3
You are too low!! My number was 5

Process completed.
```

You should always thoroughly test your project to make sure all options work. Save your project if you needed to make any changes.

Other Things to Try

A good modification would be to offer more informative messages following a guess. Have you ever played the game where you try to find something and the person who hid the item tells you, as you move around the room, that you are freezing (far away), cold (closer), warm (closer yet), hot (very close), or burning up (right on top of the hidden item)? Try to modify the Guess the Number game to give these kind of clues. That is, the closer you are to the correct number, the warmer you get. To make this change, you will need the Java **absolute value** function, **Math.abs**. Recall this function returns the value of a number while ignoring its sign (positive or negative).

In our number guessing game, we can use **Math.abs** to see how close a guess is to the actual number. One possible decision logic is:

```
if (yourGuess == computerNumber)
{
      [Java code block for correct answer]
}
else if (Math.abs(yourGuess - computerNumber) <= 1)
{
      [Java code block when burning up - within 1 of correct answer]
}
else if (Math.abs(yourGuess - computerNumber) <= 2)
{
      [Java code block when hot - within 2 of correct answer]
}
else if (Math.abs(yourGuess - computerNumber) <= 3)
{
      [Java code block when warm - within 3 of correct answer]
}
else
{
      [Java code block when freezing - more than 3 away]
}
```

I'm sure you noticed it was kind of a pain to only get one guess at the computer's number. A great modification to this program would be to add the capability of entering another guess, based on the computer's analysis. Then, you could see how many guesses it takes to "hone in" on the correct answer. To do this requires capability we haven't discussed yet in this course. But, don't worry, this idea of **looping** is covered in the next class. With looping, or the capability to repeat code, we will modify the **Guess the Number** game to allow repeated guesses until correct.

Adding the ability to enter improved guesses opens up a number of additional modifications you could make to this little game. One suggestion is to all the user to input the upper range of numbers that can be guessed. That way, the game could be played by a wide variety of players. Use a maximum value of 10 for little kids, 1000 for older kids. Implement the "hot, warm, cold" if logic discussed above. Or, perhaps make the project into a math game, and tell the guesser "how far away" the guess is. I'm sure you can think of other ways to change this game. Have fun doing it.

Summary

In this class, you learned a lot of new material. You discovered there are three types of errors that try to attack your hard work: syntax errors, run-time errors and logic errors. You learned about a key part of Java programming - decision making. You learned about logical expressions, comparison operators, logical operators, and if structures. And, you had fun with random numbers in the **Guess the Number** game. You are well on your way to being a Java programmer.

This page intentionally not left blank.

6. Java Looping, Methods

Review and Preview

The projects we build are becoming more detailed, especially with the capability to make decisions using the **if** structure.

In this class, you learn about another very important programming concept – looping, which allows you to repeat blocks of code. You also learn about methods, which are self-contained blocks of code that accomplish given tasks. And, you will build a **Lemonade Stand** simulation as your project.

Java - The Fourth Lesson

In the **Guess the Number** project built in Class 5, we noted it would be nice if we could continue to make guesses until we got the correct number. To do this requires the ability to repeat segments of code. In this Java lesson, we learn how to add this looping capability to our Java projects. We will also learn about methods, which allow us to write better, more compact projects.

Java Loops

Many (in fact, most) Java programs require repetition of certain code blocks. For example, as just noted, the **Guess the Number** game we built could really use it. Or, you may want to roll a die (simulated die of course) until it shows a six. Or, you might generate some math results until a value has been achieved. This idea of repeating code is called iteration or **looping**.

In Java, one way of looping is with the **while** loop:

```
while (expression)
{
    [Java code block to repeat while expression is true]
}
```

In this structure, all code between the curly braces is repeated **while** the given logical **expression** is **true**. Note there is no semicolon at the end of the **while** line.

Notice a **while** structure looks a lot like a simple **if** structure:

```
if (expression)
{
    [Java code block to process if expression is true]
}
```

What's the difference? In the **if** structure, the code block is processed just once if **expression** is true. In the **while** structure, the code block is continually processed as long as **expression** remains true.

Note a **while** loop structure will not execute even once if **expression** is false the first time through. If we do enter the loop (**expression** is true), it is assumed at some point **expression** will become false to allow exiting. Once this happens, code execution continues at the statement following the closing right brace. This brings up a very important point about loops – if you get in one, make sure you get out at some point. In the **while** loop, if **expression** is always true, you will loop forever – something called an infinite loop.

Let's look at a couple of examples. First, here is a loop that can be used in a rocket countdown. It repeats as long as (**while**) the variable **counter** (starting at 10) is greater than 0:

```
counter = 10;
while (counter > 0)
{
   counter = counter - 1;
}
```

Another example (assuming we have a **Random** object named **myRandom**):

```
rolls = 0;
counter = 0;
while (counter < 10)
{
  // Roll a simulated die
  roll = roll + 1;
  if ((myRandom.nextInt(6) + 1) == 6)
  {
    counter = counter + 1;
  }
}
```

This loop repeats while the **counter** variable remains less than 10. The **counter** variable is incremented (increased by one) each time a simulated die rolls a 6. The **roll** variable tells you how many rolls of the die were needed to roll 10 sixes.

As mentioned, if the logical expression used by a **while** loop is false the first time the loop is encountered, the code block in the **while** loop will not be executed. This may be acceptable behavior – it may not be. There is another looping structure in Java that will always be executed at least once. This loop is a **do/while** structure:

```
do
{
    [Java code block to process]
}
while (expression);
```

Java Looping, Methods

Notice here, unlike the **while** loop, there <u>is</u> a semicolon at the end of the **while** statement. The code block in the braces repeats 'as long as' the **boolean**-valued **expression** is true. Notice, the loop is always executed at least once. Somewhere in the loop, **expression** should be changed to false to allow exiting.

Let's look at examples of the **do/while** loop. What if we want to keep adding three to a **sum** until the value exceeds 50. This loop will do it:

```
sum = 0;
do
{
   sum = sum + 3;
}
while (sum <= 50);
```

Or, another dice example:

```
sum = 0;
roll = 0;
do
{
   //  Roll a simulated die
   sum = sum + myRandom.nextInt(6) + 1;
   roll = roll + 1;
}
while (sum <= 30);
```

This loop rolls a simulated die while the **sum** of the rolls does not exceed 30. It also keeps track of the number of rolls (**roll**) needed to achieve this sum.

You need to decide which of the loop structures (**while**, **do/while**) fits your project. Recall the major difference is that a **do/while** loop is always executed at least once; a **while** loop may never be executed. And, make sure you can always get out of a loop. In both looping structures, this means that, at some point, the checking logical expression must become false to allow exiting the loop. When you exit a **while** loop, processing continues at the next Java statement after the closing brace. In a **do/while** loop, processing continues at the Java statement after the **while** statement.

There is one other way to exit a loop. If, at some point in the code block of a loop, you decide you need to immediately leave the loop, this can be done using a Java **break** statement. When a **break** statement is encountered, processing is immediately transferred to the Java statement following the loop structure. As an example:

```
sum = 0;
roll = 0;
do
{
  //  Roll a simulated die
  die = myRandom.nextInt(6) + 1;
  if (die == 5)
  {
    break;
  }
  sum = sum + die;
  roll = roll + 1;
}
while (sum <= 30);
```

This is a modified version (new code is shaded) of the dice example we just looked at. In this example, the die value is added to the sum, unless the die rolls a 5. In that case, the loop is immediately exited via a **break** statement.

Java Looping, Methods

One other statement used in loops is the **continue** statement. It is similar to the **break** statement except, instead of leaving the loop, it just tells the computer to skip statements not yet executed in the loop and immediately return to the beginning of the loop. In a **while** loop, this means control returns to the **while** statement. In a **do** loop, control is returned to the **do** statement. What if we replace the **break** with a **continue** in the dice example (modified code is shaded):

```
sum = 0;
roll = 0;
do
{
  //  Roll a simulated die
  die = myRandom.nextInt(6) + 1;
  if (die == 5)
  {
     continue;
  }
  sum = sum + die;
  roll = roll + 1;
}
while (sum <= 30);
```

In this case, if a 5 is rolled (die == 5), that value is just not included in the sum (all lines following continue in the **do** loop are ignored). Program control transfers to the **do** statement. The big difference is that the loop continues – that's why it's called continue!

A Brief Interlude - Guess the Number Game (Revisited)

We'll return to our Java lesson in a bit. But first, let's change the **Guess the Number** game from Class 5 so a user can have repeated guesses until getting the computer's number. It's a simple application of the **do/while** loop – we want to keep guessing **while** your guess does not equal the computer's number. The modified code (changes are shaded) is:

```
/*
 *  Guess the Number
 *  Modified with Looping
 *  Java for Kids
 *  www.KIDwareSoftware.com
 */

import java.util.Random;
import java.util.Scanner;

public class GuessIt
{
  public static void main(String[] args)
    {
    int computerNumber;
    int yourGuess;
    Random myRandom = new Random();
    Scanner myScanner = new Scanner(System.in);

    // get the computer's number between 1 and 10
    computerNumber = myRandom.nextInt(10) + 1;
    System.out.println("I'm thinking of a number between 1 and 10.");

    // start do loop here
    do
    {
      // get your guess
      System.out.print("What do you think it is? ");
      yourGuess = myScanner.nextInt();

      // analyze guess and print results
      if (yourGuess == computerNumber)
      {
```

```java
      // you got it
      System.out.println("You got it!! That's my number!");
    }
    else if (yourGuess < computerNumber)
    {
      // too low
      System.out.println("You are too low!!");
    }
    else
    {
      // too high
      System.out.println("You are too high!!");
    }
  }
  while (yourGuess != computerNumber);
 }
}
```

In this code, we have made a couple of changes. We have put the code asking for your guess and checking your guess within a **do/while** loop (using the "not equals" operator in the **while** expression). And, we have removed the display of the computer's number when you are too low or too high (that would make the game too easy). We have saved this modification as **NumberProject2** in the course projects folder (**\JavaKids\JK Code**).

Open **JCreator** and load in your **Guess the Number** game project. Make the changes noted above and any others you might like. Be aware of the automatic addition of a right brace when modifying the code to add the do loop – you'll have to move it to the proper location. Compile and run the project. Here's one time I played:

```
General Output
                    --------Configuration: NumberProject2 - JDK version 1.6.
I'm thinking of a number between 1 and 10.
What do you think it is? 5
You are too high!!
What do you think it is? 3
You are too high!!
What do you think it is? 2
You got it!! That's my number!

Process completed.
```

I think you will agree that this is a much better game. The **do/while** loop has really improved this project. We often use our programming skills to improve projects we build. You can probably think of many more improvements. Maybe add another loop that, once one game ends, you are given the option to play again. With repeated guesses possible, you might like to extend the possible range for the computer's number (try it with 100). Maybe implement the "hot, warm, cold" logic outlined in Class 5. Have fun trying your own ideas!!

Now, back to the Java lesson.

Java - The Fourth Lesson (Continued)

The interlude is over. We finish this class' Java lesson with a look at a very important Java programming concept – the method.

Java Methods

In the looping discussion, we saw how code in one particular block could be repeated until some desired condition was met. Many times in Java projects, we might have a need to repeat a certain block of code at several different points in the project. Why would you want to do this? Say we had a game that requires us to roll 5 dice and add up their individual values to yield a sum. What if we needed to do this at 10 different places in our project? We could write the code, then copy and paste it to the 10 different places. I think you can see problems already. What if you need to change the code? You would need to change it in 10 different places. What if you needed to put the code in another place in your project? You would need to do another 'copy and paste' operation. There's a better way. And that way is to use a Java **method**. A method allows you to write the code to perform certain tasks just once. Then, whenever you need to access the code in your project, you can "call it," providing any information it might need to do its tasks. Methods are the building blocks of a Java program.

Actually, you've been using several methods (besides the **main** method in every project) already in this course and, whether you know it or not, have seen the big advantages to using methods. Whenever you print information using the **println** method, you are actually executing lots of code provided by the Java language. This code decides how to print the text you provide. Can you imagine replacing every reference to a **println** statement with the actual code that prints the line? Other methods you've been using include the methods in the **Scanner** class that allow us to get keyboard input and the Java **Math** functions. It's nice to have this code available for our use, rather than have to write it ourselves. Would you know how to write the code needed to find the square root of a number? When we use one of these "built-in" methods, we call it by providing information it needs (arguments). It then does its tasks. Some methods, for example the **nextInt** method of the **Scanner** class return a value for your use, while some only perform a task (**println**, for example), returning nothing to the calling program.

Using methods in your Java projects can help divide a complex application into more manageable units of code. Just think of a method as a code block you can access from anywhere in a Java project. When you call the method, program control goes to that method, performs the assigned tasks and returns to the calling program. It's that easy. Methods are also reusable, keeping you from having to rewrite code to do the same task. You can easily copy methods from one application to another. Reusability is a big advantage of object-oriented languages like Java.

Let's see how to create a method. Every method has a method declaration and the method body that contains the actual code (just like the **main** method we've been using). The form of the declaration we will use is:

```
public static type methodName(argumentList)
```

In this declaration, it says we are defining a method named **methodName**. The information needed by the method is provide in the **argumentList** (a comma-delimited list of variables). The method will return a value of **type** (if no value is returned type is **void**). We will ignore the keywords **public** and **static**.

Information is passed to the method via the **argumentList**. Notice in the **println** method, we pass the string to print, in the **Math.sqrt** function, we pass the number to find the square root of, in the **inInt** method, we pass nothing (that's okay too). The argument list is of the form:

```
type1 varName1, type2 varName2, type3 varName3, ...
```

You can have as many arguments as you like (or none). Information (if any) is returned from the method using the **return** statement:

```
return(returnedValue);
```

This **returnedValue** is then available to the calling program, either for assignment to a variable or for use in some Java expression.

Once defined, the method can be referenced in any other method in your project using:

```
returnedValue = methodName(argumentList);
```

If there is no returned value, you simply use:

```
methodName(argumentList);
```

In either case, you need to make sure the **argumentList** in the calling code matches the **argumentList** expected by the method. The list (variables or values separated by commas) must have the proper number of arguments, the proper type and they must be in the proper order.

Let's try to make this clearer by looking at a couple of method examples. First, an example that returns a value. We'll do the dice example of rolling five dice and returning their sum. The method that accomplishes this task is:

```
public static int rollDice()
{
  int die1, die2, die3, die4, die5;
  die1 = myRandom.nextInt(6) + 1;
  die2 = myRandom.nextInt(6) + 1;
  die3 = myRandom.nextInt(6) + 1;
  die4 = myRandom.nextInt(6) + 1;
  die5 = myRandom.nextInt(6) + 1;
  return (die1 + die2 + die3 + die4 + die5);
}
```

This method is named **rollDice** and has no arguments. It returns the **int** value containing the sum of the five dice.

Using this method, any time you need the sum of five dice in your project, you would use:

sum = rollDice();

Notice you need the parentheses even if there are no arguments. Once called, the variable **sum** (must be of type **int**) will have a sum of five dice.

Now, an example that returns no value. We will build a method that, given the length and width of a rectangle, prints out the area of the rectangle. Here's that method (yes, I know it's a very simple one):

```
public static void rectArea(int length, int width)
{
  System.out.println("Your rectangle has an area of " +
(length * width));
}
```

Notice use of the keyword **void** in the declaration statement to indicate no value is returned. Also, notice how the input variables (**length** and **width**) are defined in the argument list.

To use this method in code, you could use literals:

```
rectArea(13, 15);
```

This would print out the area of a rectangle of length 13 and width 15. Or, you can use variables:

```
rectArea(myLength, myWidth);
```

In each case, notice the method is expecting an integer representing the length in the first position of the argument list and an integer width in the second position. Notice, too, that the variable names used in the calling program do not (and usually don't) have to match the variable names in the method declaration. Only position within the argument list matters.

So, where do methods go in your project? By convention, they are placed after the **main** method. Make sure to put it after the closing brace of the **main** method and before the closing brace of the class definition for your project. For example:

```
public class MethodExample
{
  public static void main(String[] args)
  {
     [Main method code]
  }
```

> Your methods go here!

```
}
```

As you progress in your Java programming education, you will become more comfortable with using methods and see how useful they are. In the remainder of this course, we will use methods when needed. Study each example to help learn how to build and use methods.

Project – Lemonade Stand

A very powerful use of computers is to do something called **simulation**. Before building an actual airplane, companies "build" the plane on a computer and simulate its performance. This is much cheaper and far safer than testing actual airplanes. Engineers simulate how a building might react to an earthquake to help them design better buildings. And, businesses use computers to simulate how decisions could affect their profits. Based on computer results, they decide how and where to invest their money. In this project, we will build a small business simulation. We will simulate the operation of a backyard lemonade stand. Based on the temperature, you will set a selling price for your lemonade (the hotter it is, the more you can charge). You will then be told how many cups you sold and how much money you made. If you're too greedy, asking too much for your product, you won't sell as much. If you're too nice, you won't make as much money. It's a tough world out there! This project is saved as **LemonadeProject** in the course projects folder (**\JavaKids\JK Code**).

Project Design

You'll sell lemonade for five days (simulated days). On each day, you will be told the temperature. Based on this temperature, you set a price for your lemonade. You will be told how many cups of lemonade you sold and how much money you made. The steps to follow on each day:

1. Computer picks a random temperature.
2. You assign a price for each cup of lemonade.
3. Computer analyzes the information and computes number of cups sold.
4. Your sales are computed and displayed.

The first step is a straightforward use of the random number object. In the second step, we will use the **Scanner nextDouble** method to get the price. Step 3 is the difficult one – how does the computer determine cups sold? In this project, we will give you the code to do this (code we made up) in the form of a method you can use. This is something done all the time in programming – borrowing and using someone else's code. In this method, you provide the temperature and the price (the arguments) and the method returns the number of cups sold. Finally, the **println** method will be used to output the results of each day's sales.

Project Development

Start JCreator, open your workspace and create a new project named **LemonadeProject**. Add a blank file named **Lemonade** (the .java extension will be added).

Open the empty **Lemonade.java** file. Type the usual header information, the class definition line, the import statements needed for the **Random** and **Scanner** objects and the main method definition (along with needed braces):

```
/*
 *   Lemonade Stand
 *   Java for Kids
 *   www.KIDwareSoftware.com
 */

import java.util.Random;
import java.util.Scanner;

public class Lemonade
{
  public static void main(String[] args)
    {
    }
}
```

Java Looping, Methods

We will use several variables in this program: Type their declarations next (in the main method):

```
// define variables
int dayNumber;
int temperature;
int cupPrice;
int cupsSold;
double daySales;
double totalSales;
Random myRandom = new Random();
Scanner myScanner = new Scanner(System.in);
```

Notice with good naming practice, you can see what each variable is. One note – we will assume the **cupPrice** is an integer value in cents, while **daySales** and **totalSales** are in dollars. For our foreign readers, there are 100 cents in a dollar. Feel free to change the units to anything you want.

Now, we write the code, following the previously defined programming steps. First, initialize the **dayNumber** and **totalSales** and begin the loop over the five days of sales:

```
//  start loop of five days
dayNumber = 1;
totalSales = 0.0;
do
{
}
```

Each day (loop) begins with the computer selecting a random temperature (degrees F, you can change this if you want) between 60 and 100 degrees:

```
// pick a random temperature between 60 and 100
temperature = myRandom.nextInt(41) + 60;
System.out.println("\nWelcome to Day " + dayNumber + ", the temperature is " + temperature + " degrees.");
```

Based on this, you set the price (again, an **int** value) for each cup of lemonade:

```
// get price
System.out.print("How many cents do you want to charge for a cup of lemonade? ");
cupPrice = myScanner.nextInt();
```

With this information, the computer computes how many cups you sold and determines daily and total sales. The cups sold will be computed in a method named **getSales**, with two arguments, **temperature** and **cupPrice**. We will show you that method soon. For now, just assume it is available so it can be called. The code to report your sales is:

```
// get cups sold, provide sales report
cupsSold = getSales(temperature, cupPrice);
daySales = cupsSold * cupPrice / 100.0;
totalSales = totalSales + daySales;
System.out.println("\nYou sold " + cupsSold + " cups of lemonade, earning $" + daySales + ".");
if (dayNumber > 1)
{
  System.out.println("Total sales after " + dayNumber + " days are $" + totalSales + ".");
}
```

You should be able to see what's going on here. We find the **cupsSold**, compute daily and total sales and report the results. Notice that **totalSales** are only displayed for the second through the fifth day (since, on the first day, daily and total sales are the same). Next, increment the **dayNumber**, close out the **do/while** loop (the right brace should already be there – type the code shown before and after the brace):

```
  // go to next day
  dayNumber = dayNumber + 1;
}
while (dayNumber < 6);
System.out.println("\nThe lemonade stand is now closed.");
```

The method (**getSales**) that computes the number of cups sold is placed after the closing brace for the main method. For this method, we will just give you the code, so you can type it in. We will try to explain what's going on. Here is the complete method, including the declaration statement. Type this in, being careful to check that it is correct (note some lines are fairly long):

```
/*
 *  getSales method
 *  input temperature t and price p
 *  output number of cups sold
 *  KIDware
 */
public static int getSales(int t, double p)
{
  //  t represents temperature
  //  p represents price

  double bestPrice;
  double maxSales;
  double adjustment;
  Random anotherRandom = new Random();

  //  find best price
  bestPrice = (t - 60.0) * (45 - anotherRandom.nextInt(20)) / 40.0 + 20.0;
```

```
  // find maximum sales
  maxSales = (t - 60.0) * (230 - anotherRandom.nextInt(100))
/ 40.0 + 20.0;

  // find sales adjustment
  adjustment = 1.0 - Math.abs((p - bestPrice) / bestPrice);
  if (adjustment < 0.0)
  {
    adjustment = 0.0;
  }

   // return adjusted sales
  return((int) (adjustment * maxSales));
}
```

Make sure this is typed after the closing brace of the **main** method and before the closing right brace for the class **Lemonade**.

Let me try to explain what I'm doing here. First, I assume there is a **bestPrice** (most you can charge) for a cup of lemonade, based on the temperature (**t**). You can charge more on hotter days. The equation used assumes this **bestPrice** ranges from 20 cents at 60 degrees to a random value between 45 and 65 cents at 100 degrees. Similarly, there is a maximum number of cups you can sell (**maxSales**) based on temperature. You can sell more on hotter days. The equation used assumes **maxSales** ranges from 20 cups at 60 degrees to a random value between 150 and 250 at 100 degrees. Before returning a number of cups, I compute an **adjustment** variable. This is used to adjust your sales based on your input price. If you ask more than the **bestPrice**, sales will suffer because people will think you are asking too much for your product. Your sales will also suffer if you charge too little for lemonade! Why's that? Many people think if something doesn't cost enough, it may not be very good. You just can't win in the business world. So, adjustment is computed based on how far your set price (**p**) is from the **bestPrice**. Once **adjustment** is found, it is multiplied times the **maxSales** and returned to the calling program in this line of code:

```
return((int) (adjustment * maxSales));
```

Notice you see something you have never seen before, the words **int** in parentheses before the product. This is called a **casting** in Java and converts the product (**adjustment * maxSales**), a **double** value, to the required **int** return value for the number of cups sold. You can't sell a fraction of a cup! This brings up a good point. Many times, when using someone else's Java code, you may see things you don't recognize. What do you do? The best thing is to consult some Java reference (another Java programmer, a textbook, the Java website) and do a little research and self-study. This helps you learn more and helps you become a better Java programmer.

Notice if you play this program as a game, you wouldn't know all the details behind the rules (how **cupSales** are computed). You would learn these rules as you play. That's what happens in all computer games – the games have rules and, after many plays, you learn what rules the programmers have included. If you can't follow all the math in the **getSales** method, that's okay. You don't really need to – just trust that it does the job. Actually, Java programmers use methods all the time without an understanding of how they work (do you know how Java finds the square root of a number?). In such cases, we rely on the method writer to tell us what information is required (arguments) and what information is computed (returned value) and trust that the method works. That's the beauty of methods – we get code without doing the work.

The finished code in the JCreator view window should appear as:

```java
/*
 *   Lemonade Stand
 *   Java for Kids
 *   www.KIDwareSoftware.com
 */

import java.util.Random;
import java.util.Scanner;

public class Lemonade
{
  public static void main(String[] args)
  {
    // define variables
    int dayNumber;
    int temperature;
    int cupPrice;
    int cupsSold;
    double daySales;
    double totalSales;
    Random myRandom = new Random();
    Scanner myScanner = new Scanner(System.in);

    //  start loop of five days
    dayNumber = 1;
    totalSales = 0.0;
    do
    {
      // pick a random temperature between 60 and 100
      temperature = myRandom.nextInt(41) + 60;
      System.out.println("\nWelcome to Day " + dayNumber + ", the temperature is " + temperature + " degrees.");

      // get price
      System.out.print("How many cents do you want to charge for a cup of lemonade? ");
      cupPrice = myScanner.nextInt();

      // get cups sold, provide sales report
      cupsSold = getSales(temperature, cupPrice);
      daySales = cupsSold * cupPrice / 100.0;
      totalSales = totalSales + daySales;
      System.out.println("\nYou sold " + cupsSold + " cups of lemonade, earning $" + daySales + ".");
```

```java
      if (dayNumber > 1)
      {
        System.out.println("Total sales after " + dayNumber +
" days are $" + totalSales + ".");
      }

      // go to next day
      dayNumber = dayNumber + 1;
    }
    while (dayNumber < 6);
    System.out.println("\nThe lemonade stand is now
closed.");
  }

  /*
   * getSales method
   * input temperature t and price p
   * output number of cups sold
   * KIDware
   */
  public static int getSales(int t, double p)
  {
    //  t represents temperature
    //  p represents price

    double bestPrice;
    double maxSales;
    double adjustment;
    Random anotherRandom = new Random();

    //  find best price
    bestPrice = (t - 60.0) * (45 - anotherRandom.nextInt(20))
/ 40.0 + 20.0;

    // find maximum sales
    maxSales = (t - 60.0) * (230 -
anotherRandom.nextInt(100)) / 40.0 + 20.0;

    // find sales adjustment
    adjustment = 1.0 - Math.abs((p - bestPrice) / bestPrice);
    if (adjustment < 0.0)
    {
      adjustment = 0.0;
    }

     // return adjusted sales
    return((int) (adjustment * maxSales));
```

```
    }
}
```

Java Looping, Methods

Run the Project

Compile and run the project. Eliminate any syntax, run-time or logic errors you may encounter. You may have to recheck your typing, especially in the method. You should now see:

```
General Output
    --------------------Configuration: LemonadeProject - JDK version 1.6

Welcome to Day 1, the temperature is 78 degrees.
How many cents do you want to charge for a cup of lemonade?
```

Enter a value for cup price (in cents) and you should see something like:

```
General Output
    --------------------Configuration: LemonadeProject - JDK version 1.6.

Welcome to Day 1, the temperature is 78 degrees.
How many cents do you want to charge for a cup of lemonade? 25

You sold 67 cups of lemonade, earning $16.75.

Welcome to Day 2, the temperature is 96 degrees.
How many cents do you want to charge for a cup of lemonade?
```

Continue playing until you have run the lemonade stand for five days.

Here's my try at five days:

```
General Output
--------------------Configuration: LemonadeProject - JDK version 1.6.0

Welcome to Day 1, the temperature is 78 degrees.
How many cents do you want to charge for a cup of lemonade? 25

You sold 67 cups of lemonade, earning $16.75.

Welcome to Day 2, the temperature is 96 degrees.
How many cents do you want to charge for a cup of lemonade? 35

You sold 132 cups of lemonade, earning $46.2.
Total sales after 2 days are $62.95.

Welcome to Day 3, the temperature is 92 degrees.
How many cents do you want to charge for a cup of lemonade? 30

You sold 144 cups of lemonade, earning $43.2.
Total sales after 3 days are $106.15.

Welcome to Day 4, the temperature is 78 degrees.
How many cents do you want to charge for a cup of lemonade? 25

You sold 91 cups of lemonade, earning $22.75.
Total sales after 4 days are $128.9.

Welcome to Day 5, the temperature is 83 degrees.
How many cents do you want to charge for a cup of lemonade? 35

You sold 108 cups of lemonade, earning $37.8.
Total sales after 5 days are $166.7.

The lemonade stand is now closed.

Process completed.
```

Try several runs to see if you can improve your playing skills. Save your project if you needed to make any changes.

Other Things to Try

You have the beginnings of a fun computer simulation. Can you think of changes you would like to make? Add more days, change the rules in **getSales**? Why not add another loop so you play over and over again without having to rerun the application each time? We have some ideas.

To make lemonade, you need products: cups, lemons, sugar. These cost money and cut into your profit. A great modification would be to add the need for shopping into your simulation. You would need to figure out how much of each product you need to make a cup of lemonade. Research at a grocery store would tell you the cost to make a cup of lemonade. Then, you can determine how much profit you make on your sales. This gives the program more of a "real-world" flavor.

Add more randomness into the program. Maybe consider both temperature and weather conditions. Add a chance of precipitation into the computations. You wouldn't sell as much lemonade on a hot rainy day as you would on a hot clear day. Try these and any other ideas you have.

Summary

In this class, with the added capabilities of looping and methods, we greatly expanded our Java programming skills. Being able to repeat blocks of code lets us build far more useful programs. We used this capability to allow multiple guesses in our **Guess the Number** game and the **Lemonade Stand** program was seen to be a fun computer simulation. In the next class, we'll study another looping method that gives us even more programming power.

7. Arrays, More Java Looping

Review and Preview

In the last class, we introduced the idea of looping - repeating code blocks.

In this class' Java lesson, we look at another way to loop (the Java **for** loop) and at a new way to declare variables. And, as a project, we build a version of the card game **War**. We'll learn how to get the computer how to shuffle a deck of cards!

Java - The Fifth Lesson

In this Java lesson, we look at ways to store large numbers of variables and a technique for counting.

Variable Arrays

Your school principal has recognized your great Java programming skills and has come for your help. Everyone (352 students) in the school has just taken a basic skills test. The principal wants you to write a program that stores each student's name and score. The program should rank (put in order) the scores and compute the average score. The code to do this is not that hard. The problem we want to discuss here is how do we declare all the variables we need? To write this test score program, you need 352 **String** variables to store student names and 352 **int** variables to store student scores. We are required to declare every variable we use. Do you want to type 704 lines of code something like this?:

```
String student1;
String student2;
String student3;
    .
    .
String student352;
int score1;
int score2;
int score3;
    .
    .
int score352;
```

I don't think so.

Arrays, More Java Looping 7-3

Java provides a way to store a large number of variables under the same name - **variable arrays**. Each variable in an array, called an **element**, must have the same data type, and they are distinguished from each other by an array **index**. A variable array is declared in a way similar to other variables. To indicate the variable is an array, you use two square brackets (**[ ]**) after the type. Square brackets are used a lot with arrays. At the same time you declare an array, it is good practice to create it using the **new** keyword. For 352 student names and 352 student scores, we declare and create the needed arrays using:

```
String[] student = new String[352];
int[] score = new int[352];
```

The number in brackets is called the array **dimension**. These two lines have the same effect as the 704 declaration lines we might have had to write! And, notice how easy it would be to add 200 more variables if we needed them. You can also declare and create an array in two separate statements if you prefer. For the student name array, that code would be:

```
String[] student;  // the declaration;
student = new String[352];  // the creation
```

We now have 352 **student** variables (**String** type) and 352 **score** variables (**int** type) available for our use. A very important concept to be aware of is that Java uses what are called **zero-based** arrays. This means array indices begin with 0 and end at the dimension value minus 1, in this case 351. Each variable in an array is referred to by its declared name and index. The first student name in the array would be **student[0]** and the last name would be **student[351]**, <u>not</u> **student[352]**. If you try to refer to **student[352]**, you will get a run-time error saying an array value is out of bounds. This is a common mistake! When working with arrays in Java, always be aware they are zero-based.

As an example of using an array, to assign information to the student with index of 150 (actually, the 151st student in the array because of the zero base), we could write two lines of code like this:

```
student[150] = "Billy Gates";
score[150] = 100;
```

Array variables can be used anywhere regular variables are used. They can be used on the left side of assignment statements or in expressions. To add up the first three test scores, you would write:

```
sum = score[0] + score[1] + score[2];
```

Again, notice the first score in the array is **score[0]**, not **score[1]**. I know this is confusing, but it's something you need to remember. We still need to provide values for each element in each array, but there are also some shortcuts we can take to avoid lots of assignment statements. One such shortcut, the **for** loop, is examined next. You will find variable arrays are very useful when working with large numbers (and sometimes, not so large numbers) of similar variables.

Java for Loops

In the previous class, we looked at two methods of looping: the **while** loop and the **do/while** loop. In each of these loops, a particular code block was repeated while a certain logical **expression** remained true. In those loops, we did not know ahead of time how many times the code block would be repeated (if any). Many times, though, we might like to execute some Java code block a particular number of times. This computer programming task is called **counting**. For example, in the school score example from above, we need to go through a loop 352 times to compute an average of the 352 scores. Java offers a convenient way to do counting: the **for** loop.

The Java **for** loop has this unique structure:

```
for (initialization; expression; update)
{
    [Java code block to execute]
}
```

After the word **for** are three parts separated by semicolons: **initialization**, **expression**, and **update**. The first, **initialization**, is a step executed <u>once</u> and is used to initialize a counter variable (usually an **int** type). A very common initialization would start a counter **i** at zero:

```
i = 0
```

The second part, **expression**, is a step executed before each iteration (repetition) of the code in the loop. If **expression** is true, the code is executed; if false, program execution continues at the line following the end of the **for** loop. A common **expression** would be:

```
i < iMax
```

The final part, **update**, is a step executed after each iteration of the code in the loop; it is used to update the value of the counter variable. A common **update** would be:

```
i = i + 1
```

The functionality of a **for** loop can also be expressed as a **while** loop:

```
initialization;
while (expression)
{
      [Java code block to execute]
   update;
}
```

Maybe this helps better show you how **for** loops work. Also, like the **while** and **do/while** loops you can exit a **for** loop at any time by executing a **break** statement. Or, you can skip the rest of the statements in the loop by executing a **continue** statement. And, **for** loops can be nested (one loop in another), but that's beyond this class.

Arrays, More Java Looping

A few examples should clear things up. Assume we want to print out the 10 elements of some array, **myArray[10]**. The **for** loop that would accomplish this task is:

```
for (i = 0; i < 10; i = i + 1)
{
   System.out.println("Element " + i + " is " + myArray[i]);
}
```

In this loop, the counter variable **i** (declared to be an **int** variable prior to this statement) is initialized at 0. With each iteration, **i** is incremented by one. The loop is repeated as long as **i** remains smaller than 10 (remember **myArray[9]** is the last element of the array).

How about a rocket launch countdown? This loop will do the job:

```
for (i = 10; i <= 0; i = i - 1)
{
     [Java code block for the countdown]
}
```

Here **i** starts at 10 and goes <u>down</u> by 1 (i = i -1) each time the loop is repeated. Yes, you can decrease the counter. And, you can have counter increments that are not 1. This loop counts from 0 to 200 by 5's:

```
for (i = 0; i <= 200; i = i + 5)
{
     [Java code block to execute]
}
```

In each of these examples, it is assumed that **i** has been declared prior to these loops.

How about averaging the scores from our student example. This code will do the job:

```
scoreSum = 0;
for (studentNumber = 0; studentNumber < 352; studentNumber = studentNumber + 1)
{
   scoreSum = scoreSum + score[StudentNumber];
}
average = scoreSum / 300;
```

(Again, it is assumed that all variables have been declared to have the proper type). To find an average of a group of numbers, you add up all the numbers then divide by the number of numbers you have. In this code, **scoreSum** represents the sum of all the numbers. We set this to zero to start. Then, each time through the loop, we add the next score to that "running" sum. The loop adds up all 352 scores making use of the **score** array. The first time through it adds in **score[0]**, then **score[1]**, then **score[2]**, and so on, until it finishes by adding in **score[351]**. Once done, the average is computed by dividing **scoreSum** by 352. Do you see how the for loop greatly simplifies the task of adding up 352 numbers? This is one of the shortcut methods we can use when working with arrays. Study each of these examples so you have an idea of how the **for** loop works. Use them when you need to count.

Before leaving the **for** loop, let's examine a couple of other things. A very common update to a counter variable is to add one (increment) or subtract one (decrement). Java has special increment and decrement operators that do just that. To add one to a variable named **counterVariable**, you can simply write:

```
counterVariable++;
```

This statement is equivalent to:

```
counterVariable = counterVariable + 1;
```

Similarly, the decrement operator:

```
counterVariable--;
```

Is equivalent to:

```
counterVariable = counterVariable - 1;
```

The increment and decrement operators are not limited to **for** loops. They can be used anywhere they are needed in a Java program.

Let's address one last issue. Notice, at a minimum, the **for** loop requires the declaration of one variable, the loop counter, usually an integer variable. This variable is only used in this loop - it's value is usually of no use anywhere else. When we declare a variable at the top of a method, its value is available everywhere in that method. Such declarations are not necessary with **for** loop counters and it becomes a headache if you have lots of **for** loops. Loop counters can be declared in the initialization part of the **for** statement. We give these variables **loop level scope** - their value is only known within that loop.

As an example of declaring loop level variables, look at a modification to the student average example:

```
scoreSum = 0;
for (int studentNumber = 0; studentNumber < 352;
studentNumber = studentNumber + 1)
{
   scoreSum = scoreSum + score[StudentNumber];
}
average = scoreSum / 300;
```

Notice how the counter (**studentNumber**) is declared in the **for** statement. Once the **for** loop is complete, the value of **studentNumber** is no longer known or available. As you write Java code, you will often give your loop variables such loop level scope.

"Shuffle" Method

Let's use our new knowledge of arrays and **for** loops to write a very useful method. A common task in any computer program is to randomly sort a list of consecutive integer values. Why would you want to do this? Say you have four answers in a multiple choice quiz. Randomly sort the integers 1, 2, 3, and 4, so the answers are presented in random order. Or, you have a quiz with 30 questions. Randomly sort the questions for printing out as a worksheet. Or, the classic application is shuffling a deck of standard playing cards (there are 52 cards in such a deck). In that case, you can randomly sort the integers from 0 to 51 to "simulate" the shuffling process. Let's build a "shuffle" routine. We call it a shuffle routine, recognizing it can do more than shuffle a card deck. Our routine will sort any number of consecutive integers.

Usually when we need a computer version of something we can do without a computer, it is fairly easy to write down the steps taken and duplicate them in Java code. We've done that with the projects built so far in this course. Other times, the computer version of a process is easy to do on a computer, but hard or tedious to do off the computer. When we shuffle a deck of cards, we separate the deck in two parts, then interleaf the cards as we fan each part. I don't know how you could write Java code to do this. There is a way, however, to write Java code to do a shuffle in a more tedious way (tedious to a human, easy for a computer).

We will perform what could be called a "one card shuffle." In a one card shuffle, you pull a single card (at random) out of the deck and lay it aside on a pile. Repeat this 52 times and the cards are shuffled. Try it! I think you see this idea is simple, but doing a one card shuffle with a real deck of cards would be awfully time-consuming. We'll use the idea of a one card shuffle here, with a slight twist. Rather than lay the selected card on a pile, we will swap it with the bottom card in the stack of cards remaining to be shuffled. This takes the selected card out of the deck and replaces it with the remaining bottom card. The result is the same as if we lay it aside.

Here's how the shuffle works with n numbers:

- Start with a list of n consecutive integers.
- Randomly pick one item from the list. Swap that item with the last item. You now have one fewer items in the list to be sorted (called the remaining list), or n is now n - 1.
- Randomly pick one item from the remaining list. Swap it with the item on the bottom of the remaining list. Again, your remaining list now has one fewer items.
- Repeatedly remove one item from the remaining list and swap it with the item on the bottom of the remaining list until you have run out of items. When done, the list will have been replaced with the original list in random order.

Confusing? Let's show a simple example with n = 5 (a very small deck of cards).

The starting list is (with 5 remaining items):

| 1 | 2 | 3 | 4 | 5 |

Remaining List

We want to pick one item, at random, from this list. Using the Java random number generator, we would choose a random number from 1 to 5. Say it was 3. We take the third item in the list (the 3) and swap it with the last item in the list (the 5). We now have:

<u>1   2   5   4</u>   3
Remaining List

There are 4 items in the remaining list. Pick a random number from 1 to 4 - say it's 4. The fourth item in the remaining list is 4. Swap it with the last item in the remaining list. Wait a minute! The last item in the remaining list is the 4. In this case, we swap it with itself, or it stays put. If the random number was something other than 4, there really would have been a swap here. We now have:

<u>1   2   5</u>   4   3
Remaining List

There are 3 items in the remaining list. Pick a random number from 1 to 3 - say it's 1. The first item in the list is 1. Swap the 1 with the last item in the remaining list (the 5), giving us:

<u>5   2</u>   1   4   3
Remaining List

There are 2 items in the remaining list. Pick a random number from 1 to 2 - say it's 1. The first item in the list is 5. Swap the 5 with the last item in the remaining list (the 2), giving us the final result, the numbers 1 to 5 randomly sorted:

       2   5   1   4   3

Pretty neat how this works, huh?

We want to describe the one card shuffle with Java code. Most of the code is straightforward. The only question is how to do the swap involved in each step. This swap is easy on paper. How do we do a swap in Java? Actually, this is a common Java task and is relatively simple. At first thought, to swap variable **aVariable** with variable **bVariable**, you might write:

```
aVariable = bVariable;
bVariable = aVariable;
```

The problem with this code is that when you replace **aVariable** with **bVariable** in the first statement, you have destroyed the original value of **aVariable**. The second statement just puts the newly assigned **aVariable** value (**bVariable**) back in **bVariable**. Both **aVariable** and **bVariable** now have the original **bVariable** value!

Actually, swapping two variables is a three step process. First, put **aVariable** in a temporary storage variable (make it the same type as **aVariable** and **bVariable**). Then, replace **aVariable** by **bVariable**. Then, replace **bVariable** by the temporary variable (which holds the original **aVariable** value). If **tVariable** is the temporary variable, a swap of **aVariable** and **bVariable** is done using:

```
tVariable = aVariable;
aVariable = bVariable;
bVariable = tVariable;
```

You use swaps like this in all kinds of Java applications.

Now, we'll see the Java code (a method) that uses a one card shuffle to randomly sort n consecutive integer values. The method is named **nIntegers** and has a single **int** type argument, that being n, the number of integers to shuffle. When done, the method returns the random list of integers in an array of dimension n. Make sure you have declared such an array in your calling method. One note – recall arrays in Java are zero-based. In the **nIntegers** method, if you ask it to shuffle n consecutive integers, the indices on the returned array range from 0 to n – 1 and the randomized integers will also range from 0 to n – 1, not 1 to n. If you need integers from 1 to n, just simply add 1 to each value in the returned list! The code is:

```java
public static int[] nIntegers(int n)
{
  /*
  *  Returns n randomly sorted integers 0 -> n - 1
  */
  int nArray[] = new int[n];
  int temp, s;
  Random myRandom = new Random();
  //   initialize array from 0 to n - 1
  for (int i = 0; i < n; i++)
  {
    nArray[i] = i;
  }
  //  perform one-card shuffle
  //   i is number of items remaining in list
  //   s is the random selection from that list
  //   we swap last item i - 1 with selection s
  for (int i = n; i >= 1; i--)
  {
    s = myRandom.nextInt(i);
    temp = nArray[s];
    nArray[s] = nArray[i - 1];
    nArray[i - 1] = temp;
  }
  return(nArray);
}
```

Arrays, More Java Looping 7-17

Study this code and see how it implements the procedure followed in the simple five number example. It's not that hard to see. Understanding how such code works is a first step to becoming a good Java programmer.

Notice this bit of code uses everything we talked about in this class' Java lesson: arrays, **for** loops, and loop level variables. Let's build a quick example using JCreator to try all these new concepts and see how the shuffle routine works using 10 integers. Start JCreator, open your workspace and create a new project named **ShuffleProject**. Add a blank file named **Shuffle** (the .java extension will be added). Type this code for the **Shuffle** class:

```
/*
 *   Shuffle Test
 *   Java for Kids
 */
import java.util.Random;
public class Shuffle
{
  public static void main(String[] args)
  {
    //   declare needed array
    int[] myIntegers = new int[10];
    //   shuffle integers from 0 to 9
    myIntegers = nIntegers(10);
    //   print out results
    for (int i = 0; i < 10; i++)
    {
      System.out.println("Value is " + myIntegers[i]);
    }
  }
}
```

This code creates an array of length 10. This array is then filled with the random integers 0 to 9 by calling the **nIntegers** method. The results are printed using 10 calls to **println** in the **for** loop.

Now, type in the **nIntegers** method as shown earlier. Make sure this code goes after the **main** method closing right brace and before the **Shuffle** class closing right brace. Once this code is in, compile and run the project. Correct any errors that might occur. Double-check you have entered the **nIntegers** method correctly. When I run this little example, I get (you will get different numbers – remember they're random!):

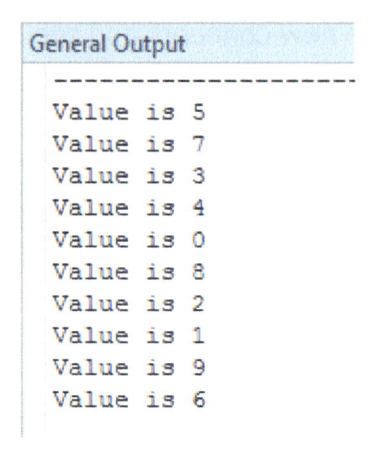

```
General Output
-------------------
Value is 5
Value is 7
Value is 3
Value is 4
Value is 0
Value is 8
Value is 2
Value is 1
Value is 9
Value is 6
```

Notice how the array (**myIntegers**) contains a random listing of the integers from 0 to 9, as desired. If I run it again, I get:

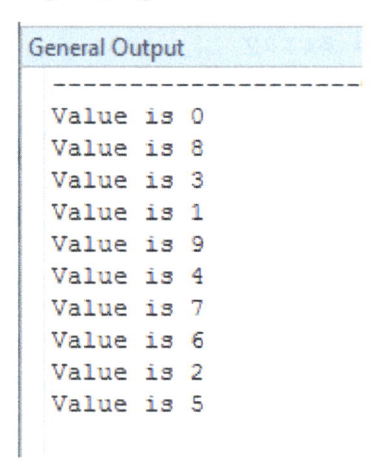

```
General Output
-------------------
Value is 0
Value is 8
Value is 3
Value is 1
Value is 9
Value is 4
Value is 7
Value is 6
Value is 2
Value is 5
```

Obviously, the list is now different. For your reference, this project has been saved as **ShuffleProject** in the course projects folder (**\JavaKids\JK Code**).

Project - Card Wars

In this project, we create a simplified version of the kid's card game - War. You play against the computer. You each get half a deck of cards (26 cards). Each player turns over one card at a time. The one with the higher card wins the other player's card. The one with the most cards at the end wins. Obviously, the shuffle routine will come in handy here. We call this project **Card Wars**! This project is saved as **CardWars** in the projects folder (**\JavaKids\JK Code**).

Project Design

The game is conceptually simple. The steps to follow are:

1. Shuffle a deck of cards.
2. Computer gives itself a card and player a card.
3. Computer compares cards, the player with the higher card wins both cards.
4. Scores are computed and displayed.
5. Process continues until all cards have been dealt from the deck.

We can use our shuffle routine to shuffle the deck of cards (compute 52 random integers from 0 to 51). Describing the handed-out cards requires converting the integer card value to an actual card in the deck (value and suit). We will create a Java method to do this. Comparing the cards is relatively easy (we'll add the capability to our card display method), as is updating and displaying the scores (we will use our old friend, the **println** method). No input is ever needed from the user (besides pressing a key on the keyboard to see the cards) - he/she merely watches the results go by.

Project Development

Before building the project, let's do a little "up front" work. In the **Project Design**, we see a need for a method that, given a card number (0 to 51), (1) determines and displays which card (**suit**, **value**) in a deck it represents, and (2) determines its corresponding **numerical** value to allow comparisons. We will create this method now.

Displaying a card consists of answering two questions: what is the card suit and what is the card value? The four suits are hearts, diamonds, clubs, and spades. The thirteen card values, from lowest to highest, are: Two, Three, Four, Five, Six, Seven, Eight, Nine, Ten, Jack, Queen, King, Ace. We've seen in our shuffle routine that a card number will range from 0 to 51. How do we translate that card number to a card suit and value? (Notice the distinction between card **number** and card **value** - card number ranges from 0 to 51, card value can only range from Two to Ace.) We need to develop some type of translation rule. This is done all the time in Java. If the number you compute with or work with does not directly translate to information you need, you need to make up rules to do the translation. For example, the numbers 1 to 12 are used to represent the months of the year. But, these numbers tell us nothing about the names of the month. We need a rule to translate each number to a month name.

We know we need 13 of each card suit. Hence, an easy rule to decide suit is: cards numbered 0 - 12 are hearts, cards numbered 13 - 25 are diamonds, cards numbered 26 - 38 are clubs, and cards numbered 39 - 51 are spades. For card values, lower numbers should represent lower cards. A rule that does this for each number in each card suit is:

Card Numbers

Hearts	Diamonds	Clubs	Spades	Card Value
0	13	26	39	Two
1	14	27	40	Three
2	15	28	41	Four
3	16	29	42	Five
4	17	30	43	Six
5	18	31	44	Seven
6	19	32	45	Eight
7	20	33	46	Nine
8	21	34	47	Ten
9	22	35	48	Jack
10	23	36	49	Queen
11	24	37	50	King
12	25	38	51	Ace

As examples, notice card 22 is a Jack of Diamonds. Card 30 is a Six of Clubs. We now have the ability to describe a card. How do we compare them?

Card comparisons must be based on a numerical value, not displayed card value - it's difficult to check if King is greater than Seven, though it can be done. So, one last rule is needed to relate card value to numerical value. It's a simple one - start with a Two having a numerical value of 0 (lowest) and go up, with an Ace having a numerical value of 12 (highest). This makes numerical card comparisons easy. Notice hearts card numbers already go from 0 to 12. If we subtract 13 from diamonds numbers, 26 from clubs numbers, and 39 from spades numbers, each of those card numbers will also range from 0 to 12. This gives a common basis for comparing cards. This all may seem complicated, but look at the Java code and you'll see it really isn't.

Here is a Java method (**cardDisplay**) that takes the card number (**n**) as an input and returns its numeric value (0 to 12) to allow comparisons. The method also prints a string description (**value** and **suit**) of the corresponding card, using the above table for translation .

```java
/*
 *  Card Display
 *  Java for Kids
 */
public static int cardDisplay(int n)
{
  // given card number n (0 - 51), prints description
  // and returns numeric value
  String suit;
  String[] value = new String[13];
  value[0] = "Two";
  value[1] = "Three";
  value[2] = "Four";
  value[3] = "Five";
  value[4] = "Six";
  value[5] = "Seven";
  value[6] = "Eight";
  value[7] = "Nine";
  value[8] = "Ten";
  value[9] = "Jack";
  value[10] = "Queen";
  value[11] = "King";
  value[12] = "Ace";
  // determine your card's suit, adjust numeric value n
  if (n >= 0 && n <= 12)
  {
    suit = "Hearts";
  }
  else if (n >= 13 && n <= 25)
  {
    suit = "Diamonds";
    n = n - 13;
  }
  else if (n >= 26 && n <= 38)
  {
    suit = "Clubs";
    n = n - 26;
  }
  else
```

```
  {
    suit = "Spades";
    n = n - 39;
  }
  // print description
  System.out.println(value[n] + " of " + suit);
  // return numeric value
  return(n);
}
```

You should be able to see how this works. With this method built, we can use it to create the complete **Card Wars** project.

Start JCreator, open your workspace and create a new project named **CardWarsProject**. Add a blank file named **CardWars** (the .java extension will be added).

Open the empty **CardWars.java** file. Type the usual header information, the class definition line, the import statements needed for the **Random** and **Scanner** objects and the **main** method definition (along with needed braces):

```
/*
 *   Card Wars
 *   Java for Kids
 *   www.KIDwareSoftware.com
 */

import java.util.Random;
import java.util.Scanner;

public class CardWars
{
   public static void main(String[] args)
   {
   }
}
```

Next, declare the needed variables (in **main** method):

```
//   declare needed variables
int cardIndex = 0;
int computerScore = 0;
int yourScore = 0;
int computerCard;
int yourCard;
int[] myCards = new int[52];
Scanner myScanner = new Scanner(System.in);
```

Again, the names tell you what the variables are. Now, shuffle the cards using the shuffle method and start the playing **do** loop:

```
//   shuffle the cards
myCards = nIntegers(52);
// do loop starting game
do
{
}
```

Now, in the **do** loop, type the code that picks and displays the cards:

```
// display computer card, then your card
System.out.print("My card:    ");
computerCard = cardDisplay(myCards[cardIndex]);
System.out.print("Your card: ");
yourCard = cardDisplay(myCards[cardIndex + 1]);
```

Arrays, More Java Looping 7-25

Next, we check to see who wins (or if there is a tie) and compute the scores:

```java
// see who won
if (yourCard > computerCard)
{
  System.out.println("You win!");
  yourScore = yourScore + 2;
}
else if (computerCard > yourCard)
{
  System.out.println("I win!");
  computerScore = computerScore + 2;
}
else
{
  System.out.println("It's a tie.");
  yourScore = yourScore + 1;
  computerScore = computerScore + 1;
}
```

Next, we print the results:

```java
System.out.println("My Score:   " + computerScore);
System.out.println("Your Score: " + yourScore);
cardIndex = cardIndex + 2;
System.out.print("There are " + (52 - cardIndex) + " cards remaining. ");
System.out.println("Press any key.");
myScanner.nextLine();
```

This closes out the do loop. After the closing brace (should be there), the **while** statement is added and a final game over message is printed:

```java
}
while ((52 - cardIndex) > 0);
System.out.println("Game over.");
```

After typing the code in the **CardWars** class, you still need to add two methods: the **displayCard** method and the **nIntegers** shuffle method. You can copy and paste **nIntegers** from the **ShuffleProject** we built earlier in this class. And, if you want, you can copy and paste **displayCard** from these notes into the editor of JCreator. That would save you lots of typing. But, go ahead and type the methods, if you'd like. In any case, make sure the two methods are there, after the closing brace of the **CardWars main** method.

For completeness, here is all the code from the JCreator view window code for the **Card Wars** project, including all methods (get ready, it's long!):

```java
/*
 *  Card Wars
 *  Java for Kids
 *  www.KIDwareSoftware.com
 */

import java.util.Random;
import java.util.Scanner;

public class CardWars
{
   public static void main(String[] args)
   {
     //  declare needed variables
     int cardIndex = 0;
     int computerScore = 0;
     int yourScore = 0;
     int computerCard;
     int yourCard;
     int[] myCards = new int[52];
     Scanner myScanner = new Scanner(System.in);

     //  shuffle the cards
     myCards = nIntegers(52);

     // do loop starting game
     do
     {
       // display computer card, then your card
```

```java
      System.out.print("My card:    ");
      computerCard = cardDisplay(myCards[cardIndex]);
      System.out.print("Your card: ");
      yourCard = cardDisplay(myCards[cardIndex + 1]);
      // see who won
      if (yourCard > computerCard)
      {
        System.out.println("You win!");
        yourScore = yourScore + 2;
      }
      else if (computerCard > yourCard)
      {
        System.out.println("I win!");
        computerScore = computerScore + 2;
      }
      else
      {
        System.out.println("It's a tie.");
        yourScore = yourScore + 1;
        computerScore = computerScore + 1;
      }
      System.out.println("My Score:   " + computerScore);
      System.out.println("Your Score: " + yourScore);
      cardIndex = cardIndex + 2;
      System.out.print("There are " + (52 - cardIndex) + " cards remaining. ");
      System.out.println("Press any key.");
      myScanner.nextLine();
    }
    while ((52 - cardIndex) > 0);
    System.out.println("Game over.");
  }

  /*
   *  Card Display
   *  Java for Kids
   */
  public static int cardDisplay(int n)
  {
    // given card number n (0 - 51), prints description and
    // returns numeric value
    String suit;
    String[] value = new String[13];
    value[0] = "Two";
    value[1] = "Three";
    value[2] = "Four";
    value[3] = "Five";
```

```java
    value[4] = "Six";
    value[5] = "Seven";
    value[6] = "Eight";
    value[7] = "Nine";
    value[8] = "Ten";
    value[9] = "Jack";
    value[10] = "Queen";
    value[11] = "King";
    value[12] = "Ace";

    // determine your card's suit, adjust numeric value n
    if (n >= 0 && n <= 12)
    {
      suit = "Hearts";
    }
    else if (n >= 13 && n <= 25)
    {
      suit = "Diamonds";
      n = n - 13;
    }
    else if (n >= 26 && n <= 38)
    {
      suit = "Clubs";
      n = n - 26;
    }
    else
    {
      suit = "Spades";
      n = n - 39;
    }
    // print description
    System.out.println(value[n] + " of " + suit);
    // return numeric value
    return(n);
  }

  /*
   *   Shuffle Method
   *   Java for Kids
   */
  public static int[] nIntegers(int n)
  {
    /*
     * Returns n randomly sorted integers 0 -> n - 1
     */
    int nArray[] = new int[n];
    int temp, s;
```

```java
    Random myRandom = new Random();
    //  initialize array from 0 to n - 1
    for (int i = 0; i < n; i++)
    {
      nArray[i] = i;
    }
    //  perform one-card shuffle
    //  i is number of items remaining in list
    //  s is the random selection from that list
    //  we swap last item i - 1 with selection s
    for (int i = n; i >= 1; i--)
    {
      s = myRandom.nextInt(i);
      temp = nArray[s];
      nArray[s] = nArray[i - 1];
      nArray[i - 1] = temp;
    }
    return(nArray);
  }
}
```

Run the Project

Compile and run the project. Eliminate any syntax, run-time or logic errors you may encounter. You may have to recheck your typing, especially in the method. You should see something like:

```
General Output
                   -------Configuration: CardWarsProject - JDK
My card:    Ten of Hearts
Your card: Queen of Spades
You win!
My Score:   0
Your Score: 2
There are 50 cards remaining. Press any key.
```

All you do at this point is press any key to see the next set of cards. You continue doing this until the card deck is empty (all 52 cards have been used). Make sure the program works correctly. Play through one game and check each comparison to make sure you get the correct result and score with each new card. Go through the usual process of making sure the program works as it should. Once you're convinced everything is okay, have fun playing the game. Share your creation with friends. If you made any changes during the running process, make sure you save the project.

Other Things to Try

Possible changes to the **Card Wars** project are obvious, but not easy. One change would be to have more than two players. Set up three and four player versions. Perhaps add another loop to allow playing another game (without restarting the application).

In **Card Wars**, we stop the game after going through the deck one time. In the real card game of War, after the first round, the players pick up the cards they won, shuffle them, and play another round. Every time a player uses all the cards in their "hand," they again pick up their winnings pile, reshuffle and continue playing. This continues until one player has lost all of their cards. Another change to **Card Wars** would be to write code that plays the game with these rules. As we said, it's not easy. You would need to add code to keep track of which cards each player won, when they ran out of cards to play, how to reshuffle their remaining cards, and new logic to see when a game was over. Such code would use more arrays, more for loops, and more variables. If you want a programming challenge, go for it!

And, while you're tackling challenges, here's another. In the usual War game, when two cards have the same value - War is declared! This means each player takes three cards from their "hand" and lays them face down. Then another card is placed face up. The higher card at that time wins all 10 cards! If it's still a tie, there's another War. Try adding this logic to the game. You'll need to check if a player has enough cards to wage War. Another difficult task, but give it a try if you feel adventurous.

Summary

This class presented one of the more challenging projects yet. The code involved in shuffling cards and displaying cards, though straightforward, was quite involved. The use of arrays and **for** loops made the coding a bit easier. If you completely understood the **Card Wars** project, you are well on your way to being a good Java programmer. Now, on to the next class, where we introduce an exciting programming area – graphics!

8. Java Graphics, Mouse Methods

Review and Preview

You've seen and learned lots of Java code by now. But, plain text console projects are a bit boring.

In this class, we begin looking at a very fun part of Java - adding graphics capabilities to our projects. We will also look at ways for Java to recognize mouse inputs and have some fun with colors. You will build an electronic blackboard project.

Graphic User Interfaces (GUI)

All the Java projects built in this course have been console applications. The computer asks some questions, you answer the questions. Because of the simplicity, using console applications is a good way to learn the Java programming language. But, let's move on. Most programs in use feature what is called a **graphic user interface**. This is abbreviated **GUI** and pronounced **"gooey."** Yes, it is pronounced "gooey." In Java, you can build GUI applications that run on your desktop or laptop computer or GUI applications that run on the Internet, so-called applets. Console applications are text-based. GUI applications are built with **frames** using **controls**, such as menus, toolbars, buttons, text boxes, selection boxes, scroll bars and other devices the user interacts with to operate the program. The primary interaction with these controls is via the computer mouse. If you've used a computer, you have used GUI applications. Examples include video games, spreadsheet programs, word processors, Internet browsers, the Windows operating system itself. In each of these applications, you would be helpless without your mouse!

Running (and building) a GUI application is different than a console application. In a console application, everything runs sequentially – you are asked a series of questions, you provide a series of answers. In a GUI application, the computer sits and waits until the user does something – clicks on a menu item, chooses an option, types somewhere, moves a scroll bar, etc. We say the application is waiting for an **event** to occur. For this reason, GUI applications are called **event-driven**. When a particular event occurs, the application processes a series of statements (Java statements, in our applications) associated with that event. That series of statements is called an **event method**. Yes, this the same kind of method we have already been using in Java. In Java, event methods are implemented in code using event listeners – they "listen" for events to occur.

Here's how it works:

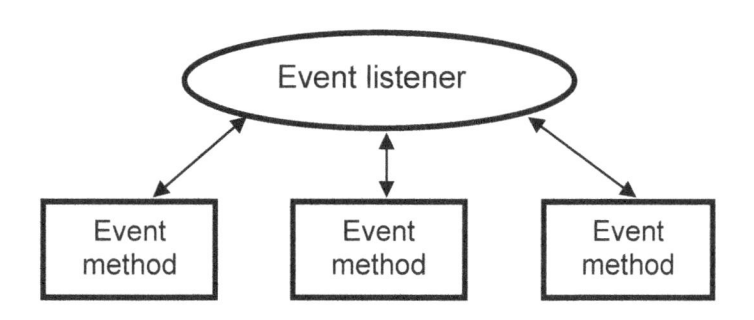

```
                    ┌─────────────────┐
                    │  Event listener │
                    └─────────────────┘
                    ↙        ↕        ↘
              ┌────────┐ ┌────────┐ ┌────────┐
              │ Event  │ │ Event  │ │ Event  │
              │ method │ │ method │ │ method │
              └────────┘ └────────┘ └────────┘
```

In this "model," the Java **listener** waits for an **event** to occur. Once an event is detected, program control transfers to the corresponding **event method**. Once that method is executed, program control returns to the listener. Each method is simply a set of Java code with instructions on what to do if the particular event occurs. So, in GUI programming, we spend most of our time writing event methods.

Let's look at some example of GUI applications and explain their use in the context of event-driven programming. Each of these examples should look very, very familiar. First, how about a **Savings Calculator** program:

As I said, these examples will look familiar. This is a GUI version of the savings calculator console application built in Class 4. This application uses controls called labels to display information and controls called text boxes for input. The user types in information in the boxes and, when done, clicks the button **Compute Savings** to get the desired results. This program has a Java method to process when it "hears" (listens for) the **click** event on this button. That method will do the multiplication of the deposit amount and the number of weeks and display that result in the text box labeled **Total Savings**. The user can continue to try new values until clicking the **Exit** button (causing an exit event method to be executed). You should see some big advantages to GUI applications – easy to use, obvious to use, and they're really not too hard to develop.

How about a GUI **Guess the Number** game (from Class 5):

[Screenshot of "Guess the Number" window displaying "I'm thinking of a number between 0 and 100" with a numeric up-down control showing 50, and buttons labeled Check Guess, Show Answer, and Exit.]

Here the computer tells you about the number it is thinking about. You enter your guess by adjusting the displayed value with the scroll bar control (causing a **scroll** event). You click the **Check Guess** button to invoke the corresponding event method where there is Java code to check your answer. At any time, you can click **Show Answer** to display the correct value or click **Exit** to stop the program. Notice GUI applications give you the ability to add more options. In the console version of this program, you could only keep guessing until you got the right answer.

Next, here's the GUI **Lemonade Stand** from Class 6:

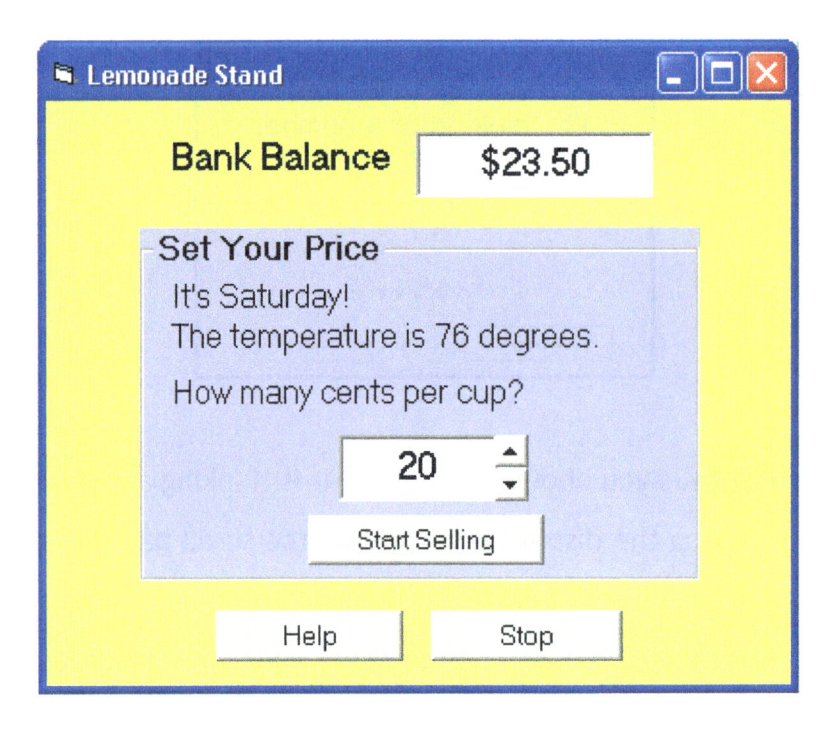

Your bank balance is displayed. You set the selling price (using a scroll bar) and click **Start Selling**. In this button's click event method is the code to compute the cups sold and present your sales results. Notice too, you can stop the application (**Stop** button) or even receive some clues (**Help** button). Again, GUI applications are very flexible.

Well, you must have known it was coming – the GUI **Card Wars** game from Class 7:

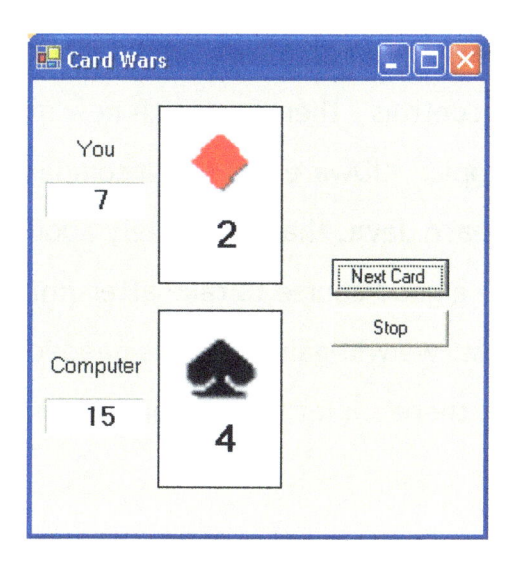

At this point in the game, you can see your score and the computer's score. And, notice rather than see a text description of the cards, a visual picture is shown! Another big advantage of GUI applications – they can show pictures! Clicking **Next Card** will process the code in the method to hand out two more cards, see who wins and adjust and display the scores.

You should be convinced by now that GUI applications are the way to go. They offer flexibility, ease of use, familiarity (every user has used a GUI application before), and they're nice to look at. In the rest of this course, we will build GUI applications. They won't be as elaborate as the examples just seen. We won't use any controls - there's enough new material to learn here without tackling such a topic. KIDware (our little company) produces a more advanced Java course, **Learn Java**, that talks solely about building Java GUI applications. It would be a good course to take after finishing **Java for Kids**. In the remainder of this class, we will gain the skills needed to build a little drawing program. Again, there's a lot to learn and we'll take it step-by-step.

Java Graphics

Java provides many classes and packages to help us with graphic user interface (GUI) applications. For our applications, we will be using something called the **Abstract Windows Toolkit** or **AWT**. We will **import** the needed parts of this toolkit. In this class, we will be looking at Java to do one primary graphics task – drawing with the mouse. There are many steps with many new terms, but I know you are up to the task.

Frames

The basic component of a GUI application is the **Frame**. It is a window with a title bar, a border and an area to build the application. We will use this area for drawing. We will use the **Frame** class to **extend** our program (our class). This simply means we can use all the properties and methods of a frame in our project. The first step in building any Java GUI application is to create a frame for our use. If your frame is named **myFrame**, the code to create a frame is:

```
Frame myFrame = new Frame();
```

Once created, we can do many things to our frame. Here, we learn the basics of sizing the frame, setting the title and making it appear. To size the frame, we need to know its width and height (in pixels). Then, to size it, we use:

```
myFrame.setSize(width, height);
```

To set the title, use:

`myFrame.setTitle(theTitle);`

where the **theTitle** is a string. Finally, to make the frame appear, a necessary step, use:

`myFrame.setVisible(true);`

With just these few steps, we can build the start of a GUI application. Let's do it.

Start JCreator, open your workspace and create a new project named **GraphicsProject**. Add a blank file named **GraphicsTest** (the .java extension will be added). Type this code:

```java
/*
 *  Graphics Test
 *  Java for Kids
 */

import java.awt.*;
import java.awt.event.*;

public class GraphicsTest extends Frame
{
  public static void main(String[] args)
  {
    // create frame
    Frame myFrame = new Frame();
    myFrame.setSize(400, 300);
    myFrame.setTitle("Graphics Testing");
    myFrame.setVisible(true);
  }
}
```

Let's go through this so you understand what we are doing. After the header comments are the two **import** statements that make the AWT available to us for graphics and processing events. These statements will always be in GUI applications. Note the program (class) declaration:

```
public class GraphicsTest extends Frame
```

Note the appending of the words **extends Frame**. This says we are extending our program (**GraphicsTest**) to allow using the **Frame** class in the AWT. After this line, the code should look pretty familiar. Notice the four lines of code in the main method here are just the frame methods we discussed. You should see we are creating a frame 400 pixels wide and 300 pixels high. Compile and run this example. After a bit, you should see your first frame:

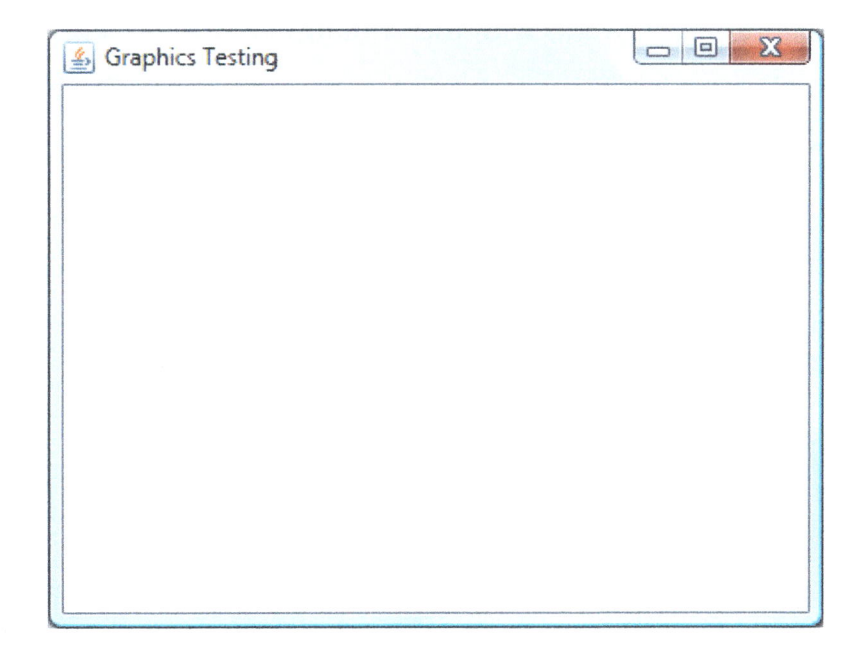

Not too hard, huh?

Event Methods

But, now we have a problem. Try clicking the "boxed X" in the upper right hand corner of the frame to stop our GUI application. Nothing happens – the frame stays there. Remember GUI applications are event-driven and each event needs an event method. There is no method (code) associated with clicking on this box, a frame closing event. We need to write it by adding a Java listener. For now, to stop the application, click **Tools** in the JCreator menu and choose **Stop Tool**. Things should stop. Let's add a listener.

Many Java **event listeners** (primarily those for mouse and keyboard inputs) are implemented using something called **adapters** (also available from the AWT). The adapter that implements events for the frame (window) is called the **WindowAdapter** and it works with the **WindowListener**. There are certain window events that can be "listened for." In our case, we want to listen for the **windowClosing** event. The code that adds this event method to our little application is (type this carefully after the lines creating the frame):

```java
// add listener for closing frame
myFrame.addWindowListener(new WindowAdapter()
{
  public void windowClosing(WindowEvent e)
  {
    System.exit(0);
  }
});
```

This is actually one very long Java statement over several lines. It calls the **addWindowListener** method and, as an argument (all in parentheses), includes a **new** instance of a **WindowAdapter** event method (the **windowClosing** event). It's really not that hard to understand when you look at it, just very long!!

Notice the code in the method itself is a single line:

```
System.exit(0);
```

This just tells Java you are done and to shut the program down. Notice too that the **windowClosing** method must have a single argument (**WindowEvent e**). In this method, we don't use this argument. In others, we will. By adding this one (long) line of Java code, our application will now know what to do when a user clicks the "close the window" X box, causing a **windowClosing** event.

After typing in this new code, recompile and rerun the **Graphics Test** program. You should now be able to stop it by clicking the X. Each of these steps for creating a window and adding a window closing event method must be taken for every GUI application you build. And, you will take similar steps to add other event methods (for other events we want to respond to) to your program.

I think you're starting to see that GUI applications are more work than console applications, but you will also see all the extra work is worth it. GUI applications are great! Before doing any drawing with Java, we need to introduce several topics: mouse events, class level variables, graphics coordinates, colors, and graphics methods. Then, we finally draw a line – yeah!

Java - The Sixth Lesson

In the Java lesson for this class, we examine how to recognize mouse events (clicking mouse buttons, moving the mouse) to help us build a drawing program using a frame. We then discuss the idea of variables with class level scope. Lastly, we talk about graphic coordinates and code to do actual drawing.

Mouse Events

The mouse is a primary interface for doing graphics in Java or any GUI application. Like the **windowClosing** event for the frame, **mouse events** are "listened for" with an **adapter**. We are interested in two mouse event methods: **mousePressed** and **mouseDragged**. Each of these methods is implemented using different adapters and different listeners.

mousePressed Event

The **mousePressed** event method is triggered whenever a mouse button is pressed while the mouse cursor is over the frame. The form of this method must be:

```
public void mousePressed(MouseEvent e)
{
      [Java code for mousePressed event]
}
```

The **MouseEvent** argument **e** provides the coordinate of the mouse cursor when a button was pressed. Those values are:

> **e.getX()**   x coordinate of mouse cursor in frame when mouse was pressed
>
> **e.getY()**   y coordinate of mouse cursor in frame when mouse was pressed

The adapter that implements the **mousePressed** event for the mouse is called the **MouseAdapter** and uses the **MouseListener**. The code to add a listener (to **myFrame**) for this event is very similar to the code used to add the **windowClosing** listener to the frame:

```
myFrame.addMouseListener(new MouseAdapter()
{
  public void mousePressed(MouseEvent e)
  {
      [Java code for mouse press]
  }
});
```

Again, this is just one very long Java statement. In drawing applications, the **mousePressed** event is used to initialize a drawing process. The point clicked is used to start drawing a line.

Example

Let's try the **mousePressed** event with the example we've been using. Open that project (**GraphicsProject**) in JCreator. Add this code after the code adding the listener for the **windowClosing** event:

```
// add listener for mouse press
myFrame.addMouseListener(new MouseAdapter()
{
  public void mousePressed(MouseEvent e)
  {
    System.out.println("Mouse pressed at x=" + e.getX() + ", y=" + e.getY());
  }
});
```

Here, we use a **println** statement to specify the x and y coordinate when the frame is clicked with the mouse.

Compile and run the project. Click the frame and notice the printed coordinate in the output window. Click various spots in the frame and see how the coordinates change. Here are a few examples:

```
General Output
--------------------Configuration: GraphicsProject - JDK version 1.6
Mouse pressed at x=200, y=120
Mouse pressed at x=286, y=187
Mouse pressed at x=148, y=213
Mouse pressed at x=110, y=146
```

Notice you cannot detect mouse clicks in the title bar area. Try to figure out the height of the title bar area by finding points you can click. Play with this example until you are comfortable with how the **mousePressed** event works and what the coordinates mean. Stop and save the project.

mouseDragged Event

The **mouseDragged** event is continuously triggered whenever the mouse is being moved while a mouse button is pressed. The event method format is:

```
public void mouseDragged(MouseEvent e)
{
    [Java code for mouseDragged event]
}
```

And, yes, the **MouseEvent** argument is the same. The x-y pair, **(e.getX(), e.getY())**, tells us the mouse position as the mouse is dragged.

The adapter that implements the **mouseDragged** event for the mouse is called the **MouseMotionAdapter** and uses the **MouseMotionListener**. The code to add a listener (to **myFrame**) for this event is:

```
myFrame.addMouseMotionListener(new MouseMotionAdapter()
{
  public void mouseDragged(MouseEvent e)
  {
      [Java code for mouse dragged]
  }
});
```

In drawing processes, the **mouseDragged** event is used to detect the continuation of a previously started line. If drawing is continuing, the current point is connected to the previous point using the **drawLine** method.

Example

Add this code to the graphics example:

```
// add listener for mouse drag
myFrame.addMouseMotionListener(new MouseMotionAdapter()
{
  public void mouseDragged(MouseEvent e)
  {
    System.out.println("Mouse dragged to x=" + e.getX() + ", y=" + e.getY());
  }
});
```

Place this code after the code adding a listener for the mouse press event. In this event method, we use a **println** statement to specify the x and y coordinate the mouse has been dragged to.

Compile and run the project. Click the frame and notice the initial point is printed in the console window. Drag the mouse around the frame. Notice the coordinates (x, y) continuously change as the mouse is moving. Here's an example:

```
General Output
-------------------Configuration: GraphicsProject - JDK version 1.
Mouse pressed at x=168, y=81
Mouse dragged to x=169, y=81
Mouse dragged to x=171, y=82
Mouse dragged to x=172, y=83
Mouse dragged to x=174, y=85
Mouse dragged to x=175, y=88
Mouse dragged to x=177, y=91
Mouse dragged to x=177, y=92
Mouse dragged to x=179, y=95
Mouse dragged to x=180, y=97
Mouse dragged to x=181, y=99
Mouse dragged to x=183, y=102
```

Notice no matter where you drag the mouse, it reports a value – in the title bar, off the frame. This is okay – in our drawing program, any point out of the frame range is ignored.

Class Level Scope Variables

Notice in the two mouse events (**mousePressed** and **mouseDragged**) that the only information available for our use is the current mouse position, given by the **MouseEvent e**. For our drawing programs, we will need more information. We will need access to the frame object, the last point drawn to, the current drawing color and other details. How can we get information into a method that is not available from that method's argument list? And, what if we need more than one result (the returned value) from a method? We use something called **class level scope variables**. Such variables can be used with any Java method, not just the event methods discussed here.

Up to now, we have seen variables with two levels of scope: **method level** scope and **loop level** scope. Variables with method level scope can only be used within the method containing their declarations. Variables with loop level scope can only be used in the particular loop with their declaration. Variables with **class level** scope can be used and modified by any method within a project (class). To give a variable such scope, it is defined outside the methods of a class. Such declarations are customarily placed after the opening left brace following the line that declares the class:

```
public class myClass
{
        [Place class level variable declarations here]
```

Variables with class level scope are declared with the same statements used for method level scope, with the prefacing word **static**. This is needed because the variables will be accessed from **static** methods. Don't worry too much about needing to know what the word static is all about.

Some examples of declaring variables with class level scope are:

```
static Frame myFrame;
static int thisInteger;
static double thisDecimal;
static String myStringVariable;
static boolean andABoolean;
static int[] myIntegerArray;
static double[] aDoubleArray;
```

Any of the above variables can be accessed and/or modified in any method within the class they are declared.

You should now know how the two mouse events work and how they differ. And, you should see how class level variables can be used to move information among various methods. Now, let's use all this new knowledge, to do some actual drawing.

More Java Graphics

With the ability to detect mouse events, let's look at some more about Java graphics.

Graphics Coordinates

We will use Java to draw using **graphics methods**. In this class, we will learn to draw lines and rectangles. Before looking at these methods, let's look at how we specify the points used to draw and connect lines. All graphics methods use a default **coordinate system**. This means we have a specific way to refer to individual points in the graphics object (from **myFrame**, in our example). The coordinate system used is:

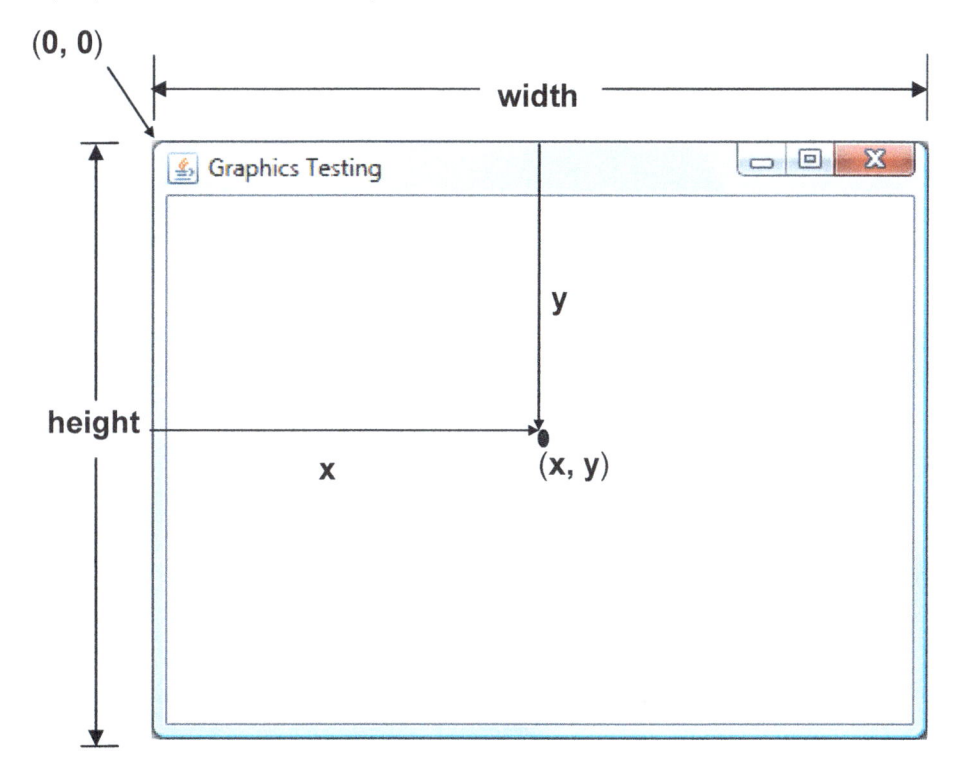

Recall the frame is **width** pixels wide and **height** pixels high. We use two values (coordinates) to identify a single point in the frame. The **x** (horizontal)

coordinate increases from left to right, starting at **0**. The **y** (vertical) coordinate increases from top to bottom, also starting at **0**. Points in the region are referred to by the two coordinates enclosed in parentheses, or **(x, y)**. All values shown are in units of **pixels**.

Notice the frame drawing area includes the title bar area. We would prefer not to draw in this area and there are ways to avoid it by **translating** the origin, (0, 0). The steps to do this are simple, but beyond our discussion here. What we will tell you is that the title bar is about 25 to 30 pixels high.

Colors

Colors play a big part in Java graphics applications. Lines, rectangles, ovals can all be drawn and filled in various colors. The background color of the frame can be set to a particular color. These colors must be defined in Java code. How do we do this? There are two approaches we will take: (1) use built-in colors and (2) create a color.

The colors built into Java are specified by the **Color** class. Such a color is specified using:

```
Color.colorName
```

where **colorName** is a reserved color name. There are thirteen standard color names:

Darker colors:

- **black**
- **blue**
- **red**
- **darkGray**
- **gray**

Lighter colors:

- white
- cyan
- lightGray
- magenta
- green
- orange
- yellow
- pink

If for some reason, the selections provided by the **Color** class do not fit your needs, you can create your own color using one of over 16 million different combinations. The code to create a color named **myColor** is:

```
Color myColor = new Color(red, green, blue);
```

where **red**, **green**, and **blue** are integer measures of intensity of the corresponding primary colors. These measures can range from 0 (least intensity) to 255 (greatest intensity). For example, **new Color(255, 255, 0)** will produce yellow.

It is easy to specify colors for graphics methods using the **Color** class. Any time you need a color, just use one of the built-in colors or create your own using different red, green, and blue values. These techniques can be used anywhere Java requires a color. For example, to change our frame's background color, we use:

```
myFrame.setBackground(Color.colorName);
```

So, you get a yellow background with:

```
myFrame.setBackground(Color.yellow);
```

Or knowing some red, green and blue combination:

```
myFrame.setBackground(new Color(red, green, blue));
```

If you want, try these with the **Graphics Test** we have been building.

Java Graphics, Mouse Methods

You can also define variables that take on color values. It is a two step process. Say we want to define a variable named **myRed** to represent the color red. First, declare your variable to be of type **Color**:

```
Color myRed;
```

Then, define your color in code using:

```
myRed = Color.red;
```

From this point on, you can use **myRed** anywhere the red color is desired. At long last, we're ready to draw some lines.

drawLine Method

To do graphics (drawing) in Java, we use the built-in **graphics methods.** In this class, we will look at graphics methods that can draw colored lines and filled rectangles. As you progress in your programming skills, you are encouraged to study the many other graphics methods that can draw rectangles, ellipses, polygons and virtually any shape, in any color. To do drawing in a frame, we reference a **Graphics** object. This is again from the AWT and provides all the methods we need for drawing. To get the **Graphics** object (we will name it **myGraphics**) from the frame (**myFrame**) we are using requires just a single line of code:

```
Graphics myGraphics = myFrame.getGraphics();
```

Once a graphics object is available, all graphics methods are applied to this newly formed object. Hence, to apply a graphics method named **graphicsMethod** to the **myGraphics** object, use:

```
myGraphics.graphicsMethod(arguments);
```

where **arguments** are any needed arguments, or information needed by the graphics method.

Java Graphics, Mouse Methods

The Java **drawLine** method is used to connect two points with a straight-line segment. It operates on a graphics object. If that object is **myGraphics** and we wish to connect the point (**x1**, **y1**) with (**x2**, **y2**), the statement is:

```
myGraphics.drawLine(x1, y1, x2, y2);
```

The line will draw in the current graphics object color. To set that color, use:

```
myGraphics.setColor(colorValue);
```

Let's modify our **Graphics Test** example to draw a black line when the frame is clicked. Make the shaded changes to the code:

```java
/*
 *  Graphics Test
 *  Java for Kids
 *  www.KIDwareSoftware.com
 */
import java.awt.*;
import java.awt.event.*;

public class GraphicsTest extends Frame
{
  static Frame myFrame;
  static Graphics myGraphics;
  public static void main(String[] args)
  {
    // create frame
    myFrame = new Frame();
    myFrame.setSize(400, 300);
    myFrame.setTitle("Graphics Testing");
    myFrame.setVisible(true);
    myGraphics = myFrame.getGraphics();
    // add listener for closing frame
    myFrame.addWindowListener(new WindowAdapter()
    {
      public void windowClosing(WindowEvent e)
      {
        System.exit(0);
      }
```

```java
    });
    // add listener for mouse press
    myFrame.addMouseListener(new MouseAdapter()
    {
      public void mousePressed(MouseEvent e)
      {
        myGraphics.setColor(Color.black);
        myGraphics.drawLine(20, 50, 380, 280);
        System.out.println("Mouse pressed at x=" + e.getX() +
", y=" + e.getY());
      }
    });
    // add listener for mouse drag
    myFrame.addMouseMotionListener(new MouseMotionAdapter()
    {
      public void mouseDragged(MouseEvent e)
      {
        System.out.println("Mouse dragged to x=" + e.getX() +
", y=" + e.getY());
      }
    });
  }
}
```

We moved the statement declaring the **Frame** object (**myFrame**) out of the main method and made it a class level variable. We also have a class level graphics object (**myGraphics**). This allows us to refer to these in the **mousePressed** event. In the main method, we add a single line of code to create the graphics object. And, in the **mousePressed** event, we added two lines set the color and draw the line.

Compile and run the project. Click the frame and the line will be drawn:

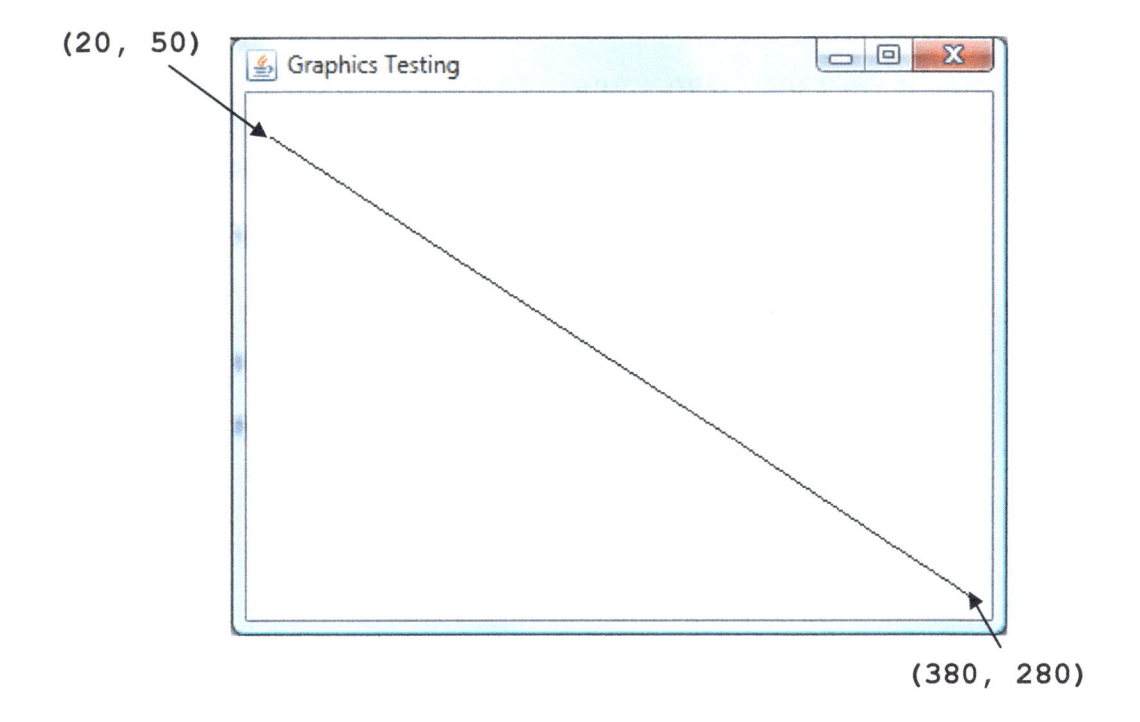

(20, 50)

(380, 280)

To connect the last point (**380, 280**) to another point (**200, 40**), add this line of code:

```
myGraphics.drawLine(380, 280, 200, 40);
```

Run the project and click the frame to see:

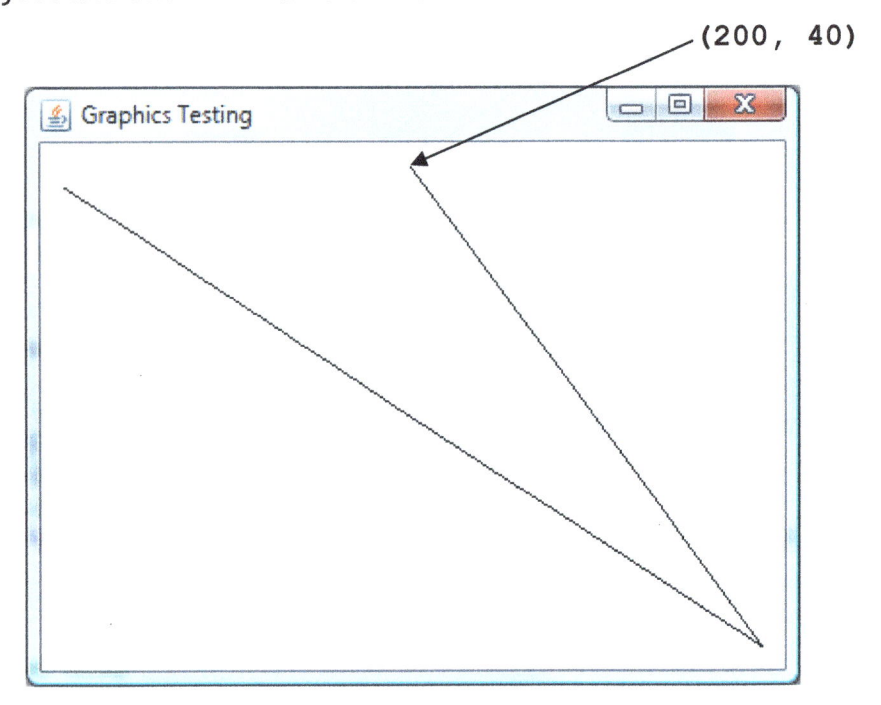

(200, 40)

Continue the line (change it to red) to point (30, 250):

```
myGraphics.setColor(Color.red);
myGraphics.drawLine(200, 40, 30, 250);
```

You will see:

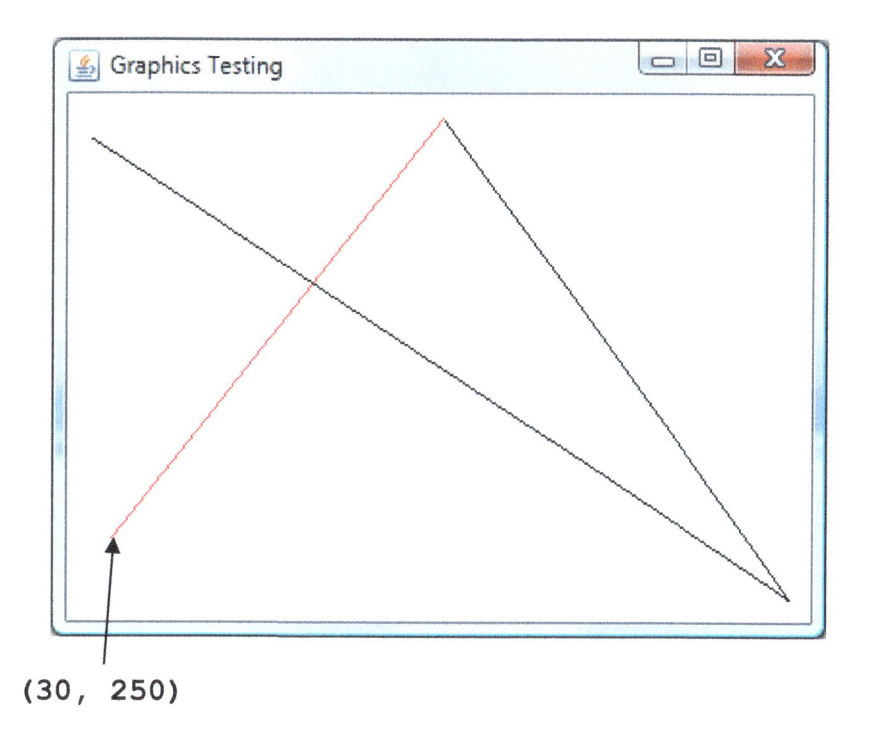

(30, 250)

Add more line segments, using other points and colors if you like. Note that for every line segment you draw, you need a separate **drawLine** statement. To connect one line segment with another, you need to save the last point drawn to in the first segment (use two integer variables, one for x and one for y). This saved point will become the starting point for the next line segment. You can choose to change the color at any time you wish. Using many line segments, with many different colors, you can draw virtually anything you want! We'll do that with the **Blackboard** project in this class. As mentioned, there are many other graphics methods. Let's look at two more (dealing with rectangles) we will use in the **Blackboard** project.

drawRect Method

The Java **drawRect** method is used to draw a rectangle. It operates on a graphics object. To draw a rectangle, we specify the upper left hand corner's coordinate (**x, y**) and the **width** and **height** of the rectangle. To draw such a rectangle on a graphics object (**myGraphics**), the statement is:

```
myGraphics.drawRect(x, y, width, height);
```

The rectangle will draw in the current graphics object color. To set that color, use:

```
myGraphics.setColor(colorValue);
```

To draw a blue rectangle with the upper left corner at (20, 50), width 150 and height 100 in our **Graphics Test** (delete the **drawLine** code), use:

```
myGraphics.setColor(Color.blue);
myGraphics.drawRect(20, 50, 150, 100);
```

This produces in the frame (don't forget to click the frame to do the drawing):

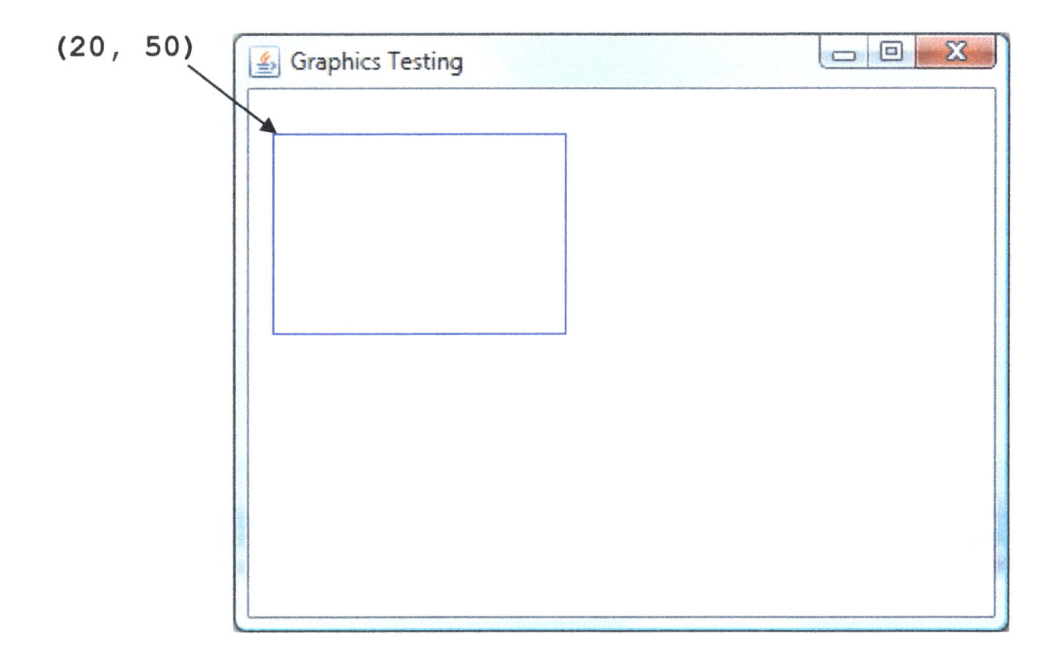

(20, 50)

And, to add a red rectangle of the same size with upper left corner at (140, 130):

```
myGraphics.setColor(Color.red);
myGraphics.drawRect(140, 130, 150, 100);
```

This yields:

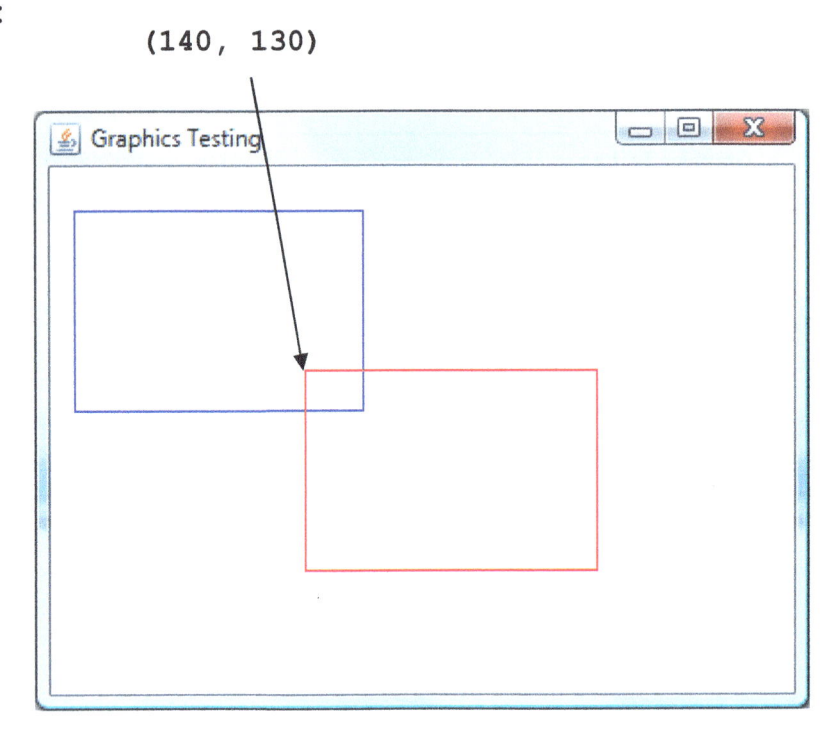

Try more rectangles if you like.

Java Graphics, Mouse Methods   8-37

fillRect Method

The Java **fillRect** method is used to fill a rectangle with the current graphics object color. To fill a rectangle, we specify the upper left hand corner's coordinate (**x**, **y**) and the **width** and **height** of the rectangle. To draw such a rectangle on a graphics object (**myGraphics**), the statement is:

```
myGraphics.fillRect(x, y, width, height);
```

The rectangle will draw and fill in the current graphics object color.

To draw a blue rectangle with the upper left corner at (20, 50), width 150 and height 100 in our Graphics Test, use:

```
myGraphics.setColor(Color.blue);
myGraphics.fillRect(20, 50, 150, 100);
```

This produces in the frame:

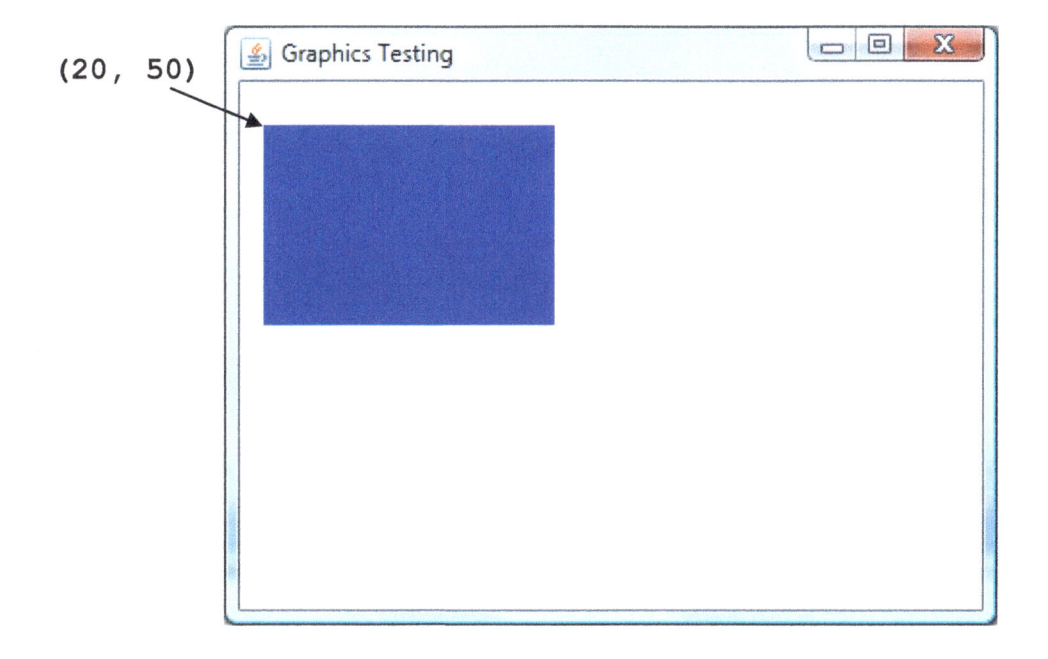

And, to add a red rectangle of the same size with upper left corner at (140, 130):

```
myGraphics.setColor(new Color(255, 0, 0));
myGraphics.fillRect(140, 130, 150, 100);
```

This yields:

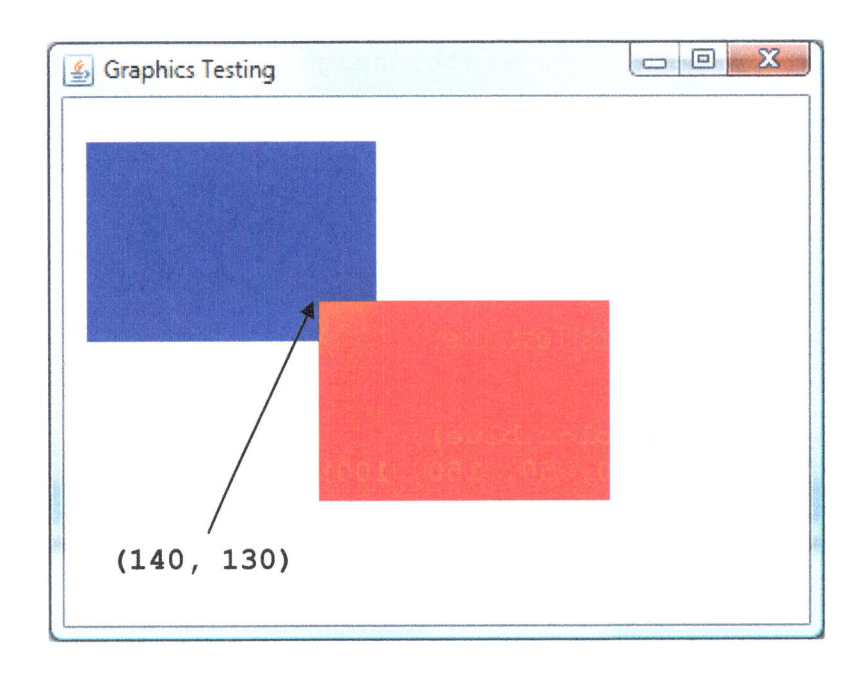

(140, 130)

Can you see that **Color(255, 0, 0)** is the same as **Color.red**? Try more rectangles if you like.

One other graphics method related to **fillRect** is the **clearRect** method. It is used to clear a rectangular region with the background color of the graphics object. The syntax for this method is:

`myGraphics.clearRect(x, y, width, height);`

This clears the region with upper left hand corner at (x, y), width pixels wide and height pixels high with the region's background color. Keep playing around with the **Graphics Test** example. Try drawing more lines and rectangles. Save this project. The last version of the **GraphicsProject** (drawing two filled rectangles) is saved in the course projects folder (**\JavaKids\JK Code**).

I think you get the idea of drawing. Just pick some points, pick some colors, and draw some lines. But, it's pretty boring to just specify points and see lines being drawn. It would be nice to have some user interaction, where points could be drawn using the mouse. And, that's just what we are going to do. We will use our newly gained knowledge about mouse events and graphics methods to build a Java drawing program.

Before leaving this example, though, try this. Run the **Graphics Test** program again. Click the frame to draw the two filled rectangles. In the upper right corner of the form is a small button with an "underscore" called the **minimize button**

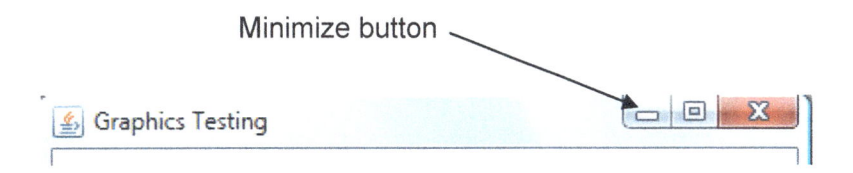

When you click this button, your application window disappears (is minimized) and is moved to the task bar at the bottom of the screen. When you click your application name in the task bar, it will return to the screen. Go ahead and try it. Where did your colored rectangles go? You need to click the frame again to redraw them.

This happens because, as coded, Java graphics objects have <u>no</u> memory. They only display what has been last drawn on them. If you reduce your form to the task bar and restore it (as we just did), the graphics object cannot remember what was displayed previously – it will be cleared. Similarly, if you switch from an active Java application to some other application, your Java form may become partially or fully obscured. When you return to your Java application, the obscured part of any graphics object will be erased. Again, there is no memory. To correct this, we need something called **persistent graphics**. Such persistence is possible, but beyond what we discuss here.

A consequence of the lack of persistent graphics is that nothing can be drawn to a frame until some event occurs. You can't put drawing commands in the main method to have some initial graphics appear. That's why in all the little graphics examples we have done, we require a mouse press to do drawing. We'll need to remember this in the drawing project we build next to get some initial things drawn.

Project - Blackboard Fun

Have you ever drawn on a blackboard with colored chalk? You'll be doing that with the "electronic" blackboard you build in this project. This project is saved as **Blackboard** in the course projects folder (**\JavaKids\JK Code**).

Project Design

This is a simple project in concept. Using the mouse, you draw colored lines on a computer blackboard. A frame will represent the blackboard. We will use rectangles drawn along the edge of the frame to choose "chalk" color. Mouse events will control the drawing and color selection process. The basic program steps are very simple:

1. Establish frame, add event methods and setup color choice rectangles.
2. Listen for mouse press, when one is detected, either change the color or initialize drawing process.
3. Listen for mouse dragging. If mouse is dragging, continue drawing line in current color.

We will write code that takes care of all the initialization steps and write code for each of three (**windowClosing**, **mousePressed**, **mouseDragged**) event methods.

Project Development

To help visualize what's going to be in this project, let's look ahead at how we want to layout the frame. We will create a frame that is 600 pixels wide and 400 pixels high. On the right-edge of the frame, we will draw 8 small filled rectangles. These rectangles will be used to select drawing color. The coordinates used for all this are:

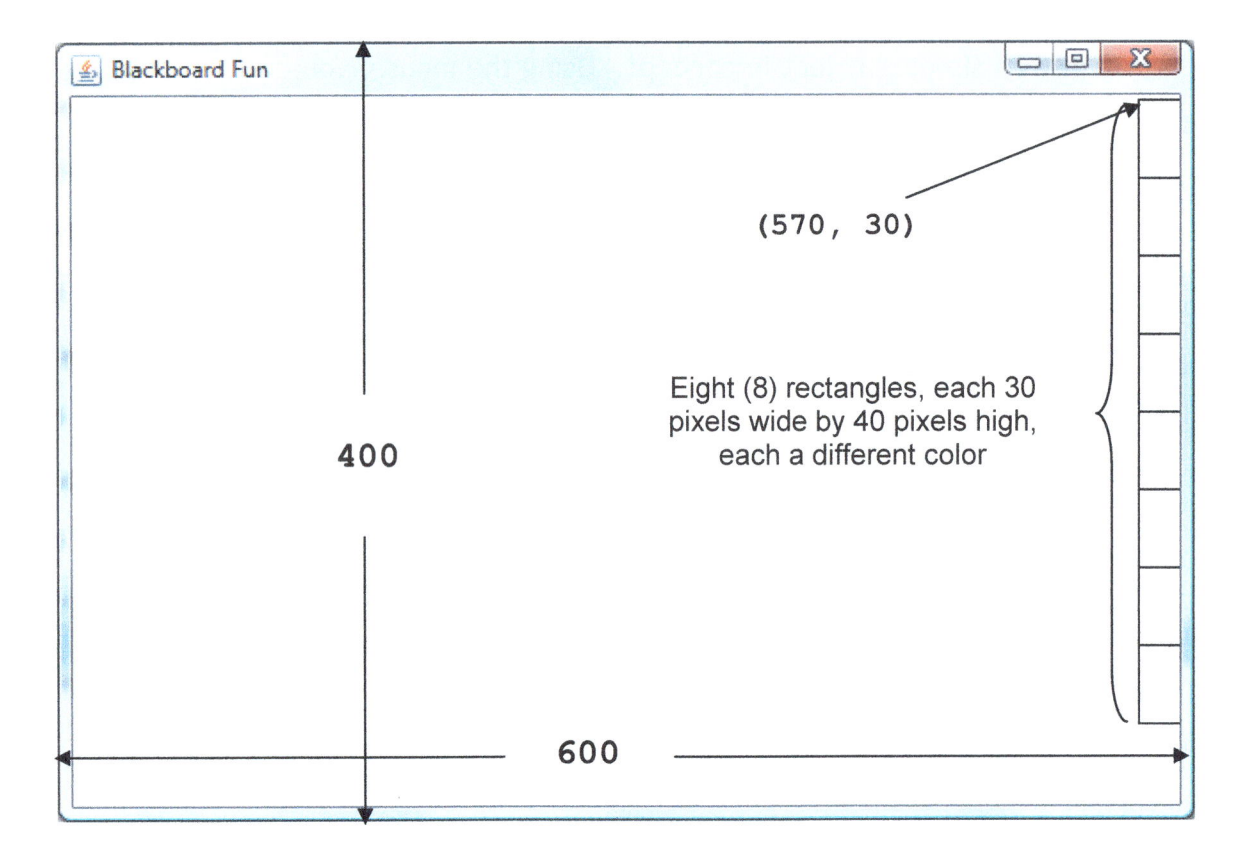

Blackboard Fun

(570, 30)

Eight (8) rectangles, each 30 pixels wide by 40 pixels high, each a different color

400

600

This project will work like any paint type program you may have used. Click on a color in one of the eight rectangles to choose a color to draw with. Then, move to the blackboard area, left-click to start the drawing process. Drag the mouse to draw lines. Release the mouse button to stop drawing. It's that easy. Clicking in the black region below the color selection rectangles will clear the blackboard and clicking the **X** in the upper right corner of the frame will stop the program. Every step, but initializing things and stopping the program, is handled by the frame mouse events.

Start JCreator, open your workspace and create a new project named **BlackboardProject**. Add a blank file named **Blackboard** (the .java extension will be added).

Open the empty **Blackboard.java** file. Build this empty framework for the project. This adds the needed import statements, sets up the class, creates the frame and graphics object and adds the three event methods (the mouse methods are empty) we will be using:

```
/*
 *  Blackboard Fun
 *  Java for Kids
 *  www.KIDwareSoftware.com
 */
import java.awt.*;
import java.awt.event.*;

public class Blackboard extends Frame
{
  static Frame myFrame;
  static Graphics myGraphics;

  public static void main(String[] args)
  {
    // create frame
    myFrame = new Frame();
    myFrame.setSize(600, 400);
    myFrame.setTitle("Blackboard Fun");
    myFrame.setBackground(Color.black);
    myFrame.setVisible(true);
    myGraphics = myFrame.getGraphics();

    //  add listener for closing frame
    myFrame.addWindowListener(new WindowAdapter()
    {
```

```
      public void windowClosing(WindowEvent e)
      {
        System.exit(0);
      }
    });

    //  add listener for clicking mouse
    myFrame.addMouseListener(new MouseAdapter()
    {
      public void mousePressed(MouseEvent e)
      {
      }
    });

    //  add listener for dragging mouse
    myFrame.addMouseMotionListener(new MouseMotionAdapter()
    {
      public void mouseDragged(MouseEvent e)
      {
      }
    });
  }
}
```

Save the file. Compile and run the project to make sure the frame appears (it should be black, like a blackboard!). In long, detailed projects like this, it is good practice to occasionally stop and try your program even if it's not complete. This gives you some confidence things are working okay and you can move on.

Notice we have given the frame **myFrame** and graphics object (**myGraphics**) class level scope. This is necessary so we can draw to the frame in the mouse methods. Five other class level variables are used in this project. We use a boolean variable (**boxesDrawn**) to tell us if we have initialized the program by drawing the color selection boxes. We use another boolean variable (**drawingOn**) that tells us if we are drawing. The Color type **drawingColor** will hold the current drawing color. And, we need two variables (**xPrevious** and **yPrevious**) that save the last point drawn in a line (we will always connect the "current" point to the "last" point). Declare these variables after the line declaring the graphics object:

```
static int previousX, previousY;
static Color drawingColor;
static boolean drawingOn = false;
static boolean boxesDrawn = false;
```

We need to establish some initial values. We need to draw the eight rectangles we will use for color selection and initialize the drawing color to white. We do this when the program first starts by clicking the frame. Recall we need to do this because graphics are not 'persistent'. Put this code in the **mousePressed** method:

```
if (!boxesDrawn)
{
  boxesDrawn = true;
  // setup color choice rectangles
  myGraphics.setColor(Color.white);
  myGraphics.fillRect(570, 30, 30, 40);
  myGraphics.setColor(Color.lightGray);
  myGraphics.fillRect(570, 70, 30, 40);
  myGraphics.setColor(Color.blue);
  myGraphics.fillRect(570, 110, 30, 40);
  myGraphics.setColor(Color.cyan);
  myGraphics.fillRect(570, 150, 30, 40);
  myGraphics.setColor(Color.green);
  myGraphics.fillRect(570, 190, 30, 40);
  myGraphics.setColor(Color.magenta);
  myGraphics.fillRect(570, 230, 30, 40);
  myGraphics.setColor(Color.yellow);
  myGraphics.fillRect(570, 270, 30, 40);
  myGraphics.setColor(Color.red);
  myGraphics.fillRect(570, 310, 30, 40);
}
```

You should see that this code just draws and fills eight rectangles along the side of the frame. The eight colors we will use are values from the **Color** class. These colors were selected to look good on a black background. Note this code will only be called the first time the frame is clicked (when **boxesDrawn** is false). We also initialized the drawing color to white:

You'll see that this is pretty cool in how it works. Compile and run to test it out. When the frame appears, click it to see:

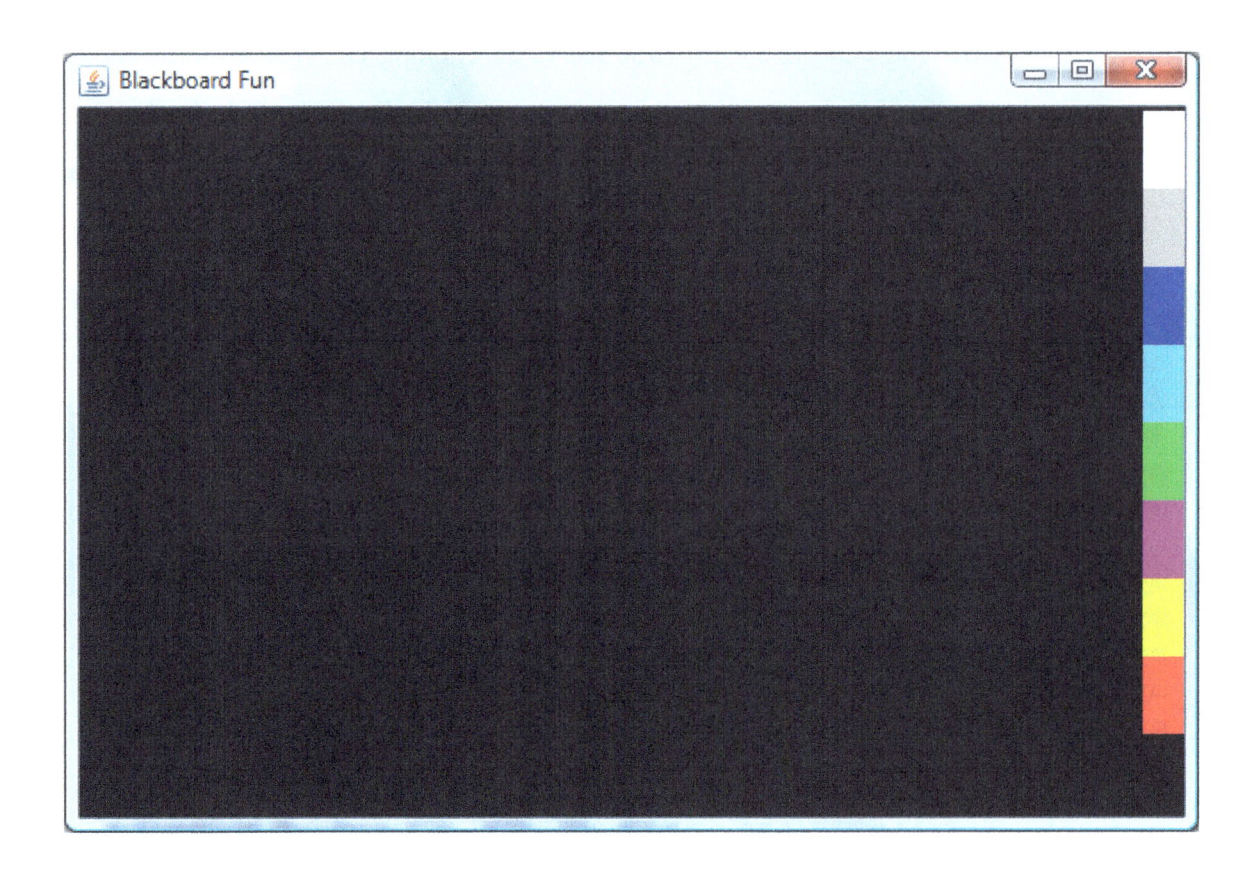

Now, we are ready to code the drawing process. There are two events we look for:

- Mouse button press – picks color or starts drawing
- Mouse dragging - continues drawing

Each of these is a separate mouse event.

The **mousePressed** event is executed when a mouse button is clicked. We just used the first click to draw the color section boxes. In all other clicks, we check the x coordinate (**e.getX()**) to see if it exceeds 570 (the boundary of the color selection rectangles). If so, we determine which rectangle has been clicked (by checking the value of **e.getY()**) and change the **drawingColor** variable. If the lowest rectangle (the black area) is selected, the frame is cleared. If the x coordinate is less than 570, we are starting to draw a line. In this case, we set **drawingOn** to **true** (we are drawing) and initialize the "last point" variables, **xPrevious** and **yPrevious**. Recall drawingColor, drawingOn, xPrevious and yPrevious (as is **myFrame** and **myGraphics**) are class level variables. Add the shaded code to the event method is (it's kind of long):

```
public void mousePressed(MouseEvent e)
{
  if (!boxesDrawn)
  {
    boxesDrawn = true;
    // setup color choice rectangles
    myGraphics.setColor(Color.white);
    myGraphics.fillRect(570, 30, 30, 40);
    myGraphics.setColor(Color.lightGray);
    myGraphics.fillRect(570, 70, 30, 40);
    myGraphics.setColor(Color.blue);
    myGraphics.fillRect(570, 110, 30, 40);
    myGraphics.setColor(Color.cyan);
    myGraphics.fillRect(570, 150, 30, 40);
```

```java
      myGraphics.setColor(Color.green);
      myGraphics.fillRect(570, 190, 30, 40);
      myGraphics.setColor(Color.magenta);
      myGraphics.fillRect(570, 230, 30, 40);
      myGraphics.setColor(Color.yellow);
      myGraphics.fillRect(570, 270, 30, 40);
      myGraphics.setColor(Color.red);
      myGraphics.fillRect(570, 310, 30, 40);
      // initialize drawing color
      drawingColor = Color.white;
      myGraphics.setColor(drawingColor);
    }
    //  drawing begins or color is changed
    if (e.getX() > 570)
    {
      drawingOn = false;
      // new color
      if (e.getY() > 350)
      {
        // clear drawing area
        myGraphics.clearRect(0, 0, 570, 400);
      }
      else if (e.getY() > 310)
      {
        drawingColor = Color.red;
      }
      else if (e.getY() > 270)
      {
        drawingColor = Color.yellow;
      }
      else if (e.getY() > 230)
      {
        drawingColor = Color.magenta;
      }
      else if (e.getY() > 190)
      {
        drawingColor = Color.green;
      }
      else if (e.getY() > 150)
      {
        drawingColor = Color.cyan;
      }
      else if (e.getY() > 110)
      {
        drawingColor = Color.blue;
      }
      else if (e.getY() > 70)
```

```
         {
            drawingColor = Color.lightGray;
         }
         else
         {
            drawingColor = Color.white;
         }
      }
      else
      {
         //  drawing begins, save point
         drawingOn = true;
         previousX = e.getX();
         previousY = e.getY();
         myGraphics.setColor(drawingColor);
      }
   }
```

Save, compile and run to make sure the code is correct.

The **mouseDragged** event is executed when the mouse is being dragged over the frame. In this event, (if **drawingOn** is true) we connect the last point (**xPrevious, yPrevious**) to the current point (**e.getX(), e.getY()**) using the **drawLine** method. Once done drawing, the "last point" becomes the "current point." This event method is:

```
public void mouseDragged(MouseEvent e)
{
  if (drawingOn)
  {
    //  drawing continues
    myGraphics.drawLine(previousX, previousY, e.getX(), e.getY());
    previousX = e.getX();
    previousY = e.getY();
  }
}
```

Again, notice the use of the class level variables and **myGraphics** object.

That's all the code. Make sure both mouse event methods are typed correctly in the proper location. Save the project by clicking the **Save all files** button in the JCreator toolbar.

Here is the complete **Blackboard Fun** Java code listing (from the JCreator file view window) - it's your biggest project yet:

```java
/*
 *  Blackboard Fun
 *  Java for Kids
 *  www.KIDwareSoftware.com
 */
import java.awt.*;
import java.awt.event.*;
public class Blackboard extends Frame
{
  static Frame myFrame;
  static Graphics myGraphics;
  static int previousX, previousY;
  static Color drawingColor;
  static boolean drawingOn = false;
  static boolean boxesDrawn = false;
  public static void main(String[] args)
  {
    // create frame
    myFrame = new Blackboard();
    myFrame.setSize(600, 400);
    myFrame.setTitle("Blackboard Fun");
    myFrame.setBackground(Color.black);
    myFrame.setVisible(true);
    myGraphics = myFrame.getGraphics();
    //  add listener for closing frame
    myFrame.addWindowListener(new WindowAdapter()
    {
      public void windowClosing(WindowEvent e)
      {
        System.exit(0);
      }
    });
    //  add listener for clicking mouse
    myFrame.addMouseListener(new MouseAdapter()
    {
      public void mousePressed(MouseEvent e)
      {
        if (!boxesDrawn)
        {
          boxesDrawn = true;
          // setup color choice rectangles
          myGraphics.setColor(Color.white);
          myGraphics.fillRect(570, 30, 30, 40);
```

```java
      myGraphics.setColor(Color.lightGray);
      myGraphics.fillRect(570, 70, 30, 40);
      myGraphics.setColor(Color.blue);
      myGraphics.fillRect(570, 110, 30, 40);
      myGraphics.setColor(Color.cyan);
      myGraphics.fillRect(570, 150, 30, 40);
      myGraphics.setColor(Color.green);
      myGraphics.fillRect(570, 190, 30, 40);
      myGraphics.setColor(Color.magenta);
      myGraphics.fillRect(570, 230, 30, 40);
      myGraphics.setColor(Color.yellow);
      myGraphics.fillRect(570, 270, 30, 40);
      myGraphics.setColor(Color.red);
      myGraphics.fillRect(570, 310, 30, 40);
      // initialize drawing color
      drawingColor = Color.white;
      myGraphics.setColor(drawingColor);
  }
  //  drawing begins or color is changed
  if (e.getX() > 570)
  {
    drawingOn = false;
    // new color
    if (e.getY() > 350)
    {
      // clear drawing area
      myGraphics.clearRect(0, 0, 570, 400);
    }
    else if (e.getY() > 310)
    {
      drawingColor = Color.red;
      System.out.println("changed");
    }
    else if (e.getY() > 270)
    {
      drawingColor = Color.yellow;
    }
    else if (e.getY() > 230)
    {
      drawingColor = Color.magenta;
    }
    else if (e.getY() > 190)
    {
      drawingColor = Color.green;
    }
    else if (e.getY() > 150)
    {
```

```java
          drawingColor = Color.cyan;
        }
        else if (e.getY() > 110)
        {
          drawingColor = Color.blue;
        }
        else if (e.getY() > 70)
        {
          drawingColor = Color.lightGray;
        }
        else
        {
          drawingColor = Color.white;
        }
      }
      else
      {
        //  drawing begins, save point
        drawingOn = true;
        previousX = e.getX();
        previousY = e.getY();
        myGraphics.setColor(drawingColor);
      }
    }
  });
  //  add listener for dragging mouse
  myFrame.addMouseMotionListener(new MouseMotionAdapter()
  {
    public void mouseDragged(MouseEvent e)
    {
      if (drawingOn)
      {
        //  drawing continues
        myGraphics.drawLine(previousX, previousY, e.getX(), e.getY());
        previousX = e.getX();
        previousY = e.getY();
      }
    }
  });
  }
}
```

Run the Project

Compile and run the project. By building and testing in stages, any errors seen now (if any) should be minimal. The finished running product should look like this (after clicking the window to draw the color selection boxes):

Choose a color by clicking one of the eight displayed rectangles. Draw a line in the frame. Try other colors. Draw something. I've had students draw perfect pictures of Fred Flintstone and Homer Simpson using this program. Make sure each color works. Make sure the clear function (click below the last colored rectangle) works. Make sure clicking the **X** box exits the application. As always, thoroughly test your project. Save it if you had to make any changes while running it.

Java Graphics, Mouse Methods 8-55

Do you see how simple the drawing part of this program is? Most of the code is used just to set and select colors. The actual drawing portion of the code (**mousePressed**, **mouseDragged** events) is only a few lines of Java! This shows two things: (1) those drawing programs you use are really not that hard to build and (2) there is a lot of power in the Java graphics methods. Here's a simple picture I drew:

Other Things to Try

The Blackboard Fun project offers lots of opportunity for improvement with added options. Add the ability to change the background color of the blackboard. Make it impossible to draw in the color selection area.

See if you can figure out ways to get special effects - we'll show you a couple. Here's a way to draw "fat lines." It uses trigonometry, but don't be scared. Place this code in the **mouseDragged** method following the line where the **drawLine** method is executed:

```
// fat lines
int x2 = e.getX();
int y2 = e.getY();
double delta = 20.0;
double slope = Math.atan2(y2 - previousY, x2 - previousX);
myGraphics.drawLine((int)(x2 - delta * Math.sin(slope)),
  (int)(y2 + delta * Math.cos(slope)), (int)(x2 + delta *
Math.sin(slope)), (int)(y2 - delta * Math.cos(slope)));
// end fat lines
```

This code draws a line (2 * **delta** long) perpendicular (at a right angle) to the drawn line. Compile and run your project to see how it works. Try different delta values.

Here's a little picture I drew:

We have left these lines of code (commented out) in the project (BlackboardProject) saved in the course projects folder (you can 'uncomment' them to add fat lines).

Here's another possibility to try. Delete (or 'comment out') these lines in the **mouseDragged** event:

```
xPrevious = e.getX();
yPrevious = e.getY();
```

By doing this, the first point clicked (in the **mousePressed** event) is always the last point and all line drawing originates from this original point. Now, run the project again. Notice the "fanning" effect. Pretty, huh? Here's one I drew:

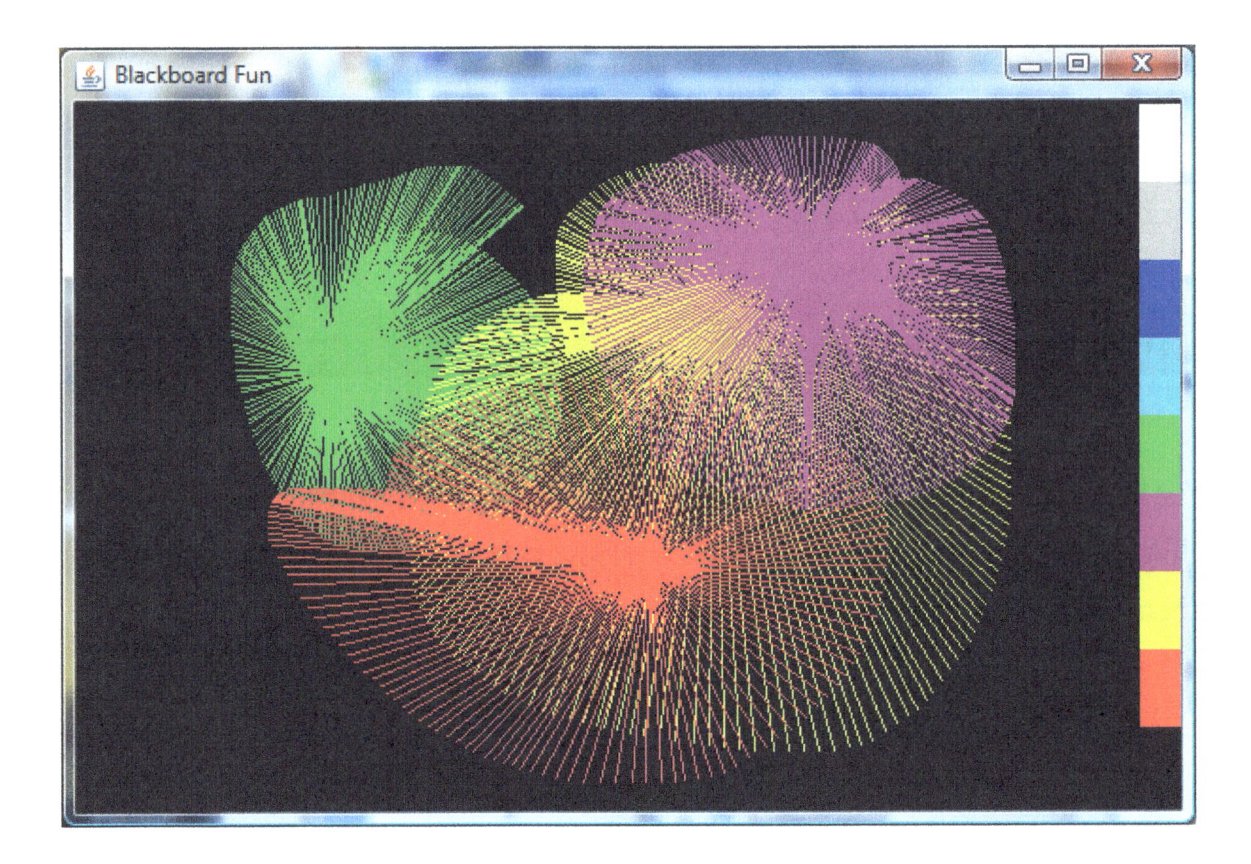

Play around and see what other effects (change colors randomly, draw little filled rectangles). Have fun! Remember to avoid the 'minimize' button or you'll lose all your hard work – graphics are not persistent!

Summary

You've now had your first experience with graphics programming in Java using the **drawLine**, **drawRect** and **fillRect** methods. You learned about two important events to help in drawing: **mousePressed** and **mouseDragged**. And, you learned about colors and class level variables. In the next class, we'll continue looking at using graphics in projects. And, we'll look at some ways to design simple computer games.

This page intentionally not left blank.

9. Timers, Animation, Keyboard Methods

Review and Preview

By now, you should have some confidence in your abilities as a Java programmer.

In this class, we'll look at another item that's a lot of fun - the **Timer** class. It's a key class for adding animation (motion) to graphics in projects. We study some animation techniques. We will also examine how to recognize user inputs from the keyboard via keyboard events. And, you'll build another project - your first video game!

Timer Class

In the Class 8, we saw that event methods were executed in a GUI application when the user caused some event to happen (usually with the mouse). The Java **Timer class** and any associated **Timer object** has an interesting feature. It can generate events without any input from the user. **Timer** objects work in your project's background, generating events at time intervals you specify. This event generation feature comes in handy for graphics animation where screen displays need to be updated at regular intervals.

The **Timer** class is part of something called the Java **Swing** package. Think of **Swing** as an updated version of the AWT (Abstract Windows Toolkit) used in the previous class. Using a **Swing** timer is simple:

- Import the proper Swing package (**javax.swing.Timer**)
- Decide how often you want to generate events; this is the timer's **delay**. The delay (an **int** value) is measured in milliseconds. There are 1000 milliseconds in one second.
- Create a timer, and write code for the event method that is to be generated every delay milliseconds.

Timers, Animation, Keyboard Methods 9-3

The first two listed steps are pretty straightforward. Let's look at how to create a **Timer** and how to add the corresponding event method. It is all done in one line of code, similar to code used to add listeners for mouse events. We construct a new timer and add its event method (**actionPerformed**), using an event listener named **ActionListener**. The code that does this for a timer named **myTimer** with a delay value **delay** is:

```
Timer myTimer = new Timer(delay, new ActionListener ()
{
  public void actionPerformed(ActionEvent e)
  {
     [Java code block to execute every delay milliseconds]
  }
});
```

Again, note this is just one long line of Java code. The method has a single argument (**ActionEvent e**), which we won't be using in our examples. For this timer, whatever Java code is included in the **actionPerformed** method will be repeated every delay milliseconds.

There are a few timer object methods we need to monitor status. To start your newly created timer, use:

```
myTimer.start();
```

You always need to start any timer object you create. By default, it is "turned off." Once started, event processing begins. To stop the timer, use:

```
myTimer.stop();
```

As a last method, to see if your timer is currently "running," check the **boolean** value:

```
myTimer.isRunning()
```

Examples

A few examples should clarify how the timer control works. It's very simple and very powerful. To review, here's what happens. If a timer control's **isRunning()** property is **true** (the timer is on), every **delay** milliseconds, Java will generate an event and execute the corresponding **actionPerformed** event method. No user interaction is needed.

The **delay** property is the most important timer object property. This property is set to the number of milliseconds between timer events. A millisecond is 1/1000th of a second, or there are 1,000 milliseconds in a second. If you want to generate N events per second, set the delay to 1000 / N. For example, if you want a timer event to occur 4 times per second, use a **delay** of 250. About the lowest practical value for **delay** is 50 and values that differ by 5, 10, or even 20 are likely to produce similar results. It all depends on your particular computer. Now, let's try some examples.

Start JCreator, open your workspace and create a new project named **TimerProject**. Add a blank file named **TimerTest**. Add this code (you should see that this code is very similar to the graphics project from Class 8 – you might like to try your copy and paste skills):

```
/*
 *   Timer Test
 *   Java for Kids
 */
import java.awt.*;
import java.awt.event.*;
import javax.swing.Timer;

public class TimerTest extends Frame
{
```

```java
  static Frame myFrame;
  static Timer myTimer;

  public static void main(String[] args)
  {
    // create frame
    myFrame = new Frame();
    myFrame.setSize(400, 300);
    myFrame.setTitle("Timer Testing");
    myFrame.setVisible(true);
    myTimer = new Timer(1000, new ActionListener ()
    {
      public void actionPerformed(ActionEvent e)
      {
        Toolkit.getDefaultToolkit().beep();
      }
    });

    // add listener for closing frame
    myFrame.addWindowListener(new WindowAdapter()
    {
      public void windowClosing(WindowEvent e)
      {
        System.exit(0);
      }
    });

    // add listener for mouse press
    myFrame.addMouseListener(new MouseAdapter()
    {
      public void mousePressed(MouseEvent e)
      {
        if (myTimer.isRunning())
        {
          myTimer.stop();
        }
        else
        {
          myTimer.start();
        }
      }
    });

  }
}
```

In this listing, all the unshaded code should be familiar and understood by you – it just creates a frame and adds a listener for the **windowClosing** and **mousePressed** events. The shaded code is concerned with the added **Timer** object. Let's discuss that code.

The first shaded line imports the needed **Swing** component. The second line declares our timer, **myTimer**, to be a class level variable. We do this because the timer will usually be referred to in several methods. After the frame is created, we add the line creating our timer:

```
myTimer = new Timer(1000, new ActionListener ()
{
  public void actionPerformed(ActionEvent e)
  {
    Toolkit.getDefaultToolkit().beep();
  }
});
```

This code creates a timer with a 1000 millisecond (1 second) delay. There is a single line of code in the method event. This line makes your computer beep, or is that obvious? The beep function uses the AWT.

The last bit of shaded code is in the **mousePressed** event method:

```
if (myTimer.isRunning())
{
  myTimer.stop();
}
else
{
  myTimer.start();
}
```

Timers, Animation, Keyboard Methods 9-7

This code is executed whenever the frame is clicked by the mouse. What does this code do? If the timer is on (**myTimer.isRunning()** is true), it stops **myTimer**, and vice versa. We say this code "toggles" the timer.

Compile and run the project. Click the frame. The timer will start and your computer will beep every second (the **actionPerformed** event is generated every 1000 milliseconds, the **delay** value) until you click the frame again. Notice it does this no matter what else is going on. It requires no input (once the timer is on) from you, the user. Click the frame. The beeping will stop. Remember to always have your Java code turn timer controls on and off. Stop the project (click the **X** in the upper right corner of the frame) when you get tired of the beeping.

Add this statement with the import statements to allow using random numbers:

```java
import java.util.Random;
```

Now, modify the timer's **actionPerformed** event, so it reads (added lines are shaded):

```java
public void actionPerformed(ActionEvent e)
{
   Random myRandom = new Random();
   Color myColor;
   Toolkit.getDefaultToolkit().beep();
   myColor = new Color(myRandom.nextInt(256),
myRandom.nextInt(256), myRandom.nextInt(256));
   myFrame.setBackground(myColor);
}
```

Can you see that this code changes the frame background color using random red, green and blue values? Notice use of the **myColor** variable. Compile and run the project. Click the frame. Now, every second, the computer beeps and the frame changes color:

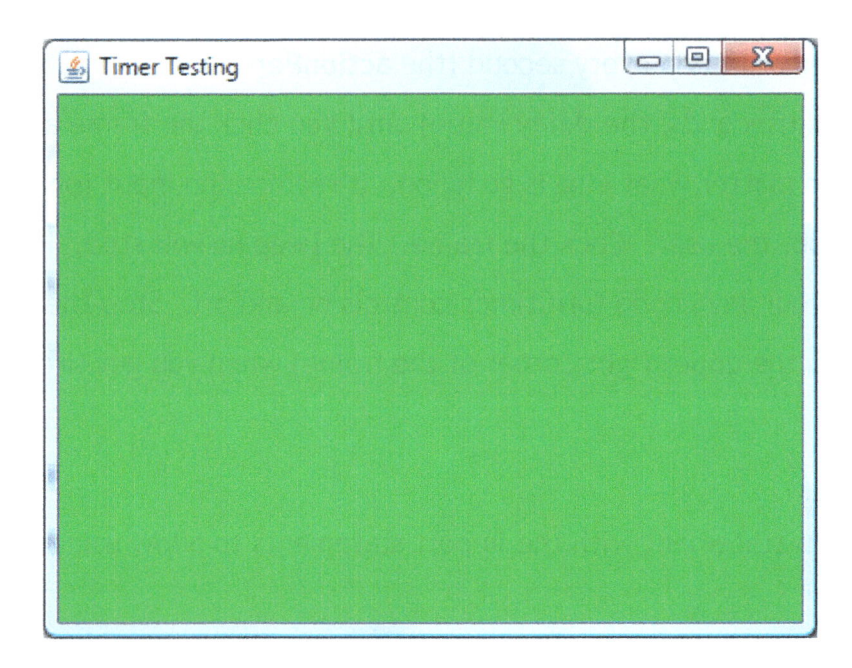

Stop the timer. Stop the project.

What if we want the computer to beep every second, but want the frame color to change four times every second? If events require different delays, each event needs its own timer object. We need to create another timer object (name it **myTimer2**), with class level scope (just like the existing timer **myTimer**). We'll use this timer to control the form color, leaving **myTimer** to only cause the beeping. We use a **delay** value of 250 (event executed every 0.25 seconds, or 4 color changes per second). We can cut and paste the code that sets color in the existing method to this new timer's method. When done, the code creating the two timer objects is:

```
myTimer = new Timer(1000, new ActionListener ()
{
  public void actionPerformed(ActionEvent e)
  {
    Toolkit.getDefaultToolkit().beep();
  }
});

myTimer2 = new Timer(250, new ActionListener ()
{
  public void actionPerformed(ActionEvent e)
  {
    Random myRandom = new Random();
    Color myColor;
    myColor = new
Color(myRandom.nextInt(256),myRandom.nextInt(256),myRandom.nextInt(256));
    myFrame.setBackground(myColor);
  }
});
```

Notice the code for **beeping** is associated with **myTimer**, the code for **color** changing is associated with **myTimer2**. Make sure you didn't forget to add this line to the declarations:

```
static Timer myTimer2;
```

We also need to add code to the **mousePressed** event to toggle (turn it on and off) this new timer. The modified code is simply (added lines shaded):

```
public void mousePressed(MouseEvent e)
{
  if (myTimer.isRunning())
  {
    myTimer.stop();
    myTimer2.stop();
  }
  else
  {
    myTimer.start();
    myTimer2.start();
  }
}
```

This code assumes both timer objects will be started and stopped simultaneously.

Compile and run the project. Click the frame. Do you see how the two timer object events are interacting? You should hear a beep every four times the screen changes color. Stop the project when you're done playing with it.

Timers, Animation, Keyboard Methods 9-11

Let's use the timer to do some flashier stuff. Declare an **int** type variable delta to have class level scope and initialize it at zero:

```
static int delta = 0;
```

Change the code that creates **myTimer2** to (modified code is shaded):

```
myTimer2 = new Timer(50, new ActionListener ()
{
  public void actionPerformed(ActionEvent e)
  {
    Random myRandom = new Random();
    Color myColor;
    myColor = new
Color(myRandom.nextInt(256),myRandom.nextInt(256),myRandom.nextInt(256));
    Graphics myGraphics = myFrame.getGraphics();
    myGraphics.setColor(myColor);
    myGraphics.drawOval(delta, delta, 400 - 2 * delta, 300 - 2 * delta);
    delta = delta + 1;
    if (delta > 150)
    {
      delta = 0;
      myGraphics.clearRect(0, 0, 400, 300);
    }
  }
});
```

You should recognize most of what's here. We've created a timer object with a **delay** of 50 milliseconds. In the event method, a random color is selected and used to draw an oval. This (**drawOval**) is a graphics method we haven't seen before. You should be able to understand it and you'll see it gives a really neat effect in this example. The **drawOval** method has the form:

```
myGraphics.DrawOval(x, y, width, height);
```

Here, **myGraphics** is the graphics object. This statement draws an oval, with a width **width** and height **height**, in the graphics object starting at the point (**x**, **y**). A picture shows the result:

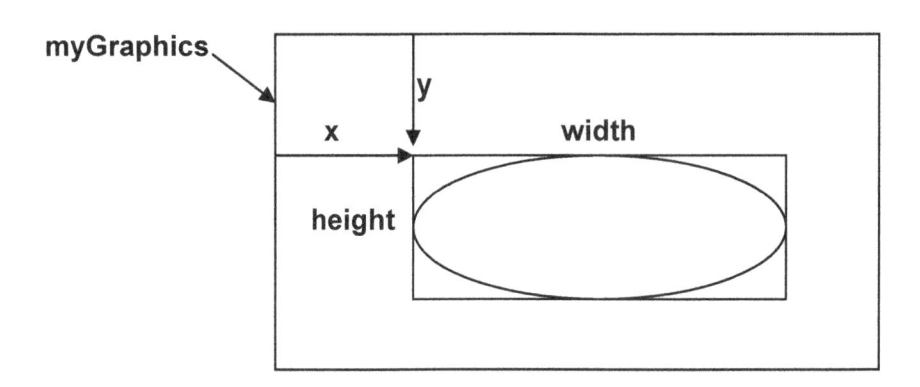

[Diagram showing myGraphics rectangle with an oval inside, labeled with x, y offsets and width, height dimensions]

In your work with Java, you will often see code you don't recognize. Use the usual reference facilities, such as other programmers, text books or the old reliable Java website in these cases. Try it with **drawOval**. Also look at **fillOval** – it has an identical form as **drawOval**, the difference being an oval filled with the current color will be drawn.

Back to the code, you should see the **drawOval** method draws the first ellipse around the border of the frame (**x** = 0 initially). The surrounding rectangle moves "in" an amount **delta** (in each direction) with each "tick" of the timer, resulting in a smaller rectangle (the width and height are decreased by both **2 * delta**). Once **delta** (incremented by one in each step) exceeds half of the frame height (150 in this case), it is reset to 0, the frame is cleared and the process starts all over.

Compile and run the project. Click the frame. Are you hypnotized?

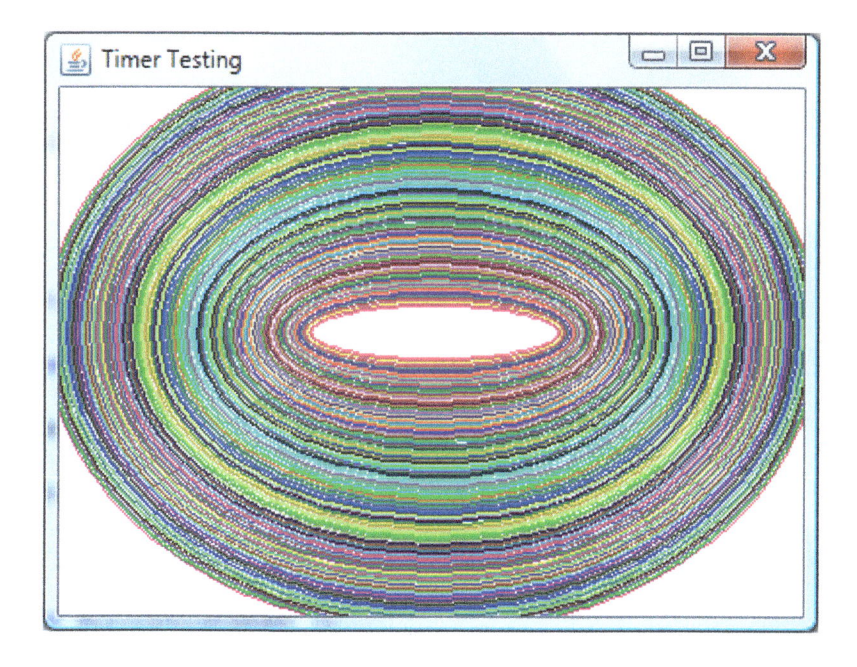

Can you think of other things you could draw using other graphics methods? Look at **drawRect** for example. Try your ideas.

In this last example, the periodic (every 0.050 seconds) changing of the display in the graphics object, imparted by the timer object, gives the appearance of motion – the ovals seem to be moving inward. This is the basic concept behind a very powerful graphics technique - **animation**. In animation, we have a sequence of pictures, each a little different from the previous one. With the ellipse example, in each picture, we add a new ellipse. By displaying this sequence over time, we can trick the viewer into thinking things are moving. It all has to do with how fast the human eye and brain can process information. That's how cartoons work - 24 different pictures are displayed every second - it makes things look like they are moving, or animated. Obviously, the timer object is a key element to animation, as well as for other Java timing tasks. In the Java lesson for this class, we will look at how to do simple animations and some other things.

For your reference, this last version of the **TimerProject** is saved in the course projects folder (**\JavaKids\JK Code**).

Java - The Final Lesson

In this last Java lesson, we look at how to add text to a graphics application, study some simple animation techniques, look at math needed with animations, and learn how to detect keyboard events.

drawString Method

We would like some capability to add text information to a frame. The method that does such a task is the **drawString** graphics method – yes, text is "drawn" to the frame. If we have a graphic object named **myGraphics**, the **drawString** method is:

```
myGraphics.drawString(stringToDisplay, x, y);
```

In this statement, **stringToDisplay** represents the string to print in the frame and the point (**x, y**) is where the string will be located. The string will draw in the current graphics object color using the default font.

Let's try an example. Follow the usual steps. Start JCreator, add a new project (name **AnimateProject**) and add an empty file (**Animate**). We will use this same example as we work through animation. Use this code (again, this should be familiar code, so copy and paste from other files will come in handy):

```java
/*
 * Animate Test
 * Java for Kids
 */

import java.awt.*;
import java.awt.event.*;

public class Animate extends Frame
{
  static Frame myFrame;
  static Graphics myGraphics;

  public static void main(String[] args)
  {
    // create frame
    myFrame = new Frame();
    myFrame.setSize(400, 300);
    myFrame.setTitle("Animation");
    myFrame.setVisible(true);
    myGraphics = myFrame.getGraphics();
    myGraphics.drawString("Isn't Java for Kids fun?", 40,100);

    // add listener for closing frame
    myFrame.addWindowListener(new WindowAdapter()
    {
      public void windowClosing(WindowEvent e)
      {
        System.exit(0);
      }
    });

  }
}
```

This code simply creates a "closeable" frame (class level scope) and displays the text information "Isn't Java for Kids fun?" Compile and run the project. You should see:

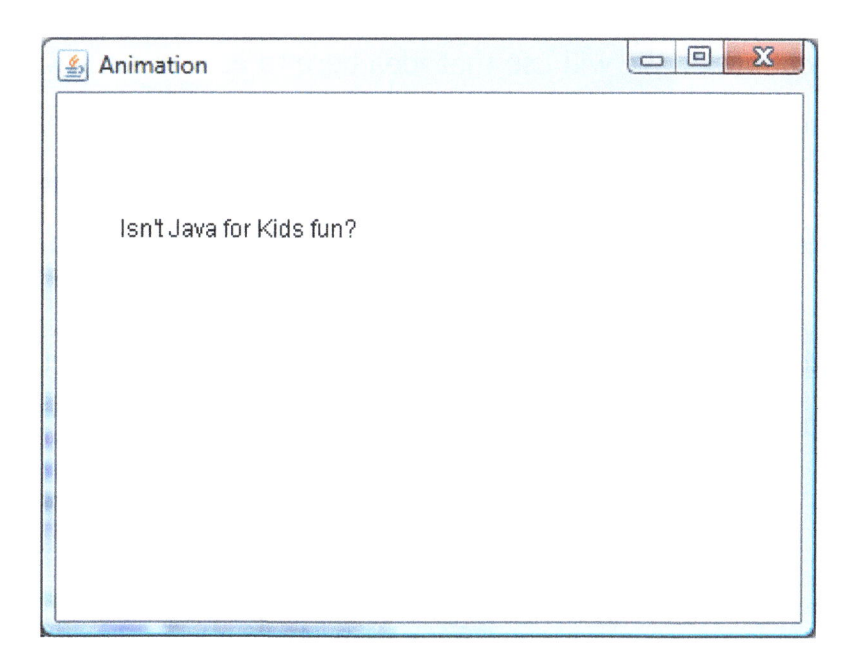

By setting the (x, y) point, you can left or right justify the text, or center it horizontally and/or vertically by knowing the frame dimensions. It is possible to change the font (type, size, style) using Java code, but that is beyond our discussion in this class. Perhaps, you can do some research on your own to figure out how to do this. It involves something called a **Font** object - what else?

One question you may be asking is how come this showed up without having to click the frame (like we did in earlier examples)? The **drawString** method is a little different than other graphics methods. It can be used in the **main** method, but is still not persistent. Minimize the form, then reopen it to see what I mean.

Animation

In an earlier example (the one with the hypnotic ovals), we saw that by using a timer to periodically change the display in a frame, a sense of motion, or animation, is obtained. We will use that idea here to do a specific kind of animation - moving objects around. This is the basis for nearly every video game ever made. The objects we move will be rectangular regions drawn with some graphics method, rectangles and ovals. As you advance in your Java programming, you will find that all graphics objects (including pictures) are rectangular, so the information here will apply when you learn how to add pictures to a project.

Moving graphics objects in a frame is easy to do. It is a simple two step process: erase it in its previous position, then redraw it in its new position. Successive transfers gives the impression of motion, or animation. Where do we put the statements implementing this erase-then-draw process? Each object to be moved must have an associated timer object. If desired, several objects can use the same timer. The "drawing" statement is placed in the corresponding timer object **actionPerformed** event. Whenever a timer event is triggered, the object is erased at its old position (by putting a "blank" object in that position, using the **clearRect** method), a new object position is computed and the corresponding graphics method to redraw the object is executed. This periodic movement is animation. Let's look at an example to see how simple it really is.

Timers, Animation, Keyboard Methods

Example

Return to JCreator and the **AnimateProject**. We will make several modifications to the code. First, remove the **drawString** line. We resize the frame to make it taller than it is wide. We add a timer object (named **myTimer**, with an empty **actionPerformed** event and a 100 millisecond delay) and a **mousePressed** event to toggle that timer. The modified code (changes are shaded) is:

```java
/*
 * Animate Test
 * Java for Kids
 */

import java.awt.*;
import java.awt.event.*;
import javax.swing.Timer;

public class Animate extends Frame
{

  static Frame myFrame;
  static myGraphics;
  static Timer myTimer;

  public static void main(String[] args)
  {
    // create frame
    myFrame = new Frame();
    myFrame.setSize(200, 400);
    myFrame.setTitle("Animation");
    myFrame.setVisible(true);
    myGraphics = myFrame.getGraphics();

    // create timer
    myTimer = new Timer(100, new ActionListener ()
    {
      public void actionPerformed(ActionEvent e)
      {
      }
    });
```

```
    // add listener for mouse press
  myFrame.addMouseListener(new MouseAdapter()
  {
    public void mousePressed(MouseEvent e)
    {
      if (myTimer.isRunning())
      {
        myTimer.stop();
      }
      else
      {
        myTimer.start();
      }
    }
  });

    // add listener for closing frame
  myFrame.addWindowListener(new WindowAdapter()
  {
    public void windowClosing(WindowEvent e)
    {
      System.exit(0);
    }
  });

  }
}
```

We will use this example a lot. Save your work.

Compile and run to make sure things look okay – the frame should appear as:

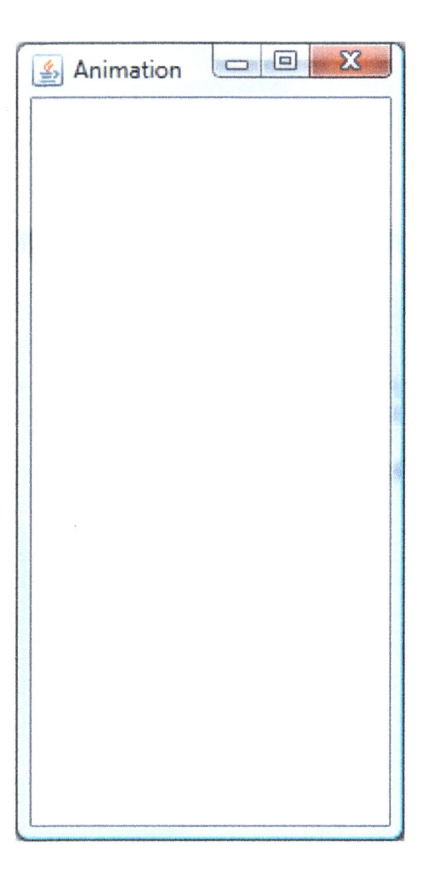

Now, let's add the code to try some animation. We will see if we can make a ball (represented by a filled oval) drop down the frame. Declare a class level variable (**objectY**) to keep track of the vertical position:

```
static int objectY;
```

Add a single line of code at the top of the **mousePressed** event method to initialize the position of the oval "ball" at the top of the frame:

```
objectY = 0;
```

Timers, Animation, Keyboard Methods 9-23

Now, use this code in the timer's **actionPerformed** event method to move the ball:

```
public void actionPerformed(ActionEvent e)
{
  int objectX = 75;
  int objectW = 50;
  int objectH = 50;
  myGraphics.clearRect(0, 0, 200, 400);
  objectY = objectY + 10;
  myGraphics.setColor(Color.red);
  myGraphics.fillOval(objectX, objectY, objectW, objectH);
}
```

In this method, we first clear the frame. The vertical position of the ball (**objectY**) is increased by 10 pixels each time the event is executed (every 0.1 seconds). The ball is moving down. The ball is 50 pixels wide and 50 pixels high (which technically makes it a circle, not an oval) and is colored red. We have horizontally centered the ball in the frame. It should take 40 executions of this routine, or about 4 seconds, for the ball to reach the bottom of the frame. Let's try it.

Compile and run the example project. Click the frame to start the timer. Watch the ball drop. Here's what it should look like:

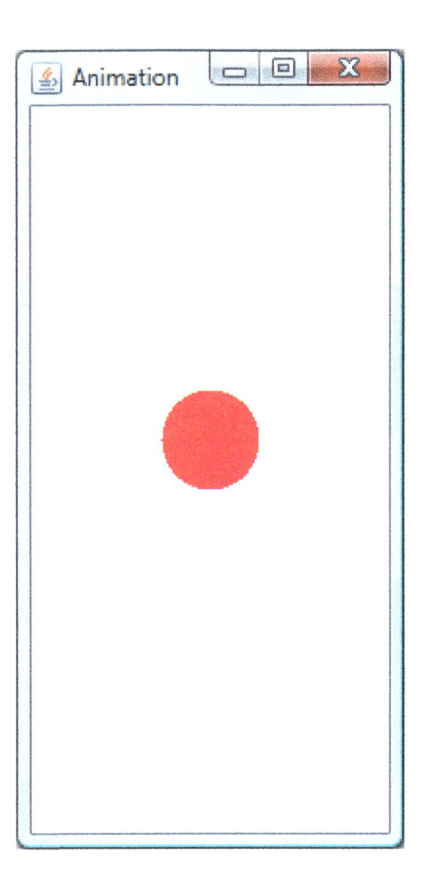

Pretty easy, wasn't it? How long does it take the ball to reach the bottom? What happens when it reaches the bottom? It just keeps on going down through the frame and out through the bottom of your computer monitor to who knows where! We need to be able to detect this disappearance and do something about it. We'll look at two ways to handle this. First, we'll make the ball reappear at the top of the frame, or scroll. Then, we'll make it bounce. Stop the project. Save it too. We'll be using it again.

Object Disappearance

When objects are moving in a frame, we need to know when they move out of the frame across a border. Such information is often needed in video type games. We just saw this need with the falling ball example. When an **object disappearance** happens, we can either ignore that object or perhaps make it "scroll" around to other side of the frame. How do we decide if an object has disappeared? It's basically a case of comparing various positions and dimensions.

We need to detect whether an object has completely moved across one of four frame borders (top, bottom, left, right). Each of these detections can be developed using this diagram of a rectangular **object** within a frame (**myFrame**):

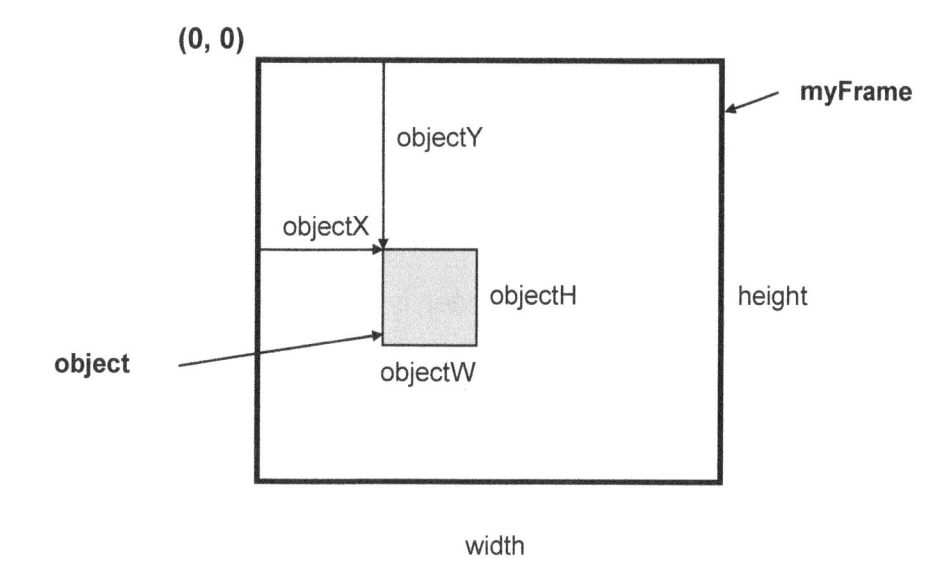

Notice the object is located at (**objectX**, **objectY**) and is **objectW** pixels wide and **objectH** pixels high. The frame is **width** pixels wide and **height** pixels high. You usually know these values from the statement that originally created the frame. To obtain these values in code, you can use (this makes your code more general):

```
width = myFrame.getWidth();
height = myFrame.getHeight();
```

If the object is moving down, it completely crosses the frame bottom border when its top (**objectY**) is lower than the bottom border. The bottom of the panel is **myFrame.getHeight()**. Java code for a bottom border disappearance is:

```
if (objectY > myFrame.getHeight())
{
    [Java code for bottom border disappearance]
}
```

If the object is moving up, the frame top border is completely crossed when the bottom of the object (**objectY** + **objectH**) becomes less than 0. In Java, this is detected with:

```
if ((objectY + objectH) < 0)
{
    [Java code for top border disappearance]
}
```

If the object is moving to the left, the frame left border is completely crossed when object right side (**objectX + objectW**) becomes less than 0. In Java, this is detected with:

```
if ((objectX + objectW) < 0)
{
      [Java code for left border disappearance]
}
```

If the object is moving to the right, it completely crosses the frame right border when its left side (**objectX**) passes the border. The right side of the frame is **myFrame.getWidth()**. Java code for a right border disappearance is:

```
if (objectX > myFrame.getWidth())
{
      [Java code for right border disappearance]
}
```

Let's add disappearance detection to our "falling ball" example. Return to that project. Say, instead of having the ball disappear when it reaches the bottom, we have it magically reappear at the top of the frame - the object is scrolling. Modify the timer's **actionPerformed** event method to this (new lines are shaded):

```
public void actionPerformed(ActionEvent e)
{
  int objectX = 75;
  int objectW = 50;
  int objectH = 50;
  myGraphics.clearRect(0, 0, myFrame.getWidth(), myFrame.getHeight());
  objectY = objectY + 10;
  if (objectY > myFrame.getHeight())
  {
    objectY = -objectH;
  }
  myGraphics.setColor(Color.red);
  myGraphics.fillOval(objectX, objectY, objectW, objectH);
}
```

We added the bottom border disappearance logic and generalized the **clearRect** method with the frame size methods. When the ball disappears, we reset its **objectY** value so it is repositioned just off the top of the frame. Compile and run the project. Watch the ball scroll. Pretty easy, wasn't it? Stop and save the project.

Border Crossing

What if, in the falling ball example, instead of scrolling, we want the ball to bounce back up when it reaches the bottom border? This is another common animation task - detecting the initiation of **border crossings**. Such crossings are used to change the direction of moving objects, that is, make them bounce. How do we detect border crossings?

The same diagram used for image disappearances can be used here. Checking to see if an image has crossed a frame border is like checking for object disappearance, except the object has not moved quite as far. For top and bottom checks, the object movement is less by an amount equal to its height (**objectH**). For left and right checks, the movement is less by an amount equal to its width (**objectW**). Look back at that diagram and you should see these code segments accomplish the respective border crossing directions:

```
if (objectY < 0)
{
     [Java code for top border crossing]
}

if ((objectY + objectH) > myFrame.getHeight())
{
     [Java code for bottom border crossing]
}

if (objectX < 0)
{
     [Java code for left border crossing]
}
```

```
if ((objectX + objectW) > myFrame.getWidth())
{
    [Java code for right border crossing]
}
```

Let's modify the falling ball example to have it bounce when it reaches the bottom of the frame. Declare a class level **int** variable **objectDir**:

```
static int objectDir;
```

objectDir is used to indicate which way the object (ball) is moving. When **objectDir** is 1, the ball is moving down (**objectY** is increasing). When **objectDir** is -1, the ball is moving up (**objectY** is decreasing). Change the **mousePressed** event to (new line is shaded):

```
public void mousePressed(MouseEvent e)
{
  objectY = 0;
  objectDir = 1;
  if (myTimer.isRunning())
  {
    myTimer.stop();
  }
  else
  {
    myTimer.start();
  }
}
```

We added a single line to initialize **objectDir** to 1 (moving down).

Change the **actionPerformed** event to this (again, changed and/or new lines are shaded):

```java
public void actionPerformed(ActionEvent e)
{
  int objectX = 75;
  int objectW = 50;
  int objectH = 50;
  myGraphics.clearRect(0, 0, myFrame.getWidth(),
myFrame.getHeight());
  objectY = objectY + objectDir * 10;
  if ((objectY + objectH) > myFrame.getHeight())
  {
    objectY = myFrame.getHeight() - objectH;
    objectDir = -1;
  }
  myGraphics.setColor(Color.red);
  myGraphics.fillOval(objectX, objectY, objectW, objectH);
}
```

We modified the calculation of **objectY** to account for the **objectDir** variable. Notice how it is used to impart the proper direction to the ball motion (down when **objectDir** is 1, up when **objectDir** is -1). We have also added the **if** structure for a bottom border crossing. Notice when a crossing is detected, the object is repositioned (by resetting **objectY**) at the bottom of the frame (**myFrame.getHeight() - objectH**) and **objectDir** is set to -1 (direction is changed so the ball will start moving up). Compile and run the project. Now when the ball reaches the bottom of the frame, it reverses direction and heads back up. We've made the image bounce! But, once it reaches the top, it's gone again!

Add top border crossing detection, so the timer **actionPerformed** event is now (changes are shaded):

```java
public void actionPerformed(ActionEvent e)
{
  int objectX = 75;
  int objectW = 50;
  int objectH = 50;
  myGraphics.clearRect(0, 0, myFrame.getWidth(),
myFrame.getHeight());
  objectY = objectY + objectDir * 10;
  if ((objectY + objectH) > myFrame.getHeight())
  {
    objectY = myFrame.getHeight() - objectH;
    objectDir = -1;
    Toolkit.getDefaultToolkit().beep();
  }
  else if (objectY < 0)
  {
    objectY = 0;
    objectDir = 1;
    Toolkit.getDefaultToolkit().beep();
  }
  myGraphics.setColor(Color.red);
  myGraphics.fillOval(objectX, objectY, objectW, objectH);
}
```

In the top crossing code (the **else if** portion), we reset **objectY** to 0 (the top of the frame) and change **objectDir** to 1. We've also added a couple of "beep" statements so there is some audible feedback when either bounce occurs. Compile and run the project again. Your ball will now bounce up and down, beeping with each bounce, until you stop it. Stop and save the project.

Timers, Animation, Keyboard Methods 9-33

The code we've developed here for checking and resetting object positions is a common task in Java. As you develop your programming skills, you should make sure you are comfortable with what all these locations and dimensions mean and how they interact. As an example, can you see why **imageX** = 75 centers the ball in the frame? The equation used was:

```
objectX = 0.5 * (myFrame.getWidth() - objectW);
```

You've now seen how to do lots of things with animations. You can make objects move, make them disappear and reappear, and make them bounce. Do you have some ideas of simple video games you would like to build? You still need two more skills – object erasure and collision detection - which are discussed next.

Object Erasure

In the little example we just did, we had to clear the frame (using the **clearRect** graphics method) prior to each **drawOval** method. This was done to erase the **object** (ball) at its previous location before drawing a new object. This "erase, then redraw" process is the secret behind animation. But, what if we are animating many objects? The **clearRect** method, as implemented, would clear all objects from the frame and require repositioning every object, even ones that haven't moved. This would be a slow, tedious and unnecessary process.

We will take a more precise approach to erasure. Instead of erasing the entire frame before moving an object, we will only erase the rectangular region previously occupied by the object. To do this, we will still use the **clearRect** graphics method, but with new arguments. We will only erase the area occupied by the object, or:

```
myGraphics.clearRect(objectX, objectY, objectW, objectH);
```

This line of code will clear a rectangular region located at (**objectX, objectY**), **objectW** wide, and **objectH** high. The region will be set to the background color of the frame, effectively erasing the object at the specified location.

Timers, Animation, Keyboard Methods

Open up the "bouncing ball" example one more time. In the timer **actionPerformed** method, change the **clearRect** statement to:

```
myGraphics.clearRect(objectX, objectY, objectW, objectH);
```

Recompile and rerun the project. You probably won't notice much difference since we only have one object moving. But, in more detailed animations, this object erasing approach is superior.

Collision Detection

Another requirement in animation is to determine if two objects have collided. This is needed in games to see if a ball hits a paddle, if an alien rocket hits its target, or if a cute little character grabs some reward. Each object is described by a rectangular area, so the **collision detection** problem is to see if two rectangles collide, or overlap. This check is done using each object's position and dimensions.

Here are two objects (**object1** and **object2**) in a frame:

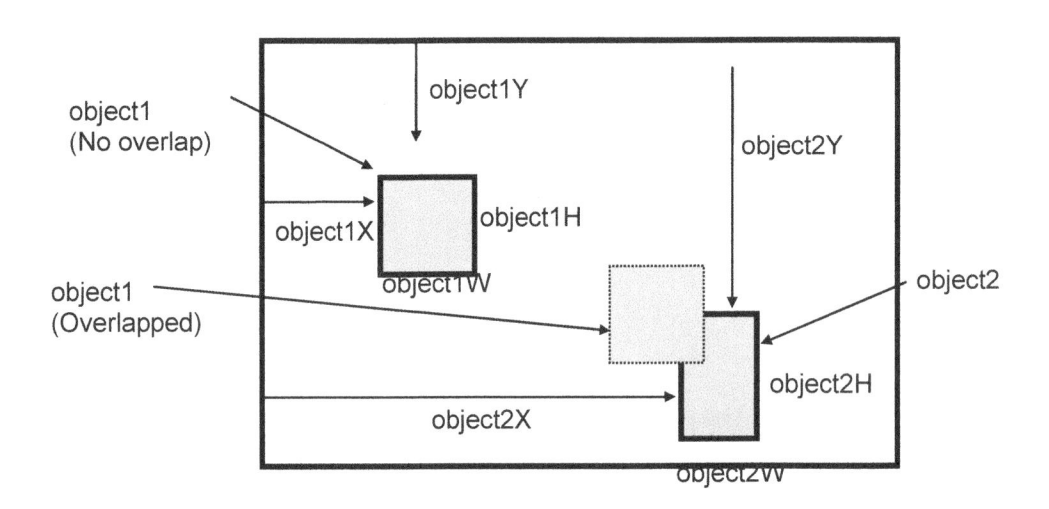

object1 is positioned at (**object1X**, **object1Y**), is **object1W** wide and **object1H** high. Similarly, **object2** is positioned at (**object2X**, **object2Y**), is **object2W** wide and **object2H** high.

Looking at this diagram, you should see there are four requirements for the two rectangles to overlap:

1. The right side of **object1** (**object1X + object1H**) must be "farther right" than the left side of **object2** (**object2X**)
2. The left side of **object1** (**object1X**) must be "farther left" than the right side of **object2** (**object2X + object2W**)
3. The bottom of **object1** (**object1Y + object1H**) must be "farther down" than the top of **object2** (**object2Y**)
4. The top of **object1** (**object1Y**) must be "farther up" than the bottom of **object2** (**object2Y + object2H**)

All four of these requirements must be met for a collision.

The Java code to check if these rectangles overlap is:

```
if ((object1X + object1W) > object2X)
{
  if (object1X < (object2X + object2W))
  {
    if ((object1Y + object1H) > object2Y)
    {
      if (object1Y < (object2Y + object2H))
      {
            [Java code for overlap, or collision]
      }
    }
  }
}
```

This code checks the four conditions for overlap using four "nested" if structures. The Java code for a collision is executed only if all four conditions are found to be true.

Let's try some collision detection with the bouncing ball example. We will draw a small rectangle near the bottom of the frame and see if the ball collides with the rectangle. Add these class level variables to establish the rectangle geometry:

```
static int rectX = 100;
static int rectY = 380;
static int rectW = 20;
static int rectH = 20;
```

Add these two lines to the **mousePressed** method after the line establishing **objectDir**:

```
myGraphics.setColor(Color.blue);
myGraphics.fillRect(rectX, rectY, rectW, rectH);
```

These two lines draw the rectangle when the frame is clicked.

Modify the timer **actionPerformed** method code to (added code is shaded):

```
public void actionPerformed(ActionEvent e)
{
  int objectX = 75;
  int objectW = 50;
  int objectH = 50;
  boolean collision;
  myGraphics.clearRect(objectX, objectY, objectW, objectH);
  objectY = objectY + objectDir * 10;
  collision = false;
  if ((objectX + objectW) > rectX)
  {
    if (objectX < (rectX + rectW))
    {
      if ((objectY + objectH) > rectY)
      {
        if (objectY < (rectY + rectH))
        {
          collision = true;
        }
      }
    }
  }
  if (collision)
  {
    objectY = rectY - objectH;
    objectDir = -1;
    Toolkit.getDefaultToolkit().beep();
  }
  else if (objectY < 0)
  {
    objectY = 0;
    objectDir = 1;
    Toolkit.getDefaultToolkit().beep();
  }
  myGraphics.setColor(Color.red);
  myGraphics.fillOval(objectX, objectY, objectW, objectH);
}
```

We declare a method level **boolean** variable **collision** to indicate an overlap (true for overlap, false for no overlap). The overlap code (using the rectangle variables **rectX**, **rectY**, **rectW**, **rectH**) precedes the **fillOval** method. If a collision is detected, the **object** (ball) is repositioned so it just touches the top of the rectangle, its direction is reversed and a beep is played. The code for bouncing off the top of the frame is unchanged.

Run the project. Click the frame to start things. You should see:

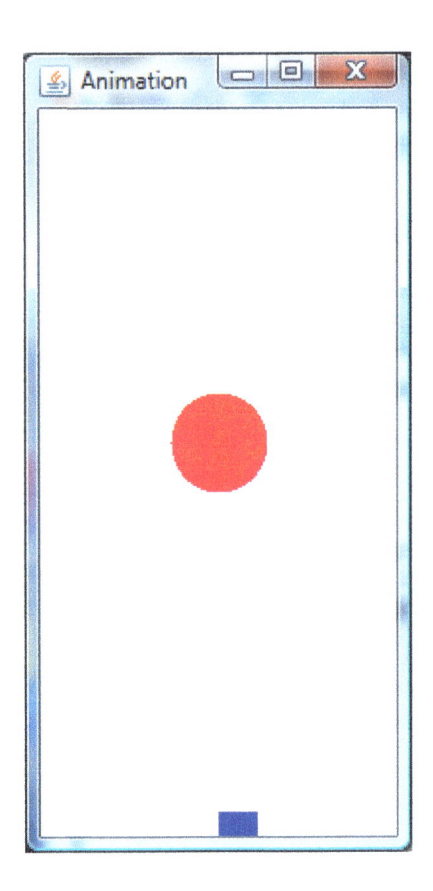

Notice the ball now bounces off the rectangle. Stop the project. Move the rectangle out of the way (set **rectX** to 0) so the ball won't collide with it. The ball should just drop off the screen. See how close the ball can pass by the rectangle without colliding to make sure the overlap routine works properly. Stop and save the project.

Now that you know how to detect collisions, you're well on your way to knowing how to build a simple video game. Next, we'll learn how to detect keyboard events from the user. One possible use for these events, among many, is to allow a user to move a little paddle to "hit" a dropping ball. The collision technique we just learned will come in handy for such a task.

Keyboard Methods

In Class 8, we looked at ways for a user to interact with a Java GUI project using the mouse for input. We studied two mouse events and associated methods: **mousePressed** and **mouseDragged**. Another input device available for use is the computer keyboard. Here we look at **keyboard events** which give our projects the ability to detect user input from the keyboard. Just one keyboard event is studied: the **keyPressed** event, which we will see is very similar to the **mousePressed** event.

In a GUI application, many objects can recognize keyboard events. Yet, only the object that has **focus** can receive a keyboard event. When trying to detect a keyboard event for a frame, we need to make sure the frame has focus. We can give the frame focus by clicking on it with the mouse. But, another way to assign focus with the **requestFocus** method. The format for such a statement is, assuming a frame named **myFrame**:

```
myFrame.requestFocus();
```

This command in Java will give the frame focus, allowing it to recognize keyboard events. It has the same effect as clicking on the frame. We use the **requestFocus** method with keyboard events to insure proper execution of each event.

keyPressed Event

The **keyPressed** event has the ability to detect the pressing of any key on the computer keyboard. It can detect:

- Special combinations of the Shift, Ctrl, and Alt keys
- Insert, Del, Home, End, PgUp, PgDn keys
- Cursor control keys
- Numeric keypad keys (it can distinguish these numbers from those on the top row of the keyboard)
- Function keys
- Letter, number and character keys

The **keyPressed** event is triggered whenever a key is pressed. The form of this method must be:

```
public void keyPressed(KeyEvent e)
{
        [Java code for keyPressed event]
}
```

The **KeyEvent** argument **e** tells us which key was pressed by providing what is called a **key code**. There is a key code value for each key on the keyboard. By evaluating the **e.getKeyCode()** argument, we can determine which key was pressed. There are over 100 values, some of which are:

e.getKeyCode()	Description
e.VK_BACK_SPACE	The BACKSPACE key.
e.VK_CANCEL	The CANCEL key.
e.VK_DELETE	The DEL key.
e.VK_DOWN	The DOWN ARROW key.
e.VK_ENTER	The ENTER key.
e.VK_ESCAPE	The ESC key.
e.VK_F1	The F1 key.
e.VK_HOME	The HOME key.
e.VK_LEFT	The LEFT ARROW key.
e.VK_NUMPAD0	The 0 key on the numeric keypad.
e.VK_PAGE_DOWN	The PAGE DOWN key.
e.VK_PAGE_UP	The PAGE UP key.
e.VK_RIGHT	The RIGHT ARROW key.
e.VK_SPACE	The SPACEBAR key.
e.VK_TAB	The TAB key.
e.VK_UP	The UP ARROW key.
e.VK_G	The letter G.
e.VK_4	The number 4.

Timers, Animation, Keyboard Methods

The adapter that implements the **keyPressed** event is called the **KeyAdapter** and uses the **KeyListener**. The code to add a listener (to **myFrame**) for this event is very similar to the code used to add the mouse events in Class 8:

```
myFrame.addKeyListener(new KeyAdapter()
{
  public void keyPressed(KeyEvent e)
  {
      [Java code for key press]
  }
});
```

Like other statements adding event listeners, this is one long line of Java code.

Using the **keyPressed** event is not easy. There is a lot of work involved in interpreting the information provided in the **keyPressed** event. For example, the **keyPressed** event cannot distinguish between an upper and lower case letter. You need to make that distinction in your Java code. You usually use an **if** structure (based on **e.getKeyCode()**) to determine which key was pressed. Let's see how to use **keyPressed** to recognize some keys.

Start JCreator and return to the **AnimateProject** we've been using. Add this code <u>after</u> the code adding the **mousePressed** event method:

```
// add listener for key press
myFrame.addKeyListener(new KeyAdapter()
{
  public void keyPressed(KeyEvent e)
  {
      System.out.println("Key pressed: " + e.getKeyCode());
  }
});
```

Here, a **println** statement will tell us which key was pressed. Place the following line of code in the main method after the line creating **myGraphics** (this line is needed to give the frame focus):

```
myFrame.requestFocus();
```

Compile and run the project. Click the frame to get the ball bouncing. Type a letter. The letter's corresponding **e.getKeyCode()** (a numeric value) are shown. (If nothing prints, click the frame to make sure it has focus.) Press the same letter while holding down the <**Shift**> key. The same code will appear – there is no distinction between upper and lower case. Press each of the four arrow keys to see their different values. Type numbers using the top row of the keyboard and the numeric keypad. Notice the keypad numbers have different key code values than the "keyboard numbers." This lets us distinguish the keypad from the keyboard. Try various keys on the keyboard to see which keys have a key code (all of them). Notice it works with function keys, cursor control keys, letters, number, everything! Stop the project.

Now, let's use the left and right cursor control keys to move the little rectangle. Change the **keyPressed** method so it is:

```
public void keyPressed(KeyEvent e)
{
  // erase rectangle
  myGraphics.clearRect(rectX, rectY, rectW, rectH);
  if (e.getKeyCode() == e.VK_LEFT)
  {
    rectX = rectX -1;
  }
  else if (e.getKeyCode() == e.VK_RIGHT)
  {
    rectX = rectX + 1;
  }
  // redraw rectangle
  myGraphics.setColor(Color.blue);
  myGraphics.fillRect(rectX, rectY, rectW, rectH);
}
```

In this code, the rectangle is first erased. Then, if either the left or right cursor key is pressed, the rectangle's x coordinate is updated. The rectangle is then redrawn. Compile and run the project. Notice how the cursor control keys move the rectangle. We have that "paddle" we've been looking for. This last version of **AnimateProject** is saved in the course project folder (**\JavaKids\JK Code**).

Project -Balloons

In this class project, we will build a little video game. Colorful balloons are dropping from the sky. You maneuver a popping device under them to make them pop and get a point. You try to pop as many balloons as you can in one minute. This project is saved as **BalloonProject** in the projects folder (**\Java Kids\JK Code**).

Project Design

All of the game action will go on in a frame. There will be five possible balloons, all drawn with **fillOval** methods. An arrow (drawn with the **drawLine** method) will be the "popping arrow." This arrow will be moved using keys on the keyboard. Clicking the frame will control starting and stopping the game. The current score (number of balloons popped) will be displayed in the frame. The steps of the project we will follow:

1. Initialize score and balloon locations; give frame focus.
2. When frame is clicked, start the timer dropping the balloons.
3. Monitor **keyPressed** event for arrow movement.
4. Monitor timer's **actionPerformed** method for collisions and misses – update score.

When writing the code, we will look at each of these steps in more detail.

Project Development

The **Balloons** game is simple, in concept. To play, click the frame. The five balloons will drop down the frame, each at a different speed. Use the left and right arrow keys to move the arrow. If the arrow is under a balloon when a collision occurs, the balloon pops and you get a point. Balloons reappear at the top after popping or after reaching the bottom of the screen without being popped. You pop as many balloons as you can in 60 seconds. At that point, the game ends.

It looks like there are only two events to code, clicking the frame to start or checking for arrow key presses. But, we will also have two timers and their associated method events. Why two timers? One timer controls the balloon animation, updating the frame 10 times a second (**delay** will be 100). Another timer controls the overall time of the game. It generates an event only once - when the game is over (**delay** will be 60000 - that's 60 seconds). So, in addition to frame clicks and key press events, we need code for two timer events. There is a substantial amount of Java code to write here, even though you will see there is a lot of repetition. We suggest writing the event methods in stages. Write one method or a part of a method. Compile and run the project. Make sure the code you wrote works. Add more code. Run the project again. Make sure the added code works. Continue adding code until complete. Building a project this way minimizes the potential for error and makes the debugging process much easier. Let's go.

Start JCreator. Open your workspace and create a new project named **BalloonProject**. Add a blank file named **Balloons**. Open the empty **Balloons.java** file. Build this empty framework. This adds needed import statements, sets up the program, creates a frame, a graphics object and adds a frame closing event method:

```java
/*
 *  Balloons
 *  Java for Kids
 */
import java.awt.*;
import java.awt.event.*;
import java.util.Random;
import javax.swing.Timer;
public class Balloons extends Frame
{
  static Frame myFrame;
  static Graphics myGraphics;

  public static void main(String[] args)
  {
    // create frame
    myFrame = new Frame();
    myFrame.setSize(400, 400);
    myFrame.setTitle("Balloons");
    myFrame.setVisible(true);
    myGraphics = myFrame.getGraphics();
    // add listener for closing frame
    myFrame.addWindowListener(new WindowAdapter()
    {
      public void windowClosing(WindowEvent e)
      {
        System.exit(0);
      }
    });
  }
}
```

Compile and run the project to insure you have a good starting point:

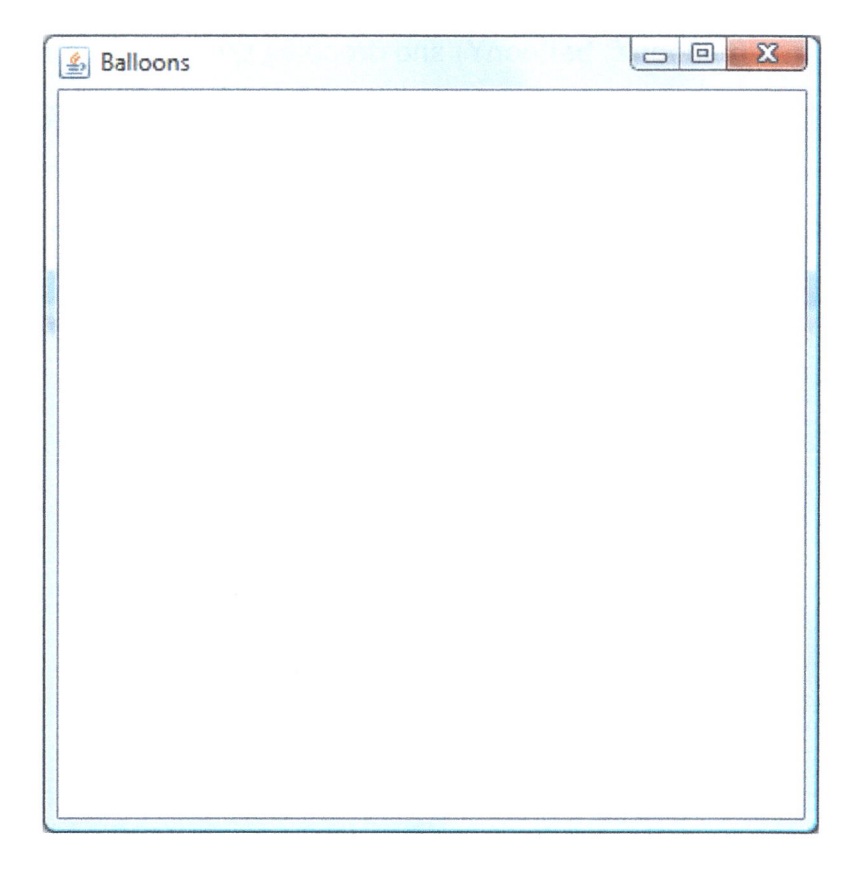

Note **myFrame** (class level scope) is 400 x 400 pixels in size. This lets us space five balloons (50 pixels wide) across the frame (with 10 pixels between each balloon). We also leave some room on the right side of the frame to print the score.

Each balloon will occupy a square region, 50 pixels wide by 50 pixels high. We need variable arrays to keep track of each balloon's color (**balloonColor**), balloon's location (**balloonX, balloonY**) and dropping speed (**balloonSpeed**). The arrow (**arrowSize**) will be half the width of a balloon and its position will be given by **arrowX**. Also, declare a variable for the score and a **Random** object to use with random numbers. These will all have class level scope. Add these declarations:

```
static int balloonSize = 50;
static Color[] balloonColor = new Color[5];
static int[] balloonX = new int[5];
static int[] balloonY = new int[5];
static int[] balloonSpeed = new int[5];
static int arrowSize = balloonSize / 2;
static int arrowX;
static int score;
static Random myRandom = new Random();
```

The array **balloonSpeed** holds the five speeds, representing the number of pixels a balloon will drop with each update of the viewing frame. We want each balloon to drop at a different rate. In code, each speed will be computed using:

```
myRandom.nextInt(4) + 3
```

Or, it will be a random value between 3 and 6. A new speed will be computed each time a balloon starts its trip down the frame. How do we know this will be a good speed, providing reasonable dropping rates? We didn't before the project began. This expression was arrived at by 'trial and error.' We built the game and tried different speeds until we found values that worked. You do this a lot in developing games. You may not know values for some numbers before you start. So, you go ahead and build the game and try all kinds of values until you find ones that work. Then, you build these numbers into your code.

When the program first starts, we need to follow these steps:

- Initialize each balloon's color and horizontal position
- Print Start message.
- Give frame focus (so **keyPressed** can be recognized)

Add this code to the **main** method to perform each of these steps. The code goes after the line creating the graphic objec:

```
balloonColor[0] = Color.red;
balloonColor[1] = Color.blue;
balloonColor[2] = Color.green;
balloonColor[3] = Color.magenta;
balloonColor[4] = Color.cyan;
// put 10 pixels between each balloon
for (int i = 0; i < 5; i++)
{
  balloonX[i] = 10 + i * (balloonSize + 10);
}
// start message
myGraphics.setColor(Color.black);
myGraphics.drawString("CLICK FRAME TO START", 100, 200);
//Give frame focus
myFrame.requestFocus();
```

Compile to make sure you have no errors. Run to see the start message.

```
Balloons

                CLICK FRAME TO START
```

Timers, Animation, Keyboard Methods

We will use two timers, named **timerBalloons** and **timerGame**. Let's create two empty event methods for these timers. First, declare them as class level objects:

```
static Timer timerBalloons;
static Timer timerGame;
```

The code to create the methods (place after the code adding the listener for the window closing event) is:

```
// create balloons timer
timerBalloons = new Timer(100, new ActionListener ()
{
  public void actionPerformed(ActionEvent e)
  {
    // empty for now
  }
});

// create game timer
timerGame = new Timer(60000, new ActionListener ()
{
  public void actionPerformed(ActionEvent e)
  {
    // empty for now
  }
});
```

Clicking the frame with the mouse initializes the game and starts the two timers. The **mousePressed** method does the work. Add this code after the code creating the timers:

```
// add listener for mouse press
myFrame.addMouseListener(new MouseAdapter()
{
  public void mousePressed(MouseEvent e)
  {
    // initializes and begins game
    myGraphics.clearRect(0, 0, myFrame.getWidth(),
myFrame.getHeight());
    score = 0;
    updateScore(score);
    for (int i = 0; i < 5; i++)
    {
      balloonY[i] = - balloonSize;
      balloonSpeed[i] = myRandom.nextInt(4) + 3;
    }
    // Set arrow near center
    arrowX = 150;
    drawArrow(arrowX);
    timerGame.start();
    timerBalloons.start();
  }
});
```

This code clears the frame, initializes the score, sets up the balloons, draws the arrow, then starts the timers.

Timers, Animation, Keyboard Methods

For this code to work, you also need to add two methods <u>after</u> the right closing brace for the **main** method, but <u>before</u> the right brace closing out the **Balloons** class (the usual place for methods). The method to update the score is:

```
public static void updateScore(int s)
{
  // draw the score
  myGraphics.setColor(Color.black);
  myGraphics.drawString("Your Score:", 320, 60);
  myGraphics.clearRect(340, 80, 400, 120);
  myGraphics.drawString(String.valueOf(score), 350, 90);
}
```

Notice how the score is converted to a string before being displayed. And the method to draw the arrow is:

```
public static void drawArrow(int x)
{
  // draw the arrow
  myGraphics.setColor(Color.black);
  myGraphics.drawLine(x, 390, x + arrowSize / 2, 370);
  myGraphics.drawLine(x + arrowSize / 2, 370, x + arrowSize, 390);
}
```

You should see that this code draws a black arrow (connecting three points) near the bottom of the frame:

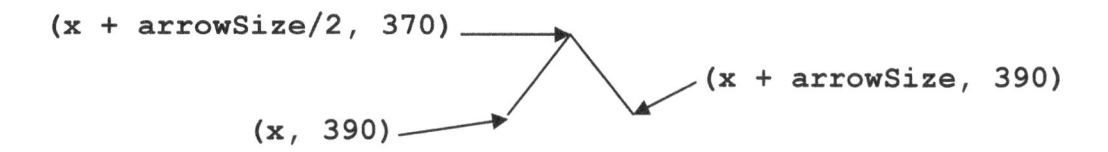

(x + arrowSize/2, 370)

(x + arrowSize, 390)

(x, 390)

Compile and run the code to check for errors. Click to see the arrow and the initial score display:

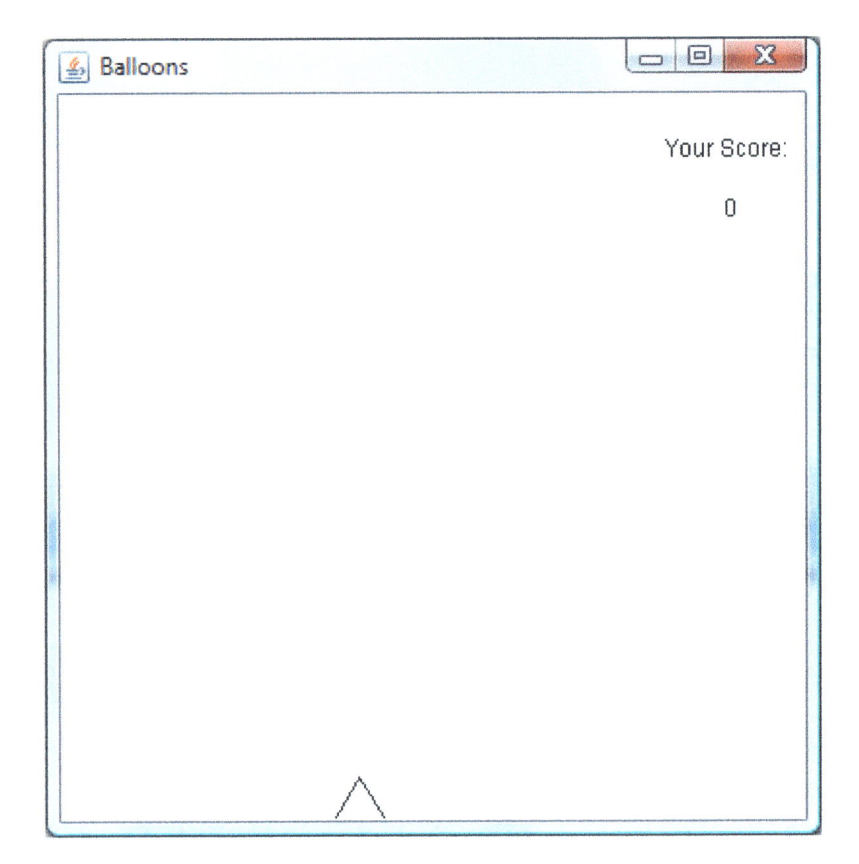

To move the arrow, we need a **keyPressed** event method Pick a key that will move the arrow to the left and a key that will move it to the right. I chose **F** for **left** movement and **J** for **right** movement. Why? The keys are in the middle of the keyboard, with F to the left of J, and are easy to reach with a natural typing position. You could pick others. The arrow keys are one possibility. I hardly ever use these because they are always at some odd location on a keyboard and just not "naturally" reached. Also, the arrow keys are often used (in more elaborate GUI projects) to move among controls in the frame and this can get confusing. The code I use to add this method is (place this after the code adding the listener for timers):

```
// add listener for keyPress
myFrame.addKeyListener(new KeyAdapter()
{
  public void keyPressed(KeyEvent e)
  {
    // Erase arrow at old location
    myGraphics.clearRect(arrowX, 370, arrowX + arrowSize, 390);
    // Check for F key (left) and J key (right) and compute arrow position
    if (e.getKeyCode() == e.VK_F)
    {
      arrowX = arrowX - 5;
    }
    else if (e.getKeyCode() == e.VK_J)
    {
      arrowX = arrowX + 5;
    }
    // Position arrow
    drawArrow(arrowX);
  }
});
```

Notice if the F key is pressed, the arrow is moved to the left by 5 pixels. The arrow is moved right by 5 pixels if the J key is pressed. Again, the 5 pixels value was found by 'trial and error' - it seems to provide smooth motion. After typing in this method, save the project, then compile and run it. Click the frame to start things. Make sure the arrow moves as expected. It should start near the middle of the frame. Notice there is no code that keeps the arrow from moving out of the frame - you could add it if you like. You would need to detect a left or right border crossing. Stop the project by clicking the X in the upper right corner of the frame.

Now, what goes on in the two timer event methods? We'll do the easy one first. Each game lasts 60 seconds. This timing is handled by the **timerGame** timer. It has a **delay** of 60000, which means it's event method is executed every 60 seconds. We'll only execute that event once - when it is executed, we stop the game and setup for another game, if desired. The **actionPerformed** event method for the **timerGame** timer (make sure you type this in the right place) should be:

```
public void actionPerformed(ActionEvent e)
{
  // game over
  timerGame.stop();
  timerBalloons.stop();
  myGraphics.clearRect(0, 0, myFrame.getWidth(),
myFrame.getHeight());
  myGraphics.drawString("Game is over. Final score is " +
String.valueOf(score) + " points.", 50, 200);
  myGraphics.drawString("Click frame to play again.", 50,
250);
}
```

Save the project. Run and compile. Play with the arrow again. After 60 seconds, you should see the **'Game Over'** notice pop up in the frame:

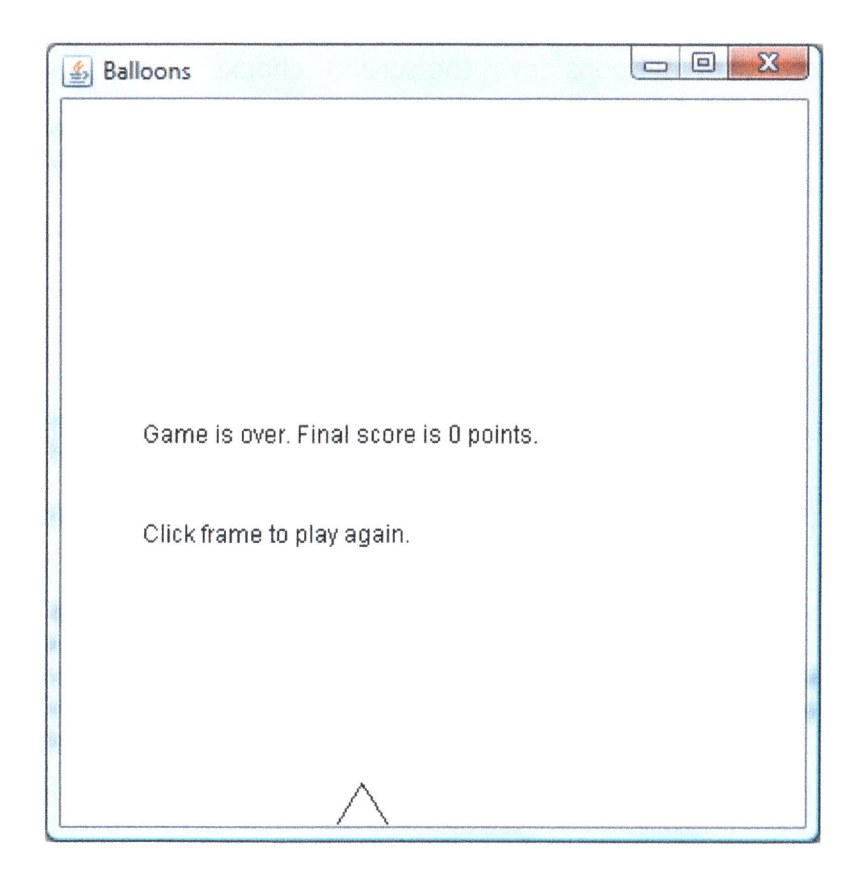

```
┌─ Balloons ─────────────────── ─ □ X ┐
│                                      │
│                                      │
│                                      │
│                                      │
│     Game is over. Final score is 0 points. │
│                                      │
│                                      │
│     Click frame to play again.       │
│                                      │
│                                      │
│                  /\                  │
└──────────────────────────────────────┘
```

If this happens, the **timerGame** timer is working. If it doesn't happen, you need to fix something.

Now, to the heart of the **Balloons** game - the event method associated with **timerBalloons**. We haven't seen any dropping balloons yet. Here's where we do that, and more. The **timerBalloons** timer handles the animation sequence. It drops the balloons down the screen, checks for popping, and checks for balloons reaching the bottom of the frame. It gets new balloons started. There's a lot going on. The procedure steps are identical for each balloon. They are:

- Move the balloon.
- Check to see if balloon has popped. If so, sound a beep, make the balloon disappear, increment score and make balloon reappear at the top with a new speed.
- Check to see if balloon has reached the bottom without being popped. If so, start a new balloon with a new speed.

The steps are easy to write, just a little harder to code. Moving a balloon simply involves erasing it at its old location and redrawing it at its new location (determined by the **balloonY** value). To check if the balloon has reached the bottom, we use the border crossing logic discussed earlier. The trickiest step is checking if a balloon has popped. One way to check for a balloon pop is to check to see if the balloon image rectangle overlaps the arrow rectangle using the collision detection logic developed earlier. This would work, but a balloon would pop if the arrow barely touched the balloon. In our code, we modify the collision logic such that we will not consider a balloon to be popped unless the entire width of the arrow is within the width of the balloon.

Here's the complete **actionPerformed** event method (for the **timerBalloons** timer) implementing these steps. The balloons are handled individually within the structure of a for loop. Make sure this is properly placed in the **timerBalloons** listener:

```java
public void actionPerformed(ActionEvent e)
{
  for (int i = 0; i < 5; i++)
  {
    // erase balloon
    myGraphics.clearRect(balloonX[i], balloonY[i],
balloonSize, balloonSize);
    // move balloon
    balloonY[i] = balloonY[i] + balloonSpeed[i];
    // check if balloon has popped
    if ((balloonY[i] + balloonSize) > 370)
    {
      if (balloonX[i] < arrowX)
      {
        if ((balloonX[i] + balloonSize) > (arrowX +
arrowSize))
        {
          // Balloon has popped
          // Increase score - move back to top
          Toolkit.getDefaultToolkit().beep();
          score = score + 1;
          updateScore(score);
          balloonY[i] = - balloonSize;
          balloonSpeed[i] = myRandom.nextInt(4) + 3;
        }
      }
    }
    // check for moving off bottom
    if ((balloonY[i] + balloonSize) > myFrame.getHeight())
    {
      // Balloon reaches bottom without popping
      // Move back to top with new speed
      balloonY[i] = - balloonSize;
      balloonSpeed[i] = myRandom.nextInt(4) + 3;
    }
    // redraw balloon at new location, redraw arrow too
    myGraphics.setColor(balloonColor[i]);
    myGraphics.fillOval(balloonX[i], balloonY[i],
balloonSize, balloonSize);
```

```
      drawArrow(arrowX);
   }
}
```

Do you see how all the steps are implemented? We added a beep statement for some audio feedback when a balloon pops.

The code is complete. Make sure you have saved the files. The **Balloons** listing from the JCreator code window is:

```
/*
 *  Balloons
 *  Java for Kids
 */
import java.awt.*;
import java.awt.event.*;
import java.util.Random;
import javax.swing.Timer;
public class Balloons extends Frame
{
  static Frame myFrame;
  static Graphics myGraphics;
  static int balloonSize = 50;
  static Color[] balloonColor = new Color[5];
  static int[] balloonX = new int[5];
  static int[] balloonY = new int[5];
  static int[] balloonSpeed = new int[5];
  static int arrowSize = balloonSize / 2;
  static int arrowX;
  static int score;
  static Random myRandom = new Random();
  static Timer timerBalloons;
  static Timer timerGame;

  public static void main(String[] args)
  {
    // create frame
    myFrame = new Frame();
    myFrame.setSize(400, 400);
    myFrame.setTitle("Balloons");
    myFrame.setVisible(true);
    myGraphics = myFrame.getGraphics();
    balloonColor[0] = Color.red;
```

```java
    balloonColor[1] = Color.blue;
    balloonColor[2] = Color.green;
    balloonColor[3] = Color.magenta;
    balloonColor[4] = Color.cyan;
    // put 10 pixels between each balloon
    for (int i = 0; i < 5; i++)
    {
      balloonX[i] = 10 + i * (balloonSize + 10);
    }
    // start message
    myGraphics.setColor(Color.black);
    myGraphics.drawString("CLICK FRAME TO START", 100, 200);

    //Give frame focus
    myFrame.requestFocus();
    // add listener for closing frame
    myFrame.addWindowListener(new WindowAdapter()
    {
      public void windowClosing(WindowEvent e)
      {
        System.exit(0);
      }
    });

    // create balloons timer
    timerBalloons = new Timer(100, new ActionListener ()
    {
      public void actionPerformed(ActionEvent e)
      {
        for (int i = 0; i < 5; i++)
        {
          // erase balloon
          myGraphics.clearRect(balloonX[i], balloonY[i],
balloonSize, balloonSize);
          // move balloon
          balloonY[i] = balloonY[i] + balloonSpeed[i];
          // check if balloon has popped
          if ((balloonY[i] + balloonSize) > 370)
          {
            if (balloonX[i] < arrowX)
            {
              if ((balloonX[i] + balloonSize) > (arrowX +
arrowSize))
              {
                // Balloon has popped
                // Increase score - move back to top
                Toolkit.getDefaultToolkit().beep();
```

```java
                    score = score + 1;
                    updateScore(score);
                    balloonY[i] = - balloonSize;
                    balloonSpeed[i] = myRandom.nextInt(4) + 3;
                  }
                }
              }
              // check for moving off bottom
              if ((balloonY[i] + balloonSize) > myFrame.getHeight())
              {
                // Balloon reaches bottom without popping
                // Move back to top with new speed
                balloonY[i] = - balloonSize;
                balloonSpeed[i] = myRandom.nextInt(4) + 3;
              }
              // redraw balloon at new location, redraw arrow too
              myGraphics.setColor(balloonColor[i]);
              myGraphics.fillOval(balloonX[i], balloonY[i], balloonSize, balloonSize);
              drawArrow(arrowX);
            }
          }
        });

        // create game timer
        timerGame = new Timer(60000, new ActionListener ()
        {
          public void actionPerformed(ActionEvent e)
          {
            // game over
            timerGame.stop();
            timerBalloons.stop();
            myGraphics.clearRect(0, 0, myFrame.getWidth(), myFrame.getHeight());
            myGraphics.drawString("Game is over. Final score is " + String.valueOf(score) + " points.", 50, 200);
            myGraphics.drawString("Click frame to play again.", 50, 250);
          }
        });

        // add listener for mouse press
        myFrame.addMouseListener(new MouseAdapter()
        {
          public void mousePressed(MouseEvent e)
          {
```

Timers, Animation, Keyboard Methods

```
      // initializes and begins game
      myGraphics.clearRect(0, 0, myFrame.getWidth(),
myFrame.getHeight());
      score = 0;
      updateScore(score);
      for (int i = 0; i < 5; i++)
      {
        balloonY[i] = - balloonSize;
        balloonSpeed[i] = myRandom.nextInt(4) + 3;
      }
      // Set arrow near center
      arrowX = 150;
      drawArrow(arrowX);
      timerGame.start();
      timerBalloons.start();
    }
  });

  // add listener for keyPress
  myFrame.addKeyListener(new KeyAdapter()
  {
    public void keyPressed(KeyEvent e)
    {
      // Erase arrow at old location
      myGraphics.clearRect(arrowX, 370, arrowX + arrowSize,
390);
      // Check for F key (left) and J key (right) and
compute arrow position
      if (e.getKeyCode() == e.VK_F)
      {
        arrowX = arrowX - 5;
      }
      else if (e.getKeyCode() == e.VK_J)
      {
        arrowX = arrowX + 5;
      }
      // Position arrow
      drawArrow(arrowX);
    }
  });
}

public static void updateScore(int s)
{
  // draw the score
  myGraphics.setColor(Color.black);
  myGraphics.drawString("Your Score:", 320, 60);
```

```
    myGraphics.clearRect(340, 80, 400, 120);
    myGraphics.drawString(String.valueOf(score), 350, 90);
  }

  public static void drawArrow(int x)
  {
    // draw the arrow
    myGraphics.setColor(Color.black);
    myGraphics.drawLine(x, 390, x + arrowSize / 2, 370);
    myGraphics.drawLine(x + arrowSize / 2, 370, x +
arrowSize, 390);
  }

}
```

I know this is lots of code, but by building in stages, using methods, the work has not been too difficult, I hope.

Timers, Animation, Keyboard Methods

Run the Project

Compile and run the project. Click the frame to get the balloons dropping. Make sure it works. Make sure each balloon falls. Make sure when a balloon reaches the bottom, a new one is initialized. Make sure you can pop each balloon. And, following a pop, make sure a new balloon appears. Make sure the score changes by one with each pop. Here's my finished version:

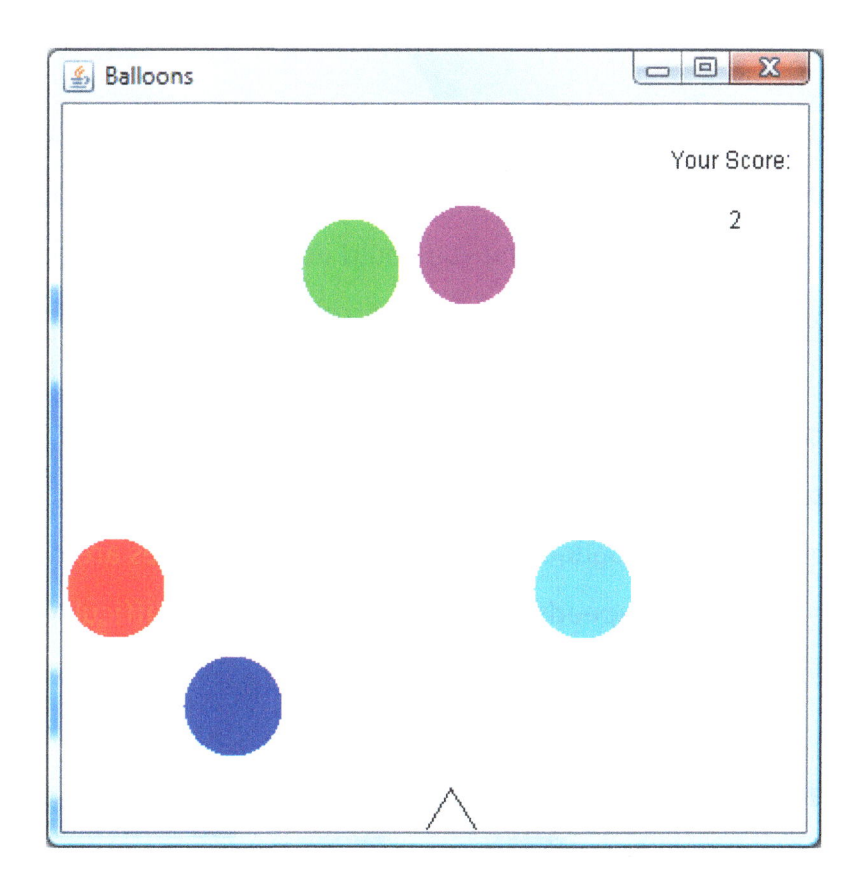

By building and testing the program in stages, you should now have a thoroughly tested, running version of **Balloons**. So relax and have fun playing it. Show your friends and family your great creation. If you do find any bugs and need to make any changes, make sure you resave your project.

Other Things to Try

I'm sure as you played the **Balloons** game, you thought of some changes you could make. Go ahead - give it a try! Here are some ideas we have.

When a balloon pops, it just disappears from the screen. Can you think of a more dramatic way to show popping? Maybe flash the frame background color. Give the balloons a random color each time a new one appears.

Add selectable difficulty levels to the game. This could be used to make the game easy for little kids and very hard for experts. What can you do to adjust the game difficulty? One thing you could do is adjust the size of the popping arrow. To pop a balloon, the entire arrow width must fit within the width of a balloon. Hence, a smaller (narrower) arrow would make it easier to pop balloons before they reach the bottom of the picture box. A larger (wider) arrow makes popping harder. The balloon dropping speed also affects game difficulty. Slowly dropping balloons are easy to pop - fast ones are not. Play with the game to see what speeds would work for different difficulty levels.

Make it possible to play longer games and, as the game goes on, make the game more difficult using some of the ideas above (smaller arrow, faster balloons). You've seen this in other games you may have played - games usually get harder as time goes on.

Timers, Animation, Keyboard Methods

Players like to know how much time they have left in a game. Add this capability to your game. Use **drawString** to print this on the frame. You'll need another timer with a **delay** of 1000 (one second). Whenever this timer's event method is executed, another second has gone by. In this event, subtract 1 from the value displayed. You should be comfortable making such a change to your project.

Another thing players like to know is the highest score on a game. Add this capability. Declare a new variable to keep track of the highest score. After each game is played, compare the current score with the highest score to see if a new high has been reached. Decide how to display the highest score. One problem, though. When you stop the program, the highest score value will be lost. A new high needs to be established each time you run the project. As you become a more advanced Java programmer, you'll learn ways to save the highest score.

Summary

In this final "official" class, we found that the **Timer** object is a key element in computer animation. By periodically changing the display in a frame, the sensation of motion was obtained. We studied "animation math" - how to detect if an object disappeared from a frame, how to detect if an object crosses the border of a frame, and how to detect if two objects (rectangles) collide. We learned how to detect keyboard events. And, you built your first video game.

The **Java for Kids** class is over. The last class will give you some more projects to build. You've come a long way. Remember back in the first class when you first learned about coding? You're a coding expert by now. But, that doesn't mean you know everything there is to know about programming. Computer programming is a never-ending educational process. There are always new things to learn - ways to improve your skills. Believe it or not, you've just begun learning about Java.

Our company, KIDware, offers another Java course that covers some more advanced topics. - **Java GUI Applications**. This course is a self-paced, study guide that provides an overview of Java for building GUI applications. What would you gain from this course? Here are a few new things you would learn:

- More Java and how to build GUI applications
- How to distribute your projects to other users
- How to read and write files to disk (this could be used to save high scores in games)
- How to do more detailed animations
- How to play elaborate sounds (the beep is pretty boring)
- How to use your printer
- How to create your own on-line help system

Contact us if you want more information. Or, visit our website - the address is on the title page for this course. Before you leave, try the bonus projects in Class 10. They give you some idea of what you can learn in the next Java class.

This page intentionally not left blank.

10. More Topics, More Projects

Preview

By now, you should feel pretty comfortable with the steps involved in building a Java project. In this last chapter, we give you more projects you can build and try.

We'll present the steps involved in building each project - **Project Design**, **Project Development**, **Run the Project**, and **Other Things to Try**. But, we won't give you detailed discussion of what's going on in the code (we will point out new ideas). You should be able to figure that out by now (with the help of the code comments). Actually, a very valuable programming skill to have is the ability to read and understand someone else's code.

The five new projects included are: **Computer Stopwatch**, **Dice Rolling**, **State Capitals**, **Tic-Tac-Toe**, and **Memory Game**. The first three projects will be console applications. **Tic-Tac-Toe** and **Memory Game** will use a GUI interface. And, as a bonus, we'll throw in a Java version of the first video game ever - **Pong!**

Project 1 - Computer Stopwatch

Project Design

In this project, we will build a computer stopwatch that measures elapsed time in seconds (to three decimal places). The steps in this program are few:

- When <**Enter**> is pressed, start stopwatch and save starting time.
- When <**Enter**> is pressed again, stop stopwatch, subtract starting time from current time and display elapsed time.

The **Scanner** object will be used for input, with **println** being used for output. The project you are about to build is saved as **StopwatchProject** in the project folder (**\JavaKids\JK Code**).

New Topic - Timing

In this project, we use a built-in Java function for timing. It is a system function and is referenced using:

```
System.currentTimeMillis()
```

This function returns the current time in milliseconds. The returned value is a **long** integer. This is a new variable type we have not seen before. It is just an integer variable that uses twice as much memory as the **int** type.

So, to use this function, first declare a variable to store the returned value:

```
long myTime;
```

Then, the time (in milliseconds) is given by:

```
myTime = System.currentTimeMillis();
```

Now, let's use it in our stopwatch project.

Project Development

Start JCreator, open your workspace and create a new project named **StopwatchProject**. Add a blank Java file named **Stopwatch**.

Open Stopwatch.java and add this basic empty framework creating the **Scanner** object:

```java
/*
 *   Stopwatch Project
 *   Java for Kids
 */
import java.util.Scanner;
public class Stopwatch
{
  public static void main(String[] args)
  {
    Scanner myScanner = new Scanner(Program.in);
  }
}
```

We will have two variables: a **long** type, **startTime**, that saves the starting time and **stopIt**, a **String** type, used to see if we should stop the program. These variables have method level scope, so declare them in the **main** method:

```
long startTime;
String stopIt = "";
```

The rest of the code is simple. Ask the user to press <**Enter**> to start and stop the stopwatch and display the results. Place this code in the main method after the variable declarations:

```
while (!stopIt.equals("0"))
{
  System.out.print("\nPress <Enter> to start stopwatch. ");
  myScanner.nextLine();
  System.out.println("Stopwatch is running ...");
  startTime = System.currentTimeMillis();
  System.out.print("Press <Enter> to stop stopwatch (enter a 0 to stop the program). ");
  stopIt = myScanner.nextLine();
  System.out.println("Elapsed time is " + (System.currentTimeMillis() - startTime) / 1000.0 + " seconds.");
}
```

The only part of this code that might be difficult to understand is displaying the elapsed time. Notice the difference in times is divided by 1000.0. This is needed to convert milliseconds to seconds. Also, notice to stop the program, the user is asked to enter a 0 (zero) when stopping the stopwatch. This loop repeats as long as the **stopIt** string is "not equal" to 0.

The complete **Stopwatch** code from the JCreator file view is:

```java
/*
 *   Stopwatch Project
 *   Java for Kids
 */
import java.util.Scanner;
public class Stopwatch
{
  public static void main(String[] args)
  {
    Scanner myScanner = new Scanner(System.in);
    long startTime;
    String stopIt = "";
    while (!stopIt.equals("0"))
    {
      System.out.print("\nPress <Enter> to start stopwatch. ");
      myScanner.nextLine();
      System.out.println("Stopwatch is running ...");
      startTime = System.currentTimeMillis();
      System.out.print("Press <Enter> to stop stopwatch (enter a 0 to stop the program). ");
      stopIt = myScanner.nextLine();
      System.out.println("Elapsed time is " + (System.currentTimeMillis() - startTime) / 1000.0 + " seconds.");
    }
  }
}
```

Run the Project

Save your work. Compile and run the project. Press <**Enter**> to start the timer. Press <**Enter**> to stop the timer. Make sure you understand how the elapsed time is computed and displayed. Here's a few of my example runs:

```
General Output
 Press <Enter> to start stopwatch.
 Stopwatch is running ...
 Press <Enter> to stop stopwatch (enter a 0 to stop the program).
 Elapsed time is 6.19 seconds.

 Press <Enter> to start stopwatch.
 Stopwatch is running ...
 Press <Enter> to stop stopwatch (enter a 0 to stop the program).
 Elapsed time is 3.992 seconds.

 Press <Enter> to start stopwatch.
 Stopwatch is running ...
 Press <Enter> to stop stopwatch (enter a 0 to stop the program). 0
 Elapsed time is 11.37 seconds.

 Process completed.
```

Stop the program when you get bored (enter a 0, instead of pressing <**Enter**> when asked to stop the stopwatch).

Other Things to Try

Many stopwatches allow you to continue timing after you've stopped one or more times. That is, you can measure total elapsed time in different segments. You'll need a variable to keep track of total elapsed time and a way to tell the stopwatch you are done timing (use some other **stopIt** value). Add a "lap timing" feature by displaying the time measured in each segment (a segment being defined as the time between each start and stop press of <**Enter**>).

Project 2 - Dice Rolling

Project Design

It happens all the time. You get your favorite game out and the dice are missing! This program comes to the rescue - it uses the Java random number generator to roll two dice for you. The program steps:

- When user presses <**Enter**>, generate two random numbers between 1 and 6.
- Display two dice using "character" graphics.
- Repeat as many times as desired.

Again, the **Scanner** object and **println** will be the input and output methods. This project is saved as **DiceRoll** in the project folder (**\JavaKids\JK Projects**).

New Topic - Switch Structure

An alternative to a complex **if** structure when simply checking the value of a single integer variable is the Java **switch** structure. The parts of the switch structure are:

- The **switch** keyword
- A controlling integer (**short, int** or **long**) **variable**
- One or more **case** statements followed by an integer value terminated by a colon (**:**). After the colon is the code to be executed if the variable equals the corresponding value.
- An optional **break** statement to leave the structure after executing the case code.
- An option **default** block to execute if none of the preceding case statements have been executed.

The general form for this statement is:

```
switch (variable)
{
case value1:
     [Java code to execute if variable == value1]
  break;
case value2:
     [Java code to execute if variable == value2]
  break;
 .
 .
default:
     [Java code to execute if no other code has been executed]
  break;
}
```

In this example, if **variable = value1**, the first code block is executed. If **variable = value2**, the second is executed. If no subsequent matches between variable and values are found, the code in the **default** block is executed. This code is equivalent to the following **if** structure:

```
If (variable == value1)
{
      [Java code to execute if variable = value1]
}
else if (variable == value2)
{
      [Java code to execute if variable = value2]
}
.
.
else
{
      [Java code to execute if no other code has been executed]
}
```

A couple of comments about **switch**. The **break** statements, though optional, will almost always be there. If a **break** statement is not seen at the end of a particular case, the following case or cases will execute until a **break** is encountered. This is different behavior than seen in **if** statements, where only one "case" could be executed. Second, all the execution blocks in a **switch** structure are enclosed in curly braces, but the blocks within each case do not have to have braces (they are optional). This is different from most code blocks in Java. Look at the use of the **switch** structure in the dice rolling project to see an example of its use.

Project Development

Start JCreator, open your workspace and create a new project named **DiceProject**. Add a blank Java file named **Dice**.

Open **Dice.java** and add this basic empty framework creating the **Scanner** object (also note the import statement needed for random numbers):

```java
/*
 * Dice Rolling Project
 * Java for Kids
 */
import java.util.Scanner;
import java.util.Random;
public class Dice
{
  public static void main(String[] args)
  {
    Scanner myScanner = new Scanner(System.in);
  }
}
```

Declare three variables in the **main** method, two for the die values and one for the random number generator:

```java
int die1;
int die2;
Random myRandom = new Random();
```

Add the **do/while** loop that controls the rolling of the die:

```
do
{
  System.out.println("\nDice are rolling ...");
  die1 = myRandom.nextInt(6) + 1;
  drawDie(die1);
  die2 = myRandom.nextInt(6) + 1;
  drawDie(die2);
  System.out.println("\nTotal is " + (die1 + die2));
  System.out.print("Press <Enter> to roll again, enter a 0 to stop ");
  stopIt = myScanner.nextLine();
}
while (!stopIt.equals("0"));
```

This code requires a method (**drawDie**) to draw a die after it rolls. Put this method after the closing brace for the main method and before the closing brace for the **Dice** class:

```
public static void drawDie(int n)
{
  // use character graphics to draw dice
  System.out.println("\n-----");
  switch (n)
  {
  case 1:
    // draw a die with one spot
    System.out.println("|   |");
    System.out.println("| * |");
    System.out.println("|   |");
    break;
  case 2:
    // draw a die with two spots
    System.out.println("|*  |");
    System.out.println("|   |");
    System.out.println("|  *|");
    break;
  case 3:
    // draw a die with three spots
    System.out.println("|*  |");
    System.out.println("| * |");
    System.out.println("|  *|");
```

```
      break;
    case 4:
      // draw a die with four spots
      System.out.println("|* *|");
      System.out.println("|   |");
      System.out.println("|* *|");
      break;
    case 5:
      // draw a die with five spots
      System.out.println("|* *|");
      System.out.println("| * |");
      System.out.println("|* *|");
      break;
    case 6:
      // draw a die with six spots
      System.out.println("|* *|");
      System.out.println("|* *|");
      System.out.println("|* *|");
      break;
    }
    System.out.println("-----");
}
```

This method "draws" a die using "character graphics," meaning we use keyboard characters. Prior to GUI applications, programmers used lots of character graphics to display their results. They got very good at producing pretty neat pictures. Note, too, how the **switch** structure makes this code look "clean," compared to using an **if** statement.

The complete **Dice** code from the JCreator file view window is:

```java
/*
 *  Dice Rolling Project
 *  Java for Kids
 */

import java.util.Scanner;
import java.util.Random;

public class Dice
{
  public static void main(String[] args)
    {
      Scanner myScanner = new Scanner(System.in);
      int die1;
      int die2;
      Random myRandom = new Random();
      String stopIt = "";
      do
      {
        System.out.println("\nDice are rolling ...");
        die1 = myRandom.nextInt(6) + 1;
        drawDie(die1);
        die2 = myRandom.nextInt(6) + 1;
        drawDie(die2);
        System.out.println("\nTotal is " + (die1 + die2));
        System.out.print("Press <Enter> to roll again, enter a 0 to stop ");
        stopIt = myScanner.nextLine();
      }
      while (!stopIt.equals("0"));
    }

    public static void drawDie(int n)
    {
      // use character graphics to draw dice
      System.out.println("\n-----");
      switch (n)
      {
        case 1:
          // draw a die with one spot
          System.out.println("|   |");
          System.out.println("| * |");
          System.out.println("|   |");
          break;
```

```java
      case 2:
        // draw a die with two spots
        System.out.println("|*  |");
        System.out.println("|   |");
        System.out.println("|  *|");
        break;
      case 3:
        // draw a die with three spots
        System.out.println("|*  |");
        System.out.println("| * |");
        System.out.println("|  *|");
        break;
      case 4:
        // draw a die with four spots
        System.out.println("|* *|");
        System.out.println("|   |");
        System.out.println("|* *|");
        break;
      case 5:
        // draw a die with five spots
        System.out.println("|* *|");
        System.out.println("| * |");
        System.out.println("|* *|");
        break;
      case 6:
        // draw a die with six spots
        System.out.println("|* *|");
        System.out.println("|* *|");
        System.out.println("|* *|");
        break;
    }
    System.out.println("-----");
  }
}
```

Run the Project

Save your work. Compile and run the project. Press **<Enter>** to see the dice roll. Look at the code to see how the random number (1 through 6) is generated and how the dice are drawn. Here's one of my runs:

```
General Output
 |* *|
 -----

Total is 11
Press <Enter> to roll again, enter a 0 to stop

Dice are rolling ...

 -----
 |*  |
 | * |
 |  *|
 -----


 -----
 |* *|
 |* *|
 |* *|
 -----

Total is 9
Press <Enter> to roll again, enter a 0 to stop 0
```

Enter a 0 whenever you want to stop.

Other Things to Try

The game of Yahtzee requires 5 dice. Modify the project to roll and display five dice. Or, let the user decide how many dice to display. A fun change would be to have the die displays delayed by some amount of time to give the appearance of rolling dice. You would need a timer object for each die. When <**Enter**> was pressed, you start the timers. Then, as each timer's delay elapses, in the corresponding timer method, you would turn off the timer and call the **drawDie** routine to display the result.

Project 3 - State Capitals

Project Design

In this project, we build a fun game for home and school. You will be given the name of a state in the United States and four possible choices for its capital city. You enter the guess of your choice to see if you are right. (We apologize to our foreign readers - perhaps you can modify this project to build a similar multiple choice type game). The program steps are:

- Initialize program with states and capitals names.
- For each question, pick a state at random and pick four possible capital cities.
- Display state and possible choices.
- Have user enter answer and check for correctness.
- Answer as many questions as desired.

Scanner methods and **println** will be used for user interaction. This project is saved as **StateCapitalsProject** in the project folder (**\JavaKids\JK Code**).

Project Development

Start JCreator, open your workspace and create a new project named **StateCapitalsProject**. Add a blank Java file named **StateCapitals**.

Open StateCapitals.java and add this basic empty framework to create the **Scanner** object and **Random** object:

```
/*
 *   State Capitals Project
 *   Java for Kids
 */
import java.util.Scanner;
import java.util.Random;

public class StateCapitals
{
  public static void main(String[] args)
  {
    Scanner myScanner = new Scanner(System.in);
    Random myRandom = new Random();
  }
}
```

Declare these variables in the **main** method:

```
int answer;
int capitalSelected = 0;
String[] state = new String[50];
String[] capital = new String[50];
int[] listedCapital = new int[4];
int[] capitalUsed = new int[50];
```

And, initialize all the states and capitals in their respective arrays (notice we put two statements on one line, an acceptable practice):

```
// initialize arrays
state[0] = "Alabama" ; capital[0] = "Montgomery";
state[1] = "Alaska" ; capital[1] = "Juneau";
state[2] = "Arizona" ; capital[2] = "Phoenix";
state[3] = "Arkansas" ; capital[3] = "Little Rock";
state[4] = "California" ; capital[4] = "Sacramento";
state[5] = "Colorado" ; capital[5] = "Denver";
state[6] = "Connecticut" ; capital[6] = "Hartford";
state[7] = "Delaware" ; capital[7] = "Dover";
state[8] = "Florida" ; capital[8] = "Tallahassee";
state[9] = "Georgia" ; capital[9] = "Atlanta";
state[10] = "Hawaii" ; capital[10] = "Honolulu";
state[11] = "Idaho" ; capital[11] = "Boise";
state[12] = "Illinois" ; capital[12] = "Springfield";
state[13] = "Indiana" ; capital[13] = "Indianapolis";
state[14] = "Iowa" ; capital[14] = "Des Moines";
state[15] = "Kansas" ; capital[15] = "Topeka";
state[16] = "Kentucky" ; capital[16] = "Frankfort";
state[17] = "Louisiana" ; capital[17] = "Baton Rouge";
state[18] = "Maine" ; capital[18] = "Augusta";
state[19] = "Maryland" ; capital[19] = "Annapolis";
state[20] = "Massachusetts" ; capital[20] = "Boston";
state[21] = "Michigan" ; capital[21] = "Lansing";
state[22] = "Minnesota" ; capital[22] = "Saint Paul";
state[23] = "Mississippi" ; capital[23] = "Jackson";
state[24] = "Missouri" ; capital[24] = "Jefferson City";
state[25] = "Montana" ; capital[25] = "Helena";
state[26] = "Nebraska" ; capital[26] = "Lincoln";
state[27] = "Nevada" ; capital[27] = "Carson City";
state[28] = "New Hampshire" ; capital[28] = "Concord";
state[29] = "New Jersey" ; capital[29] = "Trenton";
state[30] = "New Mexico" ; capital[30] = "Santa Fe";
state[31] = "New York" ; capital[31] = "Albany";
state[32] = "North Carolina" ; capital[32] = "Raleigh";
state[33] = "North Dakota" ; capital[33] = "Bismarck";
state[34] = "Ohio" ; capital[34] = "Columbus";
state[35] = "Oklahoma" ; capital[35] = "Oklahoma City";
state[36] = "Oregon" ; capital[36] = "Salem";
state[37] = "Pennsylvania" ; capital[37] = "Harrisburg";
state[38] = "Rhode Island" ; capital[38] = "Providence";
state[39] = "South Carolina" ; capital[39] = "Columbia";
state[40] = "South Dakota" ; capital[40] = "Pierre";
```

```
state[41] = "Tennessee" ; capital[41] = "Nashville";
state[42] = "Texas" ; capital[42] = "Austin";
state[43] = "Utah" ; capital[43] = "Salt Lake City";
state[44] = "Vermont" ; capital[44] = "Montpelier";
state[45] = "Virginia" ; capital[45] = "Richmond";
state[46] = "Washington" ; capital[46] = "Olympia";
state[47] = "West Virginia" ; capital[47] = "Charleston";
state[48] = "Wisconsin" ; capital[48] = "Madison";
state[49] = "Wyoming" ; capital[49] = "Cheyenne";
```

We'd suggest copy and pasting these lines from the notes into your code editor.

Now, the beginning of the game loop that generates each multiple choice question:

```
// begin questioning loop
do
{
  // Generate the next question at random
  answer = myRandom.nextInt(50);
  // Display selected state
  System.out.println("\nState is: " + state[answer] + "\n");
  // capitalUsed array is used to see which state capitals have
  //been selected as possible answers
  for (int i = 0; i < 50; i++)
  {
    capitalUsed[i] = 0;
  }
  // Pick four different state indices (J) at random
  // These are used to set up multiple choice answers
  // Stored in the listedCapital array
  for (int i = 0; i < 4; i++)
  {
    //Find value not used yet and not the answer
    int j;
    do
    {
      j = myRandom.nextInt(50);
    }
    while (capitalUsed[j] != 0 || j == answer);
    capitalUsed[j] = 1;
    listedCapital[i] = j;
```

```
  }
  // Now replace one item (at random) with correct answer
  listedCapital[myRandom.nextInt(4)] = answer;
  // Display multiple choice answers
  for (int i = 0; i < 4; i++)
  {
    System.out.println((i + 1) + " - " +
capital[listedCapital[i]]);
  }
```

See if you can see how the **do/while** loop allows us to pick four distinct capital cities for the multiple choice answers (no repeated values).

Next, the questioning loop is completed with code to check the user answer (only one try is given):

```
  System.out.print("\nWhat is the Capital? (Enter 0 to Stop) ");
  capitalSelected = myScanner.nextInt();
  // check answer
  if (capitalSelected != 0)
  {
    if (listedCapital[capitalSelected - 1] == answer)
    {
      System.out.println("That's it ... good job!");
    }
    else
    {
      System.out.println("Sorry, the answer is " +
capital[answer] +".");
    }
  }
}
while (capitalSelected != 0);
```

The complete code listing for **StateCapitals** (from the JCreator code window):

```
/*
 *   State Capitals Project
 *   Java for Kids
 */
import java.util.Scanner;
import java.util.Random;

public class StateCapitals
{
  public static void main(String[] args)
  {
    Scanner myScanner = new Scanner(System.in);
    Random myRandom = new Random();
    int answer;
    int capitalSelected = 0;
    String[] state = new String[50];
    String[] capital = new String[50];
    int[] listedCapital = new int[4];
    int[] capitalUsed = new int[50];

    // initialize arrays
    state[0] = "Alabama" ; capital[0] = "Montgomery";
    state[1] = "Alaska" ; capital[1] = "Juneau";
    state[2] = "Arizona" ; capital[2] = "Phoenix";
    state[3] = "Arkansas" ; capital[3] = "Little Rock";
    state[4] = "California" ; capital[4] = "Sacramento";
    state[5] = "Colorado" ; capital[5] = "Denver";
    state[6] = "Connecticut" ; capital[6] = "Hartford";
    state[7] = "Delaware" ; capital[7] = "Dover";
    state[8] = "Florida" ; capital[8] = "Tallahassee";
    state[9] = "Georgia" ; capital[9] = "Atlanta";
    state[10] = "Hawaii" ; capital[10] = "Honolulu";
    state[11] = "Idaho" ; capital[11] = "Boise";
    state[12] = "Illinois" ; capital[12] = "Springfield";
    state[13] = "Indiana" ; capital[13] = "Indianapolis";
    state[14] = "Iowa" ; capital[14] = "Des Moines";
    state[15] = "Kansas" ; capital[15] = "Topeka";
    state[16] = "Kentucky" ; capital[16] = "Frankfort";
    state[17] = "Louisiana" ; capital[17] = "Baton Rouge";
    state[18] = "Maine" ; capital[18] = "Augusta";
    state[19] = "Maryland" ; capital[19] = "Annapolis";
    state[20] = "Massachusetts" ; capital[20] = "Boston";
    state[21] = "Michigan" ; capital[21] = "Lansing";
```

```java
    state[22] = "Minnesota" ; capital[22] = "Saint Paul";
    state[23] = "Mississippi" ; capital[23] = "Jackson";
    state[24] = "Missouri" ; capital[24] = "Jefferson City";
    state[25] = "Montana" ; capital[25] = "Helena";
    state[26] = "Nebraska" ; capital[26] = "Lincoln";
    state[27] = "Nevada" ; capital[27] = "Carson City";
    state[28] = "New Hampshire" ; capital[28] = "Concord";
    state[29] = "New Jersey" ; capital[29] = "Trenton";
    state[30] = "New Mexico" ; capital[30] = "Santa Fe";
    state[31] = "New York" ; capital[31] = "Albany";
    state[32] = "North Carolina" ; capital[32] = "Raleigh";
    state[33] = "North Dakota" ; capital[33] = "Bismarck";
    state[34] = "Ohio" ; capital[34] = "Columbus";
    state[35] = "Oklahoma" ; capital[35] = "Oklahoma City";
    state[36] = "Oregon" ; capital[36] = "Salem";
    state[37] = "Pennsylvania" ; capital[37] = "Harrisburg";
    state[38] = "Rhode Island" ; capital[38] = "Providence";
    state[39] = "South Carolina" ; capital[39] = "Columbia";
    state[40] = "South Dakota" ; capital[40] = "Pierre";
    state[41] = "Tennessee" ; capital[41] = "Nashville";
    state[42] = "Texas" ; capital[42] = "Austin";
    state[43] = "Utah" ; capital[43] = "Salt Lake City";
    state[44] = "Vermont" ; capital[44] = "Montpelier";
    state[45] = "Virginia" ; capital[45] = "Richmond";
    state[46] = "Washington" ; capital[46] = "Olympia";
    state[47] = "West Virginia" ; capital[47] = "Charleston";
    state[48] = "Wisconsin" ; capital[48] = "Madison";
    state[49] = "Wyoming" ; capital[49] = "Cheyenne";
    // begin questioning loop
    do
    {
      // Generate the next question at random
      answer = myRandom.nextInt(50);
      // Display selected state
      System.out.println("\nState is: " + state[answer] + "\n");
      // capitalUsed array is used to see which state capitals have
      //been selected as possible answers
      for (int i = 0; i < 50; i++)
      {
        capitalUsed[i] = 0;
      }
      // Pick four different state indices (J) at random
      // These are used to set up multiple choice answers
      // Stored in the listedCapital array
      for (int i = 0; i < 4; i++)
```

```java
      {
        //Find value not used yet and not the answer
        int j;
        do
        {
          j = myRandom.nextInt(50);
        }
        while (capitalUsed[j] != 0 || j == answer);
        capitalUsed[j] = 1;
        listedCapital[i] = j;
      }
      // Now replace one item (at random) with correct answer
      listedCapital[myRandom.nextInt(4)] = answer;
      // Display multiple choice answers
      for (int i = 0; i < 4; i++)
      {
        System.out.println((i + 1) + " - " +
capital[listedCapital[i]]);
      }
      System.out.print("\nWhat is the Capital? (Enter 0 to Stop) ");
      capitalSelected = myScanner.nextInt();
      // check answer
      if (capitalSelected != 0)
      {
        if (listedCapital[capitalSelected - 1] == answer)
        {
          System.out.println("That's it ... good job!");
        }
        else
        {
          System.out.println("Sorry, the answer is " +
capital[answer] +".");
        }
      }
    }
    while (capitalSelected != 0);
  }
}
```

Run the Project

Save your work. Compile and run the project. A state name and four possible capital cities will be displayed. (Study the code used to choose and sort the possible answers – this kind of code is very useful.) Choose an answer. If correct, an encouraging message is printed and another state is displayed. If incorrect, you will be told the correct answer. Keep playing – enter a 0 as your answer to stop the program. One of my runs looks like this:

```
General Output
2 - Lincoln
3 - Madison
4 - Phoenix

What is the Capital? (Enter 0 to Stop) 3
That's it ... good job!

State is: Delaware

1 - Dover
2 - Baton Rouge
3 - Annapolis
4 - Jackson

What is the Capital? (Enter 0 to Stop) 1
That's it ... good job!

State is: Maine

1 - Hartford
2 - Lansing
3 - Augusta
4 - Raleigh

What is the Capital? (Enter 0 to Stop)
```

Other Things to Try

This would be a fun project to modify. How about changing it to display a capital city with four states as the multiple choices? Or, allow the user to type in the answer instead of picking from a list. Typing the answer brings up a host of programming problems – if not capitalized correctly, is the answer wrong? If slightly misspelled, is the answer wrong? Add some kind of scoring system. Allow more than one chance at the answer. Notice when selecting a multiple choice answer, if you pick something other than 0 through 4, an error will occur. Can you think of a way to fix this?

This program could also be used to build general multiple choice tests from any two lists. You could do language translations (given a word in English, choose the corresponding word in Spanish), given a book, choose the author, or given an invention, name the inventor. Use your imagination.

Project 4 - Tic-Tac-Toe

Project Design

In this GUI project, you build a frame where you and someone else can play the classic **Tic-Tac-Toe** game against each other. You take turns marking a 3 x 3 grid with X's and O's. The computer will monitor play. The game steps are:

- Draw grid.
- Alternate turns, placing X's and O's on the grid.
- Mark grid until someone wins or grid is full.

All selections on the grid will be made using the mouse. The project you are about to build is saved as **TicTacToeProject** in the project folder (**\JavaKids\JK Code**).

Project Development

Start JCreator, open your workspace and create a new project named **TicTacToeProject**. Add a blank Java file named **TicTacToe**.

Open **TicTacToe.java** and add this basic GUI framework:

```java
/*
 *  Tic-Tac-Toe Project
 *  Java for Kids
 */

import java.awt.*;
import java.awt.event.*;

public class TicTacToe extends Frame
{
  static Frame myFrame;
  static Graphics myGraphics;  public static void main(String[] args)
  {
    // create frame
    myFrame = new Frame();
    myFrame.setSize(300, 300);
    myFrame.setTitle("Tic-Tac-Toe");
    myFrame.setVisible(true);
    myGraphics = myFrame.getGraphics();
    myGraphics.setColor(Color.black);
    myGraphics.drawString("CLICK FRAME TO START", 50, 100);

    // add listener for closing frame
    myFrame.addWindowListener(new WindowAdapter()
    {
      public void windowClosing(WindowEvent e)
      {
        System.exit(0);
      }
    });

    // add listener for mouse press
    myFrame.addMouseListener(new MouseAdapter()
    {
      public void mousePressed(MouseEvent e)
```

```
        {
            // empty for now
        }
     });
   }
}
```

In this code, we create a frame, add a window closing event method and an empty method for mouse presses. We will use the frame title to keep track of whose turn it is. A start message is displayed. Compile and run to make sure it's working:

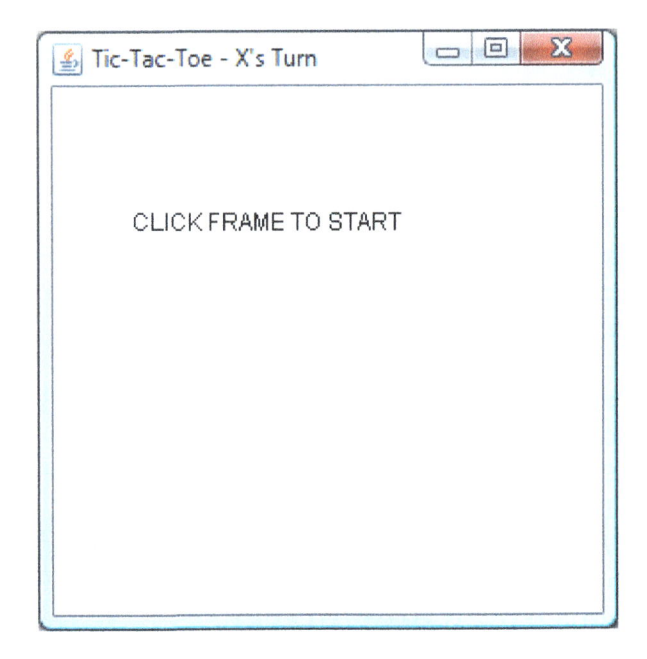

Declare the following variables to have class level scope (put them after the line declaring **myGraphics**):

```
static int[] gridMark = new int[9];
static boolean xTurn = true;
static int numberClicks = 0;
static boolean gridDrawn = false;
```

When the user first clicks the frame, we need to add code to initialize and draw the game grid. This code goes in the **mousePressed** method:

```
public void mousePressed(MouseEvent e)
{
  // if first click, draw grid and exit routine
  if (!gridDrawn)
  {
    gridDrawn = true;
    myGraphics.setColor(Color.white);
    myGraphics.clearRect(0, 0, 300, 300);
    // draw and initialize grid
    for (int i = 0; i < 9; i++)
    {
gridMark[i] = 0;
    }
    myGraphics.setColor(Color.black);
    myGraphics.drawLine(110, 40, 110, 280);
    myGraphics.drawLine(190, 40, 190, 280);
    myGraphics.drawLine(30, 120, 270, 120);
    myGraphics.drawLine(30, 200, 270, 200);
    return;
  }
}
```

Notice this code will only be executed the first time the grid is clicked.

Compile and run the program. Click the frame to make sure the grid draws:

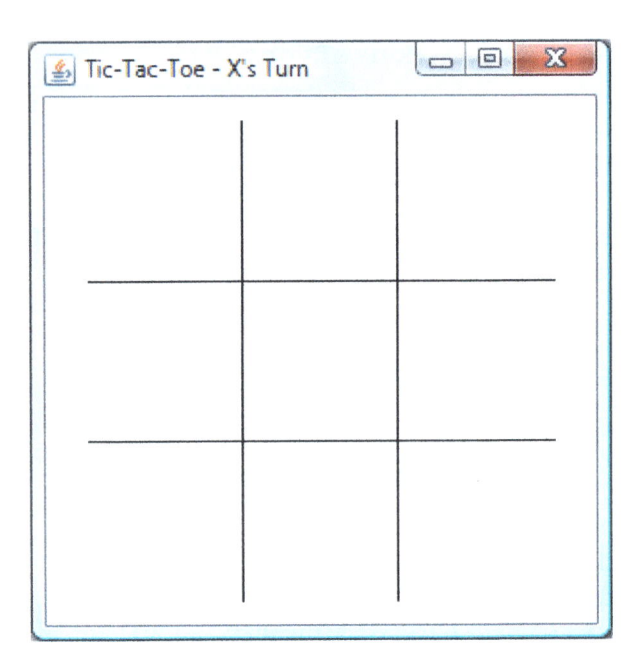

More Topics, More Projects

Once the grid is drawn, we can accept player inputs. For these, when the frame is clicked, if no mark is in the clicked position, one is drawn and it becomes the next player's turn. Add this code in mousePressed after the code just added to draw the grid:

```
int gridSelected;
int x = e.getX();
int y = e.getY();
// if we haven't clicked 9 times, can still click
if (numberClicks < 9  && x > 30 && x < 270 && y > 40 && y <
280)
{
  /* determine which grid location was clicked
   * each square is 80 pixels x 80 pixels
   * offset by 30 on right and 40 on top
   * number system:
   *   0 | 1 | 2
   *  -----------
   *   3 | 4 | 5
   *  -----------
   *   6 | 7 | 8
   */
  if (y > 200)
  {
    // one of three bottom grids
    gridSelected = 6 + (x - 30) / 80;
    y = 210;
  }
  else if (y > 120)
  {
    // one of three middle grids
    gridSelected = 3 + (x - 30) / 80;
    y = 130;
  }
  else
  {
    // one of three top grids
    gridSelected = (x - 30) / 80;
    y = 50;
  }
  // if nothing there, can draw new mark
  if (gridMark[gridSelected] == 0)
  {
```

```
      numberClicks = numberClicks + 1;
      // decide where to draw mark
      x = 40 + (gridSelected % 3) * 80;
      if (xTurn)
      {
        // draw X
        gridMark[gridSelected] = 1;
        myGraphics.setColor(Color.blue);
        myGraphics.drawLine(x, y, x + 60, y + 60);
        myGraphics.drawLine(x, y + 60, x + 60, y);
        xTurn = false;
        myFrame.setTitle("Tic-Tac-Toe - O's Turn");
      }
      else
      {
        // draw O
        gridMark[gridSelected] = 2;
        myGraphics.setColor(Color.red);
        myGraphics.drawOval(x, y, 60, 60);
        xTurn = true;
        myFrame.setTitle("Tic-Tac-Toe - X's Turn");
      }
      if (numberClicks == 9)
      {
        myFrame.setTitle("Tic-Tac-Toe - Game Over");
      }
    }
}
```

Try to understand the logic and mathematics of how I determined which grid area was clicked.

Here is the complete code listing for the **Tic-Tac-Toe** project:

```java
/*
 *  Tic-Tac-Toe Project
 *  Java for Kids
 */

import java.awt.*;
import java.awt.event.*;

public class TicTacToe extends Frame
{
  static Frame myFrame;
  static Graphics myGraphics;
  static int[] gridMark = new int[9];
  static boolean xTurn = true;
  static int numberClicks = 0;
  static boolean gridDrawn = false;

  public static void main(String[] args)
  {

    // create frame
    myFrame = new Frame();
    myFrame.setSize(300, 300);
    myFrame.setTitle("Tic-Tac-Toe - X's Turn");
    myFrame.setVisible(true);
    myGraphics = myFrame.getGraphics();
    myGraphics.setColor(Color.black);
    myGraphics.drawString("CLICK FRAME TO START", 50, 100);

    // add listener for closing frame
    myFrame.addWindowListener(new WindowAdapter()
    {
      public void windowClosing(WindowEvent e)
      {
        System.exit(0);
      }
    });

    // add listener for mouse press
    myFrame.addMouseListener(new MouseAdapter()
    {
      public void mousePressed(MouseEvent e)
      {
        int gridSelected;
```

```java
            int x = e.getX();
            int y = e.getY();
            // if first click, draw grid and exit routine
            if (!gridDrawn)
            {
              gridDrawn = true;
              myGraphics.setColor(Color.white);
              myGraphics.clearRect(0, 0, 300, 300);
              // draw and initialize grid
              for (int i = 0; i < 9; i++)
              {
                gridMark[i] = 0;
              }
              myGraphics.setColor(Color.black);
              myGraphics.drawLine(110, 40, 110, 280);
              myGraphics.drawLine(190, 40, 190, 280);
              myGraphics.drawLine(30, 120, 270, 120);
              myGraphics.drawLine(30, 200, 270, 200);
              return;
            }
             // if we haven't clicked 9 times, can still click
            if (numberClicks < 9  && x > 30 && x < 270 && y > 40 && y < 280)
            {
              /* determine which grid location was clicked
               * each square is 80 pixels x 80 pixels
               * offset by 30 on right and 40 on top
               * number system:
               *  0 | 1 | 2
               * -----------
               *  3 | 4 | 5
               * -----------
               *  6 | 7 | 8
               */

              if (y > 200)
              {
                // one of three bottom grids
                gridSelected = 6 + (x - 30) / 80;
                y = 210;
              }
              else if (y > 120)
              {
                // one of three middle grids
                gridSelected = 3 + (x - 30) / 80;
                y = 130;
              }
```

```
          else
          {
            // one of three top grids
            gridSelected = (x - 30) / 80;
            y = 50;
          }
          // if nothing there, can draw new mark
          if (gridMark[gridSelected] == 0)
          {
            numberClicks = numberClicks + 1;
            // decide where to draw mark
            x = 40 + (gridSelected % 3) * 80;
            if (xTurn)
            {
              // draw X
              gridMark[gridSelected] = 1;
              myGraphics.setColor(Color.blue);
              myGraphics.drawLine(x, y, x + 60, y + 60);
              myGraphics.drawLine(x, y + 60, x + 60, y);
              xTurn = false;
              myFrame.setTitle("Tic-Tac-Toe - O's Turn");
            }
            else
            {
              // draw O
              gridMark[gridSelected] = 2;
              myGraphics.setColor(Color.red);
              myGraphics.drawOval(x, y, 60, 60);
              xTurn = true;
              myFrame.setTitle("Tic-Tac-Toe - X's Turn");
            }
            if (numberClicks == 9)
            {
              myFrame.setTitle("Tic-Tac-Toe - Game Over");
            }

          }
        }

      }
    });
  }
}
```

Run the Project

Save your work. Compile and run the project. You should see this:

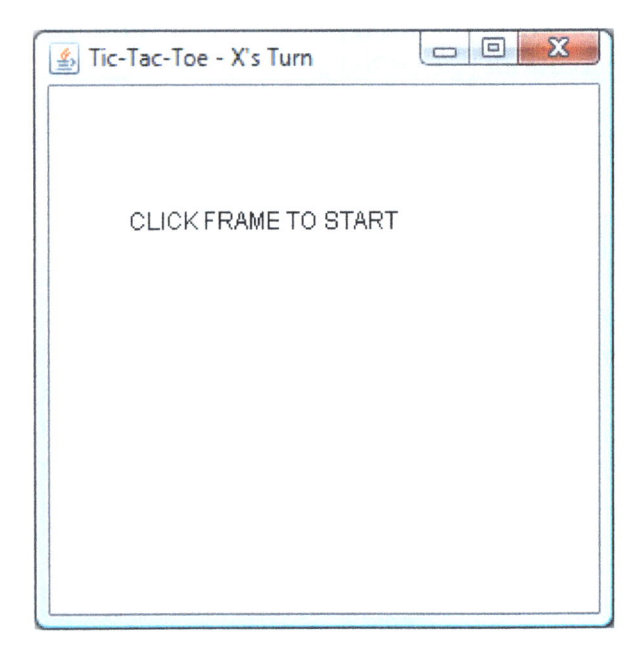

[Screenshot: Tic-Tac-Toe - X's Turn window displaying "CLICK FRAME TO START"]

Playing the game is obvious. X goes first and clicks the desired square. Then, it's O's turn. Notice the frame title bar tells you whose turn it is. Alternate turns until there is a winner or the grid is full without a winner (a tie). You must restart the program to play another game.

Here's a game I played where X is just about to win:

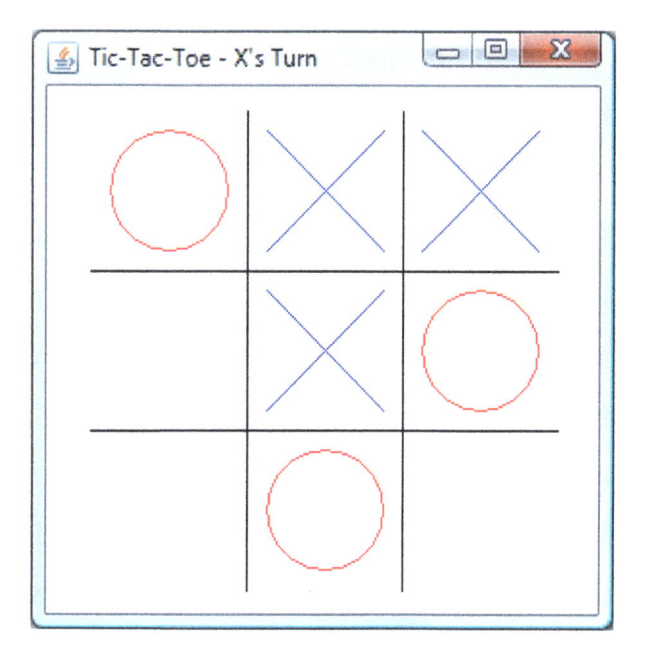

Other Things to Try

Three adaptations to this project jump out. First, can you think of a way to replay a game without rerunning the program? You would need to put all the initialization code and game play code in some kind of loop (similar to what we did for some projects in this course). Second, there is no logic to detect a win. The players must look at the grid and decide if someone has won. See if you can add logic to check if there is a winner after each move. The code would be added at the end of the existing mousePressed method. This code would see if the symbols in the three horizontal directions, three vertical directions or two diagonal directions are the same. If so, a win is declared and the game is stopped. Of use in such code would be elements of the **gridMark** array - that array has values of 0 for an empty space, 1 for an X and 2 for an O.

The last modification (a much tougher one) would be to program the computer to play the game against a human player. You could let the computer have either X's or O's and use some kind of logic (maybe even just random moves for a simple minded computer) for the computer to use in generating moves. You would probably want another a **method** to determine the computer moves. This is one of the first games ever programmed by little Billy Gates!

Project 5 - Memory Game

Project Design

In this Java GUI game for little kids, ten squares are used to hide five different pairs of shapes. The player chooses two squares on the board and the shapes behind them are revealed. If the shapes match, those squares are removed from the board. If there is no match, the shapes are recovered and the player tries again. The play continues until all five pairs are matched up. The program steps:

- Randomly sort five pairs of shapes.
- Draw game board.
- Player selects one square (using mouse) - shape is displayed.
- Player selects another square - shape is displayed.
- If match, squares are removed.
- If no match, squares are restored.
- Play ends when all matches have been found.

Selections will be made using the mouse. The game is saved as **MemoryProject** in the project folder (**\JavaKids\JK Code**).

Project Development

Start JCreator, open your workspace and create a new project named **MemoryProject**. Add a blank Java file named **Memory**.

Open **Memory.java** and add this basic GUI framework:

```java
/*
 *  Memory Project
 *  Java for Kids
 */

import java.awt.*;
import java.awt.event.*;
import java.util.Random;
import javax.swing.Timer;

public class Memory extends Frame
{
  static Frame myFrame;
  static Graphics myGraphics;
  static Timer myTimer;
  static Random myRandom = new Random();

  public static void main(String[] args)
  {
    // create frame
    myFrame = new Frame();
    myFrame.setSize(410, 220);
    myFrame.setTitle("Memory");
    myFrame.setVisible(true);
    myGraphics = myFrame.getGraphics();
    myGraphics.setColor(Color.black);
    myGraphics.drawString("CLICK FRAME TO START", 50, 100);

    // add listener for closing frame
    myFrame.addWindowListener(new WindowAdapter()
    {
      public void windowClosing(WindowEvent e)
      {
        System.exit(0);
      }
    });
```

```java
    // add listener for mouse press
    myFrame.addMouseListener(new MouseAdapter()
    {
      public void mousePressed(MouseEvent e)
      {
        // empty for now
      }
    });

    // add listener for timer method
    myTimer = new Timer(1000, new ActionListener()
    {
      public void actionPerformed(ActionEvent e)
      {
        // empty for now
      }
    });
  }
}
```

This code sets up the frame, graphics object, start message and listeners for window closing, mouse presses and timer events (used to implement a delay after displaying shapes) and adds a random number generator.

Compile and run to make sure the code is correct. You should see the start message:

Add these class level variables to the code (these keep track of what shape is behind what box, whether a box has been selected and colors):

```
static int choice;
static int remaining;
static int[] picked = new int[2];
static int[] behind = new int[10];
static boolean[] available = new boolean[10];
static Color boxColor;
static Color[] myColor = new Color[5];
static boolean boxesDrawn = false;
```

Place the following code in the **main** method after the line making the frame visible. This code decides what shape (values from 0 to 4) is behind each box:

```
// randomly sort integers from 0 to 9
behind = nIntegers(10);
// initialize available array to true
// any numbers greater than 4, reduce by 5 for matched set
for (int i = 0; i < 10; i++)
{
  available[i] = true;
  if (behind[i] > 4)
  {
    behind[i] = behind[i] - 5;
  }
}
// pick five random colors for the shapes
for (int i = 0; i < 5; i++)
{
  myColor[i] = new Color(myRandom.nextInt(255),
myRandom.nextInt(255), myRandom.nextInt(255));
}
```

Notice the hidden shapes are specified by an array of random integers. This computation uses the **nIntegers** method developed back in Class 5. Put this method after the closing brace for the main method, but before the closing brace for the **Memory** class:

```java
/*
 *   Shuffle Method
 *   Java for Kids
 */
public static int[] nIntegers(int n)
{
  /*
   *  Returns n randomly sorted integers 0 -> n - 1
   */
  int nArray[] = new int[n];
  int temp, s;
  Random myRandom = new Random();
  //   initialize array from 0 to n - 1
  for (int i = 0; i < n; i++)
  {
    nArray[i] = i;
  }
  //  perform one-card shuffle
  //   i is number of items remaining in list
  //   s is the random selection from that list
  //   we swap last item i - 1 with selection s
  for (int i = n; i >= 1; i--)
  {
    s = myRandom.nextInt(i);
    temp = nArray[s];
    nArray[s] = nArray[i - 1];
    nArray[i - 1] = temp;
  }
  return(nArray);
}
```

Make sure the code compiles successfully.

The **mousePressed** event method is used to initialize the boxes (when **boxesDrawn** is false) else it is used select boxes (each box is 70 pixels by 70 pixels in size) for display of shapes. The code for that method is:

```
public void mousePressed(MouseEvent e)
{
  // draw boxes on first click
  if (!boxesDrawn)
  {
    boxesDrawn = true;
    myGraphics.setColor(Color.white);
    myGraphics.clearRect(0, 0, 410, 220);
    // draw boxes
    int x = 10;
    int y = 50;
    boxColor =new Color(myRandom.nextInt(255),
myRandom.nextInt(255), myRandom.nextInt(255));
    myGraphics.setColor(boxColor);
    for (int i = 0; i < 10; i++)
    {
myGraphics.fillRect(x, y, 70, 70);
x = x + 80;
if (x > 330)
{
  x = 10;
  y = y + 80;
}
    }
    // set to first choice - we're ready to go
    choice = 0;
    remaining = 10;
    return;
  }
  boolean oneSelected = false;
  int temp = 0;
  // make sure clicked in box area
  if (e.getX() > 10 && e.getX() < 400 && e.getY() > 50 &&
e.getY() < 200)
  {
    oneSelected = true;
    // figure out which box was clicked
    if (e.getY() > 130)
    {
// second row (5 to 9)
```

```
temp = 5 + (e.getX() - 5) / 80;
      }
      else
      {
// first row (0 to 4)
temp = (e.getX() - 5) / 80;
      }
    }
    if (oneSelected)
    {
      picked[choice] = temp;
    }
    // only execute following code:
    // if box is selected and still available
    // and not picking same box with second choice
    if ((oneSelected && available[temp]) && (choice == 0 ||
(choice == 1 && picked[0] != picked[1])))
    {
      // draw selected shape
      drawShape(behind[picked[choice]], picked[choice]);
      if (choice == 0)
      {
// first choice - just display
choice = 1;
      }
      else
{
// Delay for one second before checking
myTimer.start();
      }
    }
  }
}
```

This code refers to a **drawShape** method. This method is used to draw a particular shape at a particular location. The code is (place this after the **nIntegers** method):

```
public static void drawShape(int s, int n)
{
  // draw selected shape s at location n
  int x;
  int y;
  // get coordinates of n
  if (n > 4)
  {
    y = 130;
    x = 10 + (n - 5) * 80;
  }
  else
  {
    y = 50;
    x = 10 + n * 80;
  }
  // clear region
  Graphics myGraphics = myFrame.getGraphics();
  myGraphics.clearRect(x, y, 70, 70);
  switch (s)
  {
    case 0:
      // circle
      myGraphics.setColor(myColor[0]);
      myGraphics.fillOval(x, y, 70, 70);
      break;
    case 1:
      // plus sign
      myGraphics.setColor(myColor[1]);
      myGraphics.fillRect(x, y + 25, 70, 20);
      myGraphics.fillRect(x + 25, y, 20, 70);
      break;
    case 2:
      // rectangle
      myGraphics.setColor(myColor[2]);
      myGraphics.fillRect(x + 20, y, 30, 70);
      break;
    case 3:
      // open square
      myGraphics.setColor(myColor[3]);
```

```
          myGraphics.fillRect(x, y, 70, 70);
          myGraphics.clearRect(x + 20, y + 20, 30, 30);
          break;
        case 4:
          // oval
          myGraphics.setColor(myColor[4]);
          myGraphics.fillOval(x + 20, y, 30, 70);
          break;
        case -1:
          // restore box
          myGraphics.setColor(boxColor);
          myGraphics.fillRect(x, y, 70, 70);
          break;
        case -2:
          // erase shape
          myGraphics.clearRect(x, y, 70, 70);
          break;
      }
  }
```

Compile and run. Click the frame to draw the boxes, then make sure when you click a box, a shape appears:

Finally, the timer's method is where we check for a match between selected shapes. The timer is used in the project to insert a one second delay between the time the last shape selected is displayed and a decision is made about a match. Use this code in the timer **actionPerformed** method:

```
public void actionPerformed(ActionEvent e)
{
  myTimer.stop();
  // After delay, check for match
  if (behind[picked[0]] == behind[picked[1]])
  {
    // If match, remove shapes
    remaining = remaining - 2;
    available[picked[0]] = false;
    available[picked[1]] = false;
    drawShape(-2, picked[0]);
    drawShape(-2, picked[1]);
    if (remaining == 0)
    {
      myFrame.setTitle("Memory Game Over");
    }
  }
  else
  {
    // If no match, restore boxes
    drawShape(-1, picked[0]);
    drawShape(-1, picked[1]);
  }
  choice = 0;
}
```

The complete code for the **Memory** project is:

```
/*
 *  Memory Project
 *  Java for Kids
 */

import java.awt.*;
import java.awt.event.*;
import java.util.Random;
import javax.swing.Timer;

public class Memory extends Frame
{
  static Frame myFrame;
  static Graphics myGraphics;
  static Timer myTimer;
  static Random myRandom = new Random();
  static int choice;
  static int remaining;
  static int[] picked = new int[2];
  static int[] behind = new int[10];
  static boolean[] available = new boolean[10];
  static Color boxColor;
  static Color[] myColor = new Color[5];
  static boolean boxesDrawn = false;


  public static void main(String[] args)
  {
    // create frame
    myFrame = new Frame();
    myFrame.setSize(410, 220);
    myFrame.setTitle("Memory");
    myFrame.setVisible(true);
    myGraphics = myFrame.getGraphics();
    myGraphics.setColor(Color.black);
    myGraphics.drawString("CLICK FRAME TO START", 50, 100);

    // randomly sort integers from 0 to 9
    behind = nIntegers(10);
    // initialize available array to true
    // any numbers greater than 4, reduce by 5 for matched set
    for (int i = 0; i < 10; i++)
    {
```

```java
      available[i] = true;
      if (behind[i] > 4)
      {
        behind[i] = behind[i] - 5;
      }
    }
    // pick five random colors for the shapes
    for (int i = 0; i < 5; i++)
    {
      myColor[i] = new Color(myRandom.nextInt(255),
myRandom.nextInt(255), myRandom.nextInt(255));
    }

    // add listener for closing frame
    myFrame.addWindowListener(new WindowAdapter()
    {
      public void windowClosing(WindowEvent e)
      {
        System.exit(0);
      }
    });

    // add listener for mouse press
    myFrame.addMouseListener(new MouseAdapter()
    {
      public void mousePressed(MouseEvent e)
      {
        // draw boxes on first click
        if (!boxesDrawn)
        {
          boxesDrawn = true;
          myGraphics.setColor(Color.white);
          myGraphics.clearRect(0, 0, 410, 220);
          // draw boxes
          int x = 10;
          int y = 50;
          boxColor =new Color(myRandom.nextInt(255),
myRandom.nextInt(255), myRandom.nextInt(255));
          myGraphics.setColor(boxColor);
          for (int i = 0; i < 10; i++)
          {
            myGraphics.fillRect(x, y, 70, 70);
            x = x + 80;
            if (x > 330)
            {
              x = 10;
              y = y + 80;
```

```java
          }
        }
        // set to first choice - we're ready to go
        choice = 0;
        remaining = 10;
        return;
      }
      boolean oneSelected = false;
      int temp = 0;
      // make sure clicked in box area
      if (e.getX() > 10 && e.getX() < 400 && e.getY() > 50
&& e.getY() < 200)
      {
        oneSelected = true;
        // figure out which box was clicked
        if (e.getY() > 130)
        {
          // second row (5 to 9)
          temp = 5 + (e.getX() - 5) / 80;
        }
        else
        {
          // first row (0 to 4)
          temp = (e.getX() - 5) / 80;
        }
      }
      if (oneSelected)
      {
        picked[choice] = temp;
      }
      // only execute following code:
      // if box is selected and still available
      // and not picking same box with second choice
      if ((oneSelected && available[temp]) && (choice == 0
|| (choice == 1 && picked[0] != picked[1])))
      {
        // draw selected shape
        drawShape(behind[picked[choice]], picked[choice]);
        if (choice == 0)
        {
          // first choice - just display
          choice = 1;
        }
        else
          {
          // Delay for one second before checking
          myTimer.start();
```

```
          }
        }
      }
    });

    // add listener for timer method
    myTimer = new Timer(1000, new ActionListener()
    {
      public void actionPerformed(ActionEvent e)
      {
        myTimer.stop();
        // After delay, check for match
        if (behind[picked[0]] == behind[picked[1]])
        {
          // If match, remove shapes
          remaining = remaining - 2;
          available[picked[0]] = false;
          available[picked[1]] = false;
          drawShape(-2, picked[0]);
          drawShape(-2, picked[1]);
          if (remaining == 0)
          {
            myFrame.setTitle("Memory Game Over");
          }
        }
        else
        {
          // If no match, restore boxes
          drawShape(-1, picked[0]);
          drawShape(-1, picked[1]);
        }
        choice = 0;
      }
    });
}

/*
 *   Shuffle Method
 *   Java for Kids
 */
public static int[] nIntegers(int n)
  {
  /*
   *   Returns n randomly sorted integers 0 -> n - 1
   */
  int nArray[] = new int[n];
  int temp, s;
```

```java
    Random myRandom = new Random();
    //  initialize array from 0 to n - 1
    for (int i = 0; i < n; i++)
    {
      nArray[i] = i;
    }
    //  perform one-card shuffle
    //  i is number of items remaining in list
    //  s is the random selection from that list
    //  we swap last item i - 1 with selection s
    for (int i = n; i >= 1; i--)
    {
      s = myRandom.nextInt(i);
      temp = nArray[s];
      nArray[s] = nArray[i - 1];
      nArray[i - 1] = temp;
    }
    return(nArray);
  }

  public static void drawShape(int s, int n)
  {
    // draw selected shape s at location n
    int x;
    int y;
    // get coordinates of n
    if (n > 4)
    {
      y = 130;
      x = 10 + (n - 5) * 80;
    }
    else
    {
      y = 50;
      x = 10 + n * 80;
    }
    // clear region
    myGraphics.clearRect(x, y, 70, 70);
    switch (s)
    {
      case 0:
        // circle
        myGraphics.setColor(myColor[0]);
        myGraphics.fillOval(x, y, 70, 70);
        break;
      case 1:
        // plus sign
```

```
        myGraphics.setColor(myColor[1]);
        myGraphics.fillRect(x, y + 25, 70, 20);
        myGraphics.fillRect(x + 25, y, 20, 70);
        break;
      case 2:
        // rectangle
        myGraphics.setColor(myColor[2]);
        myGraphics.fillRect(x + 20, y, 30, 70);
        break;
      case 3:
        // open square
        myGraphics.setColor(myColor[3]);
        myGraphics.fillRect(x, y, 70, 70);
        myGraphics.clearRect(x + 20, y + 20, 30, 30);
        break;
      case 4:
        // oval
        myGraphics.setColor(myColor[4]);
        myGraphics.fillOval(x + 20, y, 30, 70);
        break;
      case -1:
        // restore box
        myGraphics.setColor(boxColor);
        myGraphics.fillRect(x, y, 70, 70);
        break;
      case -2:
        // erase shape
        myGraphics.clearRect(x, y, 70, 70);
        break;
    }
  }
}
```

Run the Project

Save your work. Compile and run the project. Click the frame. Ten boxes appear. Click on one and view the shape. Click on another. If there is a match, the two shapes are removed (after a delay). If there is no match, the boxes are restored (also after a delay). The game stops when all matching shape pairs have been found. Here's what the frame looks like in the middle of a game:

Other Things to Try

Some things to help improve or change this game: add a scoring system to keep track of how many tries you took to find all the matches, make it a two player game where you compete against another player or the computer, or set it up to match other items (colors, upper and lower case letters, numbers and objects, etc.). You might also add logic to let you play again (without rerunning the program), once a game is finished. And, the colors selected are random – what happens if white is selected? See if you can figure out a way to avoid choosing colors that don't look good on a white background.

Bonus Project - Pong!

In the early 1970's, while Bill Gates and Paul Allen were still in high school, a man named Nolan Bushnell began the video game revolution. He invented a very simple game - a computer version of Ping Pong. There were two paddles, one on each side of the screen. Players then bounced the ball back and forth. If you missed the ball, the other player got a point.

This first game was called **Pong**. And, Nolan Bushnell was the founder of Atari - the biggest video game maker for many years. (Nolan Bushnell also founded Chucky Cheese's Pizza Parlors, but that's another story!) In this bonus project, I give you my version of **Pong** written with Java. This is a project built in KIDware's **Learn Java** course. I don't expect you to build this project, but you can if you want. Just load the project (named **Pong**) and run it. Skim through the code - you should be able to understand a lot of it. The idea of giving you this project is to let you see what can be done with Java.

In this version of **Pong**, a ball moves from one end of a panel to the other, bouncing off side walls. Players try to deflect the ball at each end using a controllable paddle. In my simple game, the left paddle is controlled with the A and Z keys on the keyboard, while the right paddle is controlled with the K and M keys (detected using **KeyPress** events). My solution freely borrows code and techniques from several reference sources. The project relies heavily on lots of coding techniques you haven't seen yet.

More Topics, More Projects   10-61

Start JCreator. Open the **JK Code** workspace (in **\JavaKids\JK Code** folder). Make **PongProject** your active project. Compile and run. Here's the game:

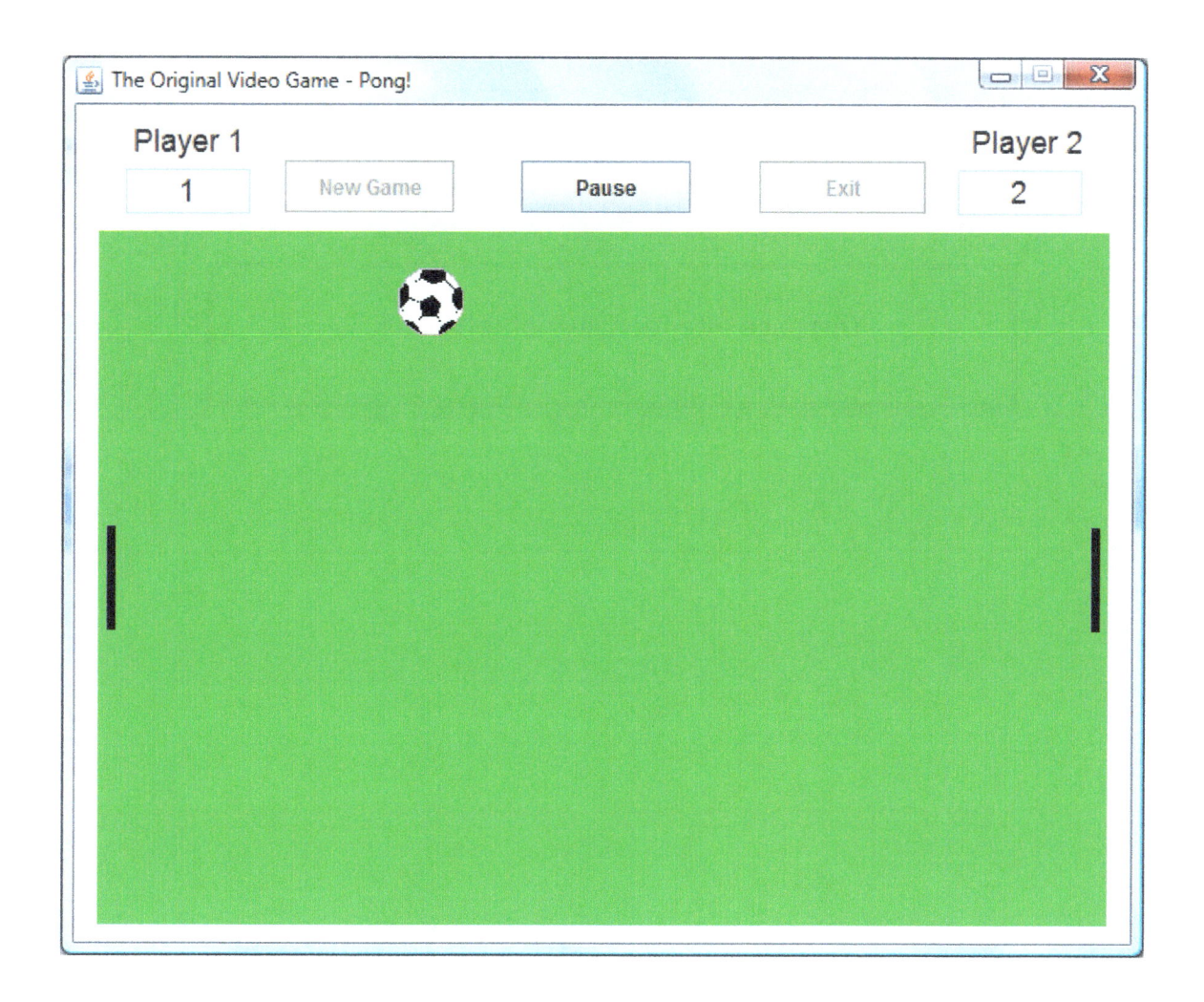

The graphics (paddles and ball) are loaded from files stored with the application. Notice the cool sounds (if you have a sound card in your computer). This is something that should be a part of any Java project - an advanced topic. Have fun with **Pong**! Can you believe people used to spend hours mesmerized by this game? It seems very tame compared to today's video games, but it holds a warm spot in many people's gaming hearts.

This page intentionally not left blank.

We publish several Self-Study or Instructor-Led Computer Programming Tutorials for Microsoft® Small Basic:

Small Basic For Kids is an illustrated introduction to computer programming that provides an interactive, self-paced tutorial to the new Small Basic programming environment. The book consists of 30 short lessons that explain how to create and run a Small Basic program. Elementary students learn about program design and many elements of the Small Basic language. Numerous examples are used to demonstrate every step in the building process. The tutorial also includes two complete games (Hangman and Pizza Zapper) for students to build and try. Designed for kids ages 8 and up.

The Beginning Microsoft Small Basic Programming Tutorial is a self-study first semester "beginner" programming tutorial consisting of 11 chapters explaining (in simple, easy-to-follow terms) how to write Microsoft Small Basic programs. Numerous examples are used to demonstrate every step in the building process. The last chapter of this tutorial shows you how four different Small Basic games could port to Visual Basic, Visual C# and Java. This beginning level self-paced tutorial can be used at home or at school. The tutorial is simple enough for kids ages 10 and above yet engaging enough for beginning adults.

Programming Games with Microsoft Small Basic is a self-paced second semester "intermediate" level programming tutorial consisting of 10 chapters explaining (in simple, easy-to-follow terms) how to write video games in Microsoft Small Basic. The games built are non-violent, family-friendly, and teach logical thinking skills. Students will learn how to program the following Small Basic video games: Safecracker, Tic Tac Toe, Match Game, Pizza Delivery, Moon Landing, and Leap Frog. This intermediate level self-paced tutorial can be used at home or school. The tutorial is simple enough for kids yet engaging enough for beginning adults.

Programming Home Projects with Microsoft Small Basic is a self-paced programming tutorial explains (in simple, easy-to-follow terms) how to build Small Basic Windows applications. Students learn about program design, Small Basic objects, many elements of the Small Basic language, and how to debug and distribute finished programs. Sequential file input and output is also introduced.. The projects built include a Dual-Mode Stopwatch, Flash Card Math Quiz, Multiple Choice Exam, Blackjack Card Game, Weight Monitor, Home Inventory Manager and a Snowball Toss Game.

The Developer's Reference Guide to Microsoft Small Basic
While developing all the different Microsoft Small Basic tutorials we found it necessary to write The Developer's Reference Guide to Microsoft Small Basic . The Developer's Reference Guide to Microsoft Small Basic is over 500 pages long and includes over 100 Small Basic programming examples for you to learn from and include in your own Microsoft Small Basic programs. It is a detailed reference guide for new developers.

David Ahl's Small Basic Computer Adventures is a Microsoft Small Basic re-make of the classic *Basic Computer Games* programming *book* originally written by David H. Ahl. This new book includes the following classic adventure simulations; Marco Polo, Westward Ho!, The Longest Automobile Race, The Orient Express, Amelia Earhart: Around the World Flight, Tour de France, Subway Scavenger, Hong Kong Hustle, and Voyage to Neptune. Learn how to program these classic computer simulations in Microsoft Small Basic. This "intermediate" level self-paced tutorial can be used at home or school.

Basic Computer Games - Small Basic Edition is a re-make of the classic BASIC COMPUTER GAMES book originally edited by David H. Ahl. It contains 100 of the original text based BASIC games that inspired a whole generation of programmers. Now these classic BASIC games have been re-written in Microsoft Small Basic for a new generation to enjoy! The new Small Basic games look and act like the original text based games. The book includes all the original spaghetti code GOTO commands and it will make you appreciate the structured programming techniques found in our other tutorials.

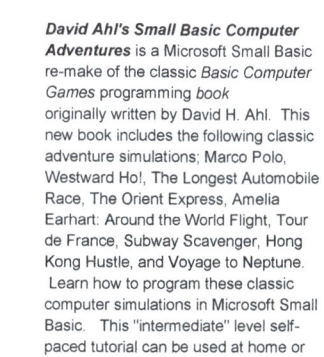

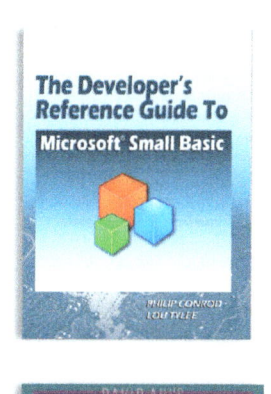

We also publish several Self-Study or Instructor-Led Computer Programming Tutorials for Microsoft® Visual Basic® Express and Visual C#® Express:

Visual Basic® Express For Kids is a beginning programming tutorial consisting of 10 chapters explaining (in simple, easy-to-follow terms) how to build a Visual Basic Express Windows application. Students learn about project design, the Visual Basic Express toolbox, and many elements of the BASIC language. The tutorial also includes several detailed computer projects for students to build and try. These projects include a number guessing game, a card game, an allowance calculator, a drawing program, a state capitals game, Tic-Tac-Toe and even a simple video game. Designed for kids ages 12 and up.

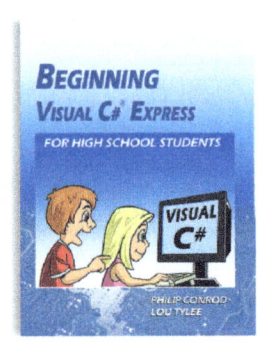

Beginning Visual Basic® Express is a semester long self-paced "beginner" programming tutorial consisting of 10 chapters explaining (in simple, easy-to-follow terms) how to build a Visual Basic Express Windows application. The tutorial includes several detailed computer projects for students to build and try. These projects include a number guessing game, card game, allowance calculator, drawing program, state capitals game, and a couple of video games like Pong. We also include several college prep bonus projects including a loan calculator, portfolio manager, and checkbook balancer. Designed for students age 15 and up.

Programming Games with Visual Basic® Express is a semester long "intermediate" programming tutorial consisting of 10 chapters explaining (in simple, easy-to-follow terms) how to build Visual Basic Video Games. The games built are non-violent, family-friendly, and teach logical thinking skills. Students will learn how to program the following Visual Basic video games: Safecracker, Tic Tac Toe, Match Game, Pizza Delivery, Moon Landing, and Leap Frog. This intermediate level self-paced tutorial can be used at home or school. The tutorial is simple enough for kids yet engaging enough for beginning adults.

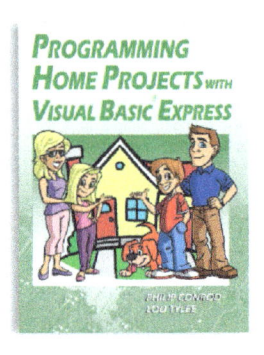

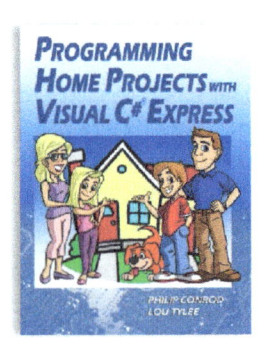

Programming Home Projects with Visual Basic® Express is a semester long self-paced programming tutorial explains (in simple, easy-to-follow terms) how to build a Visual Basic Express Windows project. Students learn about project design, the Visual Basic Express toolbox, many elements of the Visual Basic language, and how to debug and distribute finished projects. The projects built include a Dual-Mode Stopwatch, Flash Card Math Quiz, Multiple Choice Exam, Blackjack Card Game, Weight Monitor, Home Inventory Manager and a Snowball Toss Game.

Visual C#® Express For Kids is a beginning programming tutorial consisting of 10 chapters explaining (in simple, easy-to-follow terms) how to build a Visual C# Express Windows application. Students learn about project design, the Visual C# Express toolbox, and many elements of the C# language. Numerous examples are used to demonstrate every step in the building process. The projects include a number guessing game, a card game, an allowance calculator, a drawing program, a state capitals game, Tic-Tac-Toe and even a simple video game. Designed for kids ages 12 and up.

Beginning Visual C#® Express is a semester long "beginning" programming tutorial consisting of 10 chapters explaining (in simple, easy-to-follow terms) how to build a C# Express Windows application. The tutorial includes several detailed computer projects for students to build and try. These projects include a number guessing game, card game, allowance calculator, drawing program, state capitals game, and a couple of video games like Pong. We also include several college prep bonus projects including a loan calculator, portfolio manager, and checkbook balancer. Designed for students age 15 and up.

Programming Games with Visual C#® Express is a semester long "intermediate" programming tutorial consisting of 10 chapters explaining (in simple, easy-to-follow terms) how to build a Visual C# Video Games. The games built are non-violent, family-friendly and teach logical thinking skills. Students will learn how to program the following Visual C# video games: Safecracker, Tic Tac Toe, Match Game, Pizza Delivery, Moon Landing, and Leap Frog. This intermediate level self-paced tutorial can be used at home or school. The tutorial is simple enough for kids yet engaging enough for beginning adults.

Programming Home Projects with Visual C#® Express is a semester long self-paced programming tutorial explains (in simple, easy-to-follow terms) how to build a Visual C# Express Windows project. Students learn about project design, the Visual C# Express toolbox, many elements of the Visual C# language, and how to debug and distribute finished projects. The projects built include a Dual-Mode Stopwatch, Flash Card Math Quiz, Multiple Choice Exam, Blackjack Card Game, Weight Monitor, Home Inventory Manager and a Snowball Toss Game.

We also publish several Self-Study or Instructor-Led Computer Programming Tutorials for Oracle® Java® :

Java™ For Kids is a beginning programming tutorial consisting of 10 chapters explaining (in simple, easy-to-follow terms) how to build a Java application. Students learn about project design, object-oriented programming, console applications, graphics applications and many elements of the Java language. Numerous examples are used to demonstrate every step in the building process. The projects include a number guessing game, a card game, an allowance calculator, a state capitals game, Tic-Tac-Toe, a simple drawing program, and even a basic video game. Designed for kids ages 12 and up.

Beginning Java™ is a semester long "beginning" programming tutorial consisting of 10 chapters explaining (in simple, easy-to-follow terms) how to build a Java application. The tutorial includes several detailed computer projects for students to build and try. These projects include a number guessing game, card game, allowance calculator, drawing program, state capitals game, and a couple of video games like Pong. We also include several college prep bonus projects including a loan calculator, portfolio manager, and checkbook balancer. Designed for students age 15 and up.

Learn Java™ GUI Applications is a 9 lesson Tutorial covering object-oriented programming concepts, using a integrated development environment to create and test Java projects, building and distributing GUI applications, understanding and using the Swing control library, exception handling, sequential file access, graphics, multimedia, advanced topics such as printing, and help system authoring. **Our Beginning Java tutorial is a pre-requisite for this tutorial.**

Programming Games with Java™ is a semester long "intermediate" programming tutorial consisting of 10 chapters explaining (in simple, easy-to-follow terms) how to build a Visual C# Video Games. The games built are non-violent, family-friendly and teach logical thinking skills. Students will learn how to program the following Visual C# video games: Safecracker, Tic Tac Toe, Match Game, Pizza Delivery, Moon Landing, and Leap Frog. This intermediate level self-paced tutorial can be used at home or school. The tutorial is simple enough for kids yet engaging enough for beginning adults. **Our Beginning Java and Learn Java GUI Applications tutorials are required pre-requisites for this tutorial.**

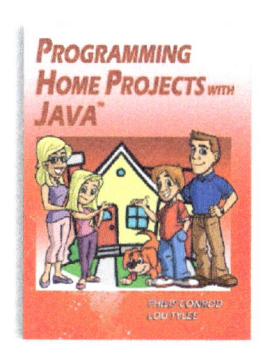

Programming Home Projects with Java™ is a Java GUI Swing tutorial covering object-oriented programming concepts. It explains (in simple, easy-to-follow terms) how to build Java GUI project to use around the home. Students learn about project design, the Java Swing controls, many elements of the Java language, and how to distribute finished projects. The projects built include a Dual-Mode Stopwatch, Flash Card Math Quiz, Multiple Choice Exam, Blackjack Card Game, Weight Monitor, Home Inventory Manager and a Snowball Toss Game. **Our Beginning Java and Learn Java GUI Applications tutorials are pre-requisites for this tutorial.**

We also publish several advanced Honors Level Self-Study or Instructor-Led "College-Prep" Computer Programming Tutorials for Microsoft® Visual Basic® Professional Edition and Visual C#® Professional Edition:

LEARN VISUAL BASIC PROFESSIONAL EDITION is a comprehensive college prep programming tutorial covering object-oriented programming, the Visual Basic integrated development environment, building and distributing Windows applications using the Windows Installer, exception handling, sequential file access, graphics, multimedia, advanced topics such as web access, printing, and HTML help system authoring. The tutorial also introduces database applications (using ADO .NET) and web applications (using ASP.NET).

VISUAL BASIC AND DATABASES PROFESSIONAL EDITION is a tutorial that provides a detailed introduction to using Visual Basic for accessing and maintaining databases for desktop applications. Topics covered include: database structure, database design, Visual Basic project building, ADO .NET data objects (connection, data adapter, command, data table), data bound controls, proper interface design, structured query language (SQL), creating databases using Access, SQL Server and ADOX, and database reports. Actual projects developed include a books tracking system, a sales invoicing program, a home inventory system and a daily weather monitor.

LEARN VISUAL C# PROFESSIONAL EDITION is a comprehensive college prep computer programming tutorial covering object-oriented programming, the Visual C# integrated development environment and toolbox, building and distributing Windows applications (using the Windows Installer), exception handling, sequential file input and output, graphics, multimedia effects (animation and sounds), advanced topics such as web access, printing, and HTML help system authoring. The tutorial also introduces database applications (using ADO .NET) and web applications (using ASP.NET).

VISUAL C# AND DATABASES PROFESSIONAL EDITION is a tutorial that provides a detailed introduction to using Visual C# for accessing and maintaining databases for desktop applications. Topics covered include: database structure, database design, Visual C# project building, ADO .NET data objects (connection, data adapter, command, data table), data bound controls, proper interface design, structured query language (SQL), creating databases using Access, SQL Server and ADOX, and database reports. Actual projects developed include a books tracking system, a sales invoicing program, a home inventory system and a daily weather monitor.